MOVING THE BAR

MOVING THE BAR

MY LIFE AS A RADICAL LAWYER

MICHAEL RATNER

OR Books

New York · London

All rights information: rights@orbooks.com
Visit our website at www.orbooks.com

First printing 2021

© 2021 Michael Ratner

Published by OR Books, New York and London

Library of Congress Cataloging-in-Publication Data: A catalog record for this book is available from the Library of Congress.

Typeset by Lapiz Digital.

paperback ISBN 978-1-68219-309-9 • ebook ISBN 978-1-68219-250-4

CONTENTS

Foreword   1

1. Truth-Tellers   9

2. In the Beginning   57

3. Days of Law and Rage   79

4. Working for the Judge   111

5. In the Center of the Seventies   131

6. The Reagan Years   181

7. The End of the Twentieth Century   215

8. Guantánamo   243

9. New Projects   291

10. A Visit to Palestine   321

11. Viva Cuba Libre!   345

FOREWORD

This is the story of a first-generation Jewish kid from a huge Polish immigrant family in Cleveland who was radicalized in the sixties, settled in New York, and became one of the great civil and human rights attorneys of his generation: truly a widely beloved lawyer for the left.

After law school Michael was expected to go back to Cleveland to join the family building supply business. His uncle advised against becoming a lawyer, warning that a lawyer "always works for someone else." With great pain, Michael ignored his uncle's advice. He began working for someone else. That someone else was the left.

Michael worked for some 40 years at the Center for Constitutional Rights, first as a staff attorney, then litigation director and finally its president. He liked to refer to the Center, in Alexander Cockburn's words, as "a small band of tigerish people." He put the CCR on firm financial footing, enabling it to continue its work for human rights and social justice as a robust supporter of grassroots organizations. Michael went on to help his friend and colleague, the Berlin attorney Wolfgang Kaleck, establish the European Center for Human and Constitutional Rights as a kind of sister organization of the CCR. Back home he helped establish Palestine Legal to defend supporters of the Palestinian people against what Michael called "the Palestine exception to the first amendment."

MOVING THE BAR

I first met Michael Ratner 35 years ago when we lived around the corner from each other in Greenwich Village. He had just been elected president of the National Lawyers Guild and came over to ask me to be on the editorial board of the organization's magazine *Guild Notes*. We became dear friends and worked together over many years.

Michael admired people who acted on their convictions, people who lived their lives, he told me, "without any contradictions." John Brown, who attempted to support a slave uprising, was such a person. Vladimir Ilych Lenin was another (an oil portrait of Lenin hung in Michael's living room). And especially Che Guevara.

Together we wrote two books on Che and traveled to Havana twice to research and promote them. On the second trip when working on our book *Who Killed Che?: How the CIA Got Away with Murder* we met with General Harry "Pombo" Villegras. Pombo started fighting alongside Che as a shoeless peasant boy during the Cuban revolution (1956-59) and fought with him in Bolivia 10 years later. He was one of the three who escaped capture and execution by managing to walk over the Andes mountains into Chile. For our interview, Pombo wore a T-shirt and a baseball cap. When it ended, we offered him a car ride home but he declined, telling us he would walk back. Michael admired Pombo's modesty, as well as his courage.

Michael himself was a modest person. In all the years I knew him he never told me that he had finished first in his class at Columbia Law School. Michael was also unfailingly generous. When I asked him once whom he helped out, he replied, "Anyone who asks me." Michael was playful and funny and fun to be around. We used to tease him saying that there was no joke too silly, too puerile, for him not to relate. He loved his children and being with his family. Indeed, he loved all children, whom he called "darlings."

In 2004 we started the radio show *Law and Disorder* on WBAI in New York City with Heidi Boghosian and Dalia Hashad. It is now broadcast nationally on 120 stations. Doing the show with Michael was really a pleasure. And easy. He was so smart we could ad lib. When Heidi and I do the show now, we prepare a written introduction and a list of questions for our guests.

Five years ago, Michael wrote a chapter for *Imagine: Living in a Socialist USA*, a book I co-edited with Frances Goldin and Debby Smith. Michael's chapter was called "What I Would Do As Attorney General." His opening sentence was "It will be a cold day in hell when a person with my politics is appointed to be attorney general of the United States." He wrote that "If I did get to take office, I would begin by not enforcing certain laws, which I have a right to do. Then I would investigate and prosecute the real bad guys."

Michael taught human rights law to students at Columbia Law School with his friend Reed Brody. Then he began commuting from New York to New Haven where he taught at an international human rights clinic. It was there that he and his class won an historic victory protecting Haitians infected with HIV virus who were initially confined by the U.S. at its military base in Guantánamo, Cuba.

Perhaps Michael's greatest victory came in his initiating and organizing some 600 lawyers in firms large and small across the country to come to the defense of Muslim prisoners accused of terrorism and held at Guantánamo after 9/11. The government invented an indefinite detention scheme claiming the captives had no right to be brought before a judge, charged, and brought to trial, that neither international nor American law applied to them, that they had no right to habeas corpus. The team Michael assembled took the case all the way up to the United States Supreme Court, where they won. Nevertheless, the offshore prison camp of Guantánamo remains open to this day.

"Justice is a constant struggle." This is the motto of the National Lawyers Guild. Michael's friend and colleague Bill Kunstler used to say that there are no green pastures, that every generation has its own battles to wage. That is why Michael wrote this book. He meant it to be both instructive and inspirational, especially for law students and young lawyers. When he died of cancer three years ago in May of 2016, Michael hadn't been able to finish the book. As sick as he was, he had gotten up to the year 2000. Karen Ranucci, Michael's wife and comrade, asked their friend, the writer Zachary Sklar, to finish the project, bringing it up to 2016. Zach was able to do this using Michael's notes and articles, previous interviews with Michael, and the recollections of his family members and legal colleagues.

As a lawyer and as an activist, Michael participated in the essential struggles of his times. He came to be, in the words of Lenin, "as radical as reality itself." He could "sense the future in the instant," as Shakespeare wrote. He understood that those who are above the struggles are also beside the point.

Michael was a Jew, but came to reject the idea that it was racial ties or bonds of blood that made up the Jewish community. He rejected Jewish nationalism in favor of an unconditional solidarity with the persecuted and exterminated. Michael had no funeral. He wasn't religious. Religion to him was superstition. The Jewish heretic who transcends Jewry belongs to a Jewish tradition— "the non-Jewish Jew," in the words of historian Isaac Deutscher. Michael was in line with the great revolutionaries of modern thought who went beyond the boundaries of Judaism: Spinoza, Heine, Marx, Luxembourg, Freud, and Einstein.

I do not wish to stretch the comparison. Michael was not as much a radical thinker as a man of action. But his intellectual understanding powered his activity. He had in common with these great thinkers the idea that knowledge, to be real, must be acted upon. As Marx observed: "Hitherto the philosophers have only interpreted the world, the point is to change it."

Like his intellectual predecessors, Michael was aware of the constantly changing and contradictory nature of society. He was essentially an optimist and shared with the great revolutionaries an optimistic belief in humanity and a belief in the solidarity of humankind.

One of the last times I saw Michael was via FaceTime. He was out of the hospital once again and back in the living room of his Greenwich Village home. I was on the Upper West Side with Michael's son Jake and his companion Elena, his daughter Ana, his friend Jen, and my wife Debby. We all took a class together called "Anyone Can Sing" from our singing teacher Elissa, and during this second meeting, we connected with Michael over an iPhone and sang him "The Internationale," his favorite song. We could see Michael lying back in his lounger. We sang the first verse:

> "Arise you prisoners of starvation,
> Arise ye wretched of the earth,
> For justice thunders condemnation
> A better world's in birth."

He could see and hear us and we could see him. So we sang the second verse.

> "No more tradition's chains shall bind us,
> Arise you slaves no more in thrall,
> The earth shall rise and new foundations,
> We have been naught, we shall be all."

Michael knew the history of this anthem of the international working class. Perhaps, as he listened to our passionate rendition, he was recalling that Eugène Pottier wrote the words even as the Paris Commune was being crushed, gun smoke in the air, its leaders lined up against the wall at Père Lachaise cemetery in Paris and executed. The Commune endured for 91 days. It was the first Socialist uprising of modern times. This was the rebel tradition with which Michael identified.

We arrived at the last verse:

"'Tis the final conflict,
Let each stand in their place,
International solidarity,
Shall be the human race."

Michael teared up and joined in the singing with us. He sang in the original French. From his chair he raised his right fist in the air, sharing that moment with his children and friends.

Michael believed in democracy and in the rule of law, but did not believe that either was compatible with capitalism. "Law is a villainess," he wrote. "Social equality will never be achieved under capitalism." Before and especially after 9/11, Michael feared the threat of fascism. It was the government which Michael fought, in court, in the media, in the streets, and in the classroom, striving tirelessly to expose its lies, its cruelty, its racism, and its imperial reach.

Michael died in the hospital on a spring afternoon in May 2016. He had hoped to go up to his place in the Catskill Mountains. He would have gone fly fishing for trout on one of the little streams up there while his wife Karen put in a large vegetable garden and hunted for mushrooms in the woods. He would've gone jogging or biking or sat in his screened-in living room looking out at the yard full of chickens and guinea hens and a black-and-white lamb born unexpectedly that spring. Later he would've joined his family and friends at a large round table where we frequently met for dinner. But this was not to be.

Michael and Karen created and formed the center of a large movement community, a community that is carrying on Michael's work and memory. This is his legacy. Michael had a piece of paper taped on the wall next to his desk. It read:

Four key principles of being a radical lawyer:

1. Do not refuse to take a case just because it has long odds of winning in court.
2. Use cases to publicize a radical critique of U.S. policy and to promote revolutionary transformation.
3. Combine legal work with political advocacy.
4. Love people.

Michael will be remembered as a generous, loyal friend and a gentle and kind person. He was a compelling speaker, an acute observer of the political scene, and a farsighted visionary. Professionally, Michael will live on as one of the great advocates for justice of his time.

Thanks are due to Zach Sklar who so ably picked up the baton when Michael became too ill to complete this book and fashioned it into a finished work of which he would have been proud.

Michael Steven Smith
October 2020

1
TRUTH TELLERS

On the mild sunny day of June 19, 2012, a motorcycle wove through traffic in London's tony Knightsbridge neighborhood. It passed fashionable boutiques and shiny, chauffeur-driven Rolls Royces owned by billionaire sheikhs. Less than a block from Harrods luxury department store, it turned onto a quiet cul de sac and stopped in front of a four-story red brick building at 3 Hans Crescent. A tall, wire-thin man, disguised as a courier, got off the motorcycle and entered the building, which housed the Ecuadorian Embassy.

The man was Julian Assange, 40-year-old founder and publisher of WikiLeaks, who had stunned the world with the online publication of hundreds of thousands of previously secret U.S. war logs and diplomatic cables. Wanted for questioning in Sweden about two sexual assault allegations, he was aware that if he traveled to Sweden to talk to prosecutors, he could be imprisoned, extradited to the United States, and charged with espionage there. In the lobby of the Ecuadorian embassy he explained to the doorman that he was not a courier delivering a package. He was a publisher and an activist who had come to seek political asylum.

Later that day I got a text message from Amy Goodman, host of *Democracy Now!:* "Julian Assange has gone into the Ecuadorian Embassy."

Soon the story went out on the wires and the internet, and I watched on TV as new bits of information emerged.

Like everyone else, I had no idea that Assange was going to do this. But unlike everyone else, I was one of Julian Assange's principal lawyers. And more than that, I had also become a close confidant and friend.

The Iraq War had begun in March 2003 when U.S. forces landed in Baghdad. For the same reasons I had opposed the Afghan War two years earlier, I opposed this one too. On February 18, a week before the impending intervention, 30 million people around the world had poured into the streets, protesting it. We felt like an international force, rising up to say no to war. For a brief moment we thought we could prevent this madness, but the Bush administration went ahead anyway, acting again, as it had in Afghanistan, under the Authorization of the Use of Military Force (AUMF) of 2001. It justified the war on the basis of two claims: 1. that Saddam Hussein had nuclear and chemical weapons; and 2. that Saddam Hussein and al-Qaeda were somehow linked.

Mainstream media, most prominently Judith Miller in the *New York Times*, supported these administration assertions. But both were lies. U.N. inspectors had found no evidence of nuclear or chemical weapons in Iraq. Nor was there any hint of collusion between Hussein and al-Qaeda. On the contrary, each of them seemed to have zero patience with the other.

Ignoring the evidence, the Bush administration proceeded with its longtime goal of regime change in Iraq. It toppled Hussein, but chaos ensued and the war dragged on year after year. By November 2007, 170,300 U.S. troops were in Iraq, not to mention untold numbers of private military contractors. Depending on whose figures you believed, casualties from 2003-2009 reached anywhere from 110,000 to 650,000 deaths, most of them innocent civilians, with millions more left wounded and homeless.

When WikiLeaks posted its *Collateral Murder* video in April 2010, it instantly sent shock waves around the world. Millions of people saw it, and social media exploded with expressions of sorrow and outrage. Virtually overnight, WikiLeaks and Julian Assange had skyrocketed from relative cyber obscurity to worldwide celebrity.

Though of course I knew war atrocities were happening daily, when I watched the video I was sickened. It became, for me and many others, the equivalent of the iconic 1972 photo of a nine-year-old Vietnamese girl running down a street naked, on fire after being napalmed. Like that photo which encapsulated the Vietnam War, the *Collateral Murder* video captured in horrifying images the disaster that the Iraq War had become not just for Iraqi civilians, but for U.S. soldiers and for the soul of America itself.

The video, recorded by a camera mounted inside a U.S. military Apache helicopter on July 12, 2007 during the height of the Iraq War, is profoundly disturbing, but I believe every American should see it. It shows U.S. soldiers indiscriminately firing on unarmed Iraqi civilians as if they're playing a video game, killing 12 people, including two Reuters journalists, then laughing and bragging about it.

As the video begins, we can hear the soldiers joking and cursing while their helicopter hovers over an open square in a neighborhood called New Baghdad. Below, people walk around doing their business. Then the soldiers spot the two Reuters journalists and mistakenly think their cameras are weapons.

"Have five to six individuals with AK-47s," says one U.S. soldier, requesting permission to engage, which is granted. And then the soldiers open fire with 30-millimeter cannons, devastating the whole area, as they cheer each other on. The innocent civilians below are slaughtered. It's like shooting ducks in a barrel. When you see the picture afterwards, there is a pool of blood at least 50 feet across and 20 feet wide. The soldiers then congratulate each other.

U.S. Soldier 1: Oh, yeah, look at those dead bastards.

U.S. Soldier 2: Nice. Good shootin'.

But the carnage isn't over yet. The driver of the Reuters journalists is hit but tries to crawl away, and a van pulls up to help him and the rest of the wounded. The soldiers in the helicopter receive permission to open fire again, killing the driver and several others. The ground is strewn with dead bodies, and a U.S. Bradley tank moves in and runs over a dead body. The soldiers in the helicopter laugh. This is when they hear from soldiers on the ground that a child inside the van has been shot through the windshield. Their response is chilling.

U.S. Soldier 3: ...We need—we need a—to evac this child. She's got a wound to the belly. I can't do anything here. She needs to get evaced. Over.

U.S. Soldier 1: Well, it's their fault for bringing their kids into a battle.

U.S. Soldier 2: That's right.

Actually, two children were critically wounded in the attack. Their father was taking them to school when he came upon the bloody scene and stopped his van to help rescue the wounded. Fortunately, the children survived. Their father, an unarmed civilian, didn't.

WikiLeaks had received the uploaded video in early 2010. Working with a small team, Assange spent a couple of months digitally clarifying it and verifying its authenticity. On April 5, 2010 he introduced the 17-minute video at a press conference at the National Press Club in Washington. Both that version and a 37-minute version were posted to the WikiLeaks website.

The Pentagon had investigated the incident but concluded that none of the pilots and gunners had violated the rules of engagement. Following the deaths of its two employees, Reuters had asked for a copy of the video, but the Pentagon would not disclose it.

When asked where he got the video, Assange said only that the source was anonymous. But a month later, the U.S. Army arrested

22-year-old Chelsea (then known as Bradley) Manning, a private first class assigned to Forward Operating Base Hammer just east of Baghdad. She was charged with leaking the video and hundreds of thousands of classified documents to WikiLeaks.

As an intelligence analyst, Manning had access to classified databases that U.S. agencies and armed forces had begun sharing in the wake of the World Trade Center attacks of 2001. In January 2010, Manning downloaded documents she believed the public had a right to see, saving them to CD-RWs that she smuggled out of security by labeling them "Lady Gaga." She then copied them to her personal computer.

Manning contacted both the *Washington Post* and the *New York Times* to offer them the files, but the *Post* reporter wasn't interested and the *Times* didn't respond. Frustrated, Manning then contacted WikiLeaks via anonymous online chats. In February, she anonymously uploaded to WikiLeaks the *Collateral Murder* video and documents that were eventually released as the *Afghan War Logs* and the *Iraq War Logs*.

Troubled by what she had seen of the war, and isolated, lonely, and confused about her sexual identity, Manning confided in online chats to a cyber "friend," a convicted hacker named Adrian Lamo, that she had blown the whistle. Lamo ratted Manning out to the Army's Criminal Investigation Command. Arrested and initially flown to Camp Arijan in Kuwait, Manning was transferred to the Marine Corps Brig in Quantico, Virginia in July 2010, where she was held in solitary confinement.

Damning as it was, the *Collateral Murder* video was just the beginning. More important to the government, Manning admitted that she had uploaded much, much more to WikiLeaks, including many thousands of State Department cables later labeled *Cablegate.*

On July 25, 2010, Assange held a press conference at the Frontline Club in London to announce the publication of the *Afghan War Logs* in conjunction with the *New York Times*, the *Guardian* in London, and *Der*

Spiegel in Germany. The 91,000 internal secret documents provide a never-seen history of the Afghan War from 2004 to 2009.

It was not a pretty picture. The documents included detailed records about the deaths of nearly 20,000 people. Civilian casualties in Afghanistan were far higher than previously reported to the public. A number of deaths of coalition soldiers resulting from friendly fire from U.S. forces were also previously unreported. The documents revealed that Pakistan, an ally receiving aid from the U.S., was working with the Taliban to plan attacks in Afghanistan. The logs also exposed a secret American assassination squad operating in Afghanistan that had killed innocent civilian women and children.

The *Times, Guardian,* and *Der Spiegel* redacted the documents to withhold the names of confidential civilian informants who could be endangered if exposed. Although WikiLeaks was philosophically committed to transparency and publication of documents in full, Assange agreed to withhold 15,000 documents for redaction.

Nonetheless, the U.S. government, politicians, and mainstream media immediately denounced WikiLeaks for publishing the war logs and endangering U.S. and allied troops and informants. The day after publication of the *Afghan War Logs*, White House Press Secretary Robert Gibbs stated that WikiLeaks "poses a very real and potential threat." Senator Lindsey Graham, member of the Armed Services Committee, stated, "WikiLeaks has blood on its hands."

The fierce media attacks focused exclusively on WikiLeaks and Assange. Three highly respected mainstream newspapers in three different western countries had published the same secret information as WikiLeaks, yet no one was attacking them, or calling for their printing presses to be shut down, or talking about blood on their hands.

It was clear to me that WikiLeaks and Julian Assange were going to need help. So I called the brilliant political lawyer Len Weinglass, who had spent his entire career representing activists. Most relevant to WikiLeaks' situation, he had defended Daniel Ellsberg in the Pentagon Papers case during the Vietnam War, perhaps the most famous leak of classified information in the history of the United States.

Len proposed that we alert WikiLeaks to the risks they were running, and I agreed. So I sent a blind e-mail to their website. I introduced myself, Len Weinglass, and the Center for Constitutional Rights, and wrote: "We have been looking at the legal situation regarding Wiki for some time and have researched the various issues. ... if and when you want to speak with us, we would be glad to travel to U.K. or otherwise."

The website was then receiving more than 600 e-mails per day, so it was lucky that WikiLeaks ambassador Joseph Farrell actually read mine and replied: "Julian would like to discuss this further. Preferably in the U.K."

Len and I started to look into flights to London, but before we could book one, our proposed meeting ran into a major snag.

In early August, after the release of the *Afghan War Logs*, the FBI had enlisted local authorities in Wales to raid the home of Manning's mother, who was living there. Assange wrote of this time, "I followed closely how pressure mounted on U.S. allies to track my movements and to stop our publications."

Hoping to put in place a legal strategy to protect WikiLeaks' servers in Sweden, Assange flew to Stockholm on August 11. Shortly after his arrival, his personal bank cards were blocked, leaving him with no money and totally dependent on the kindness of virtual strangers. Two of these strangers were women who offered their homes and had consensual sex with him. Just before Assange was scheduled to leave Sweden, he awoke to find headlines saying that he was wanted for questioning on allegations of rape and that police were hunting all over Stockholm for him.

The two women had been concerned about sexually transmitted diseases and had gone to the police to seek advice on compelling Assange to take an STD test. "I did not want to put any charges on Julian Assange," texted one of them on August 20 while she was still at the police station, but "the police were keen on getting their hands on him." She told her friend she felt "railroaded by the police."

Less than 24 hours after the warrant for Assange's arrest was issued, the chief prosecutor of Stockholm took over the preliminary investigation and dropped the rape accusation, stating "I don't believe there is any reason to suspect that he has committed rape." But by then the story of "rape" had been put out to the press and had circulated all over the world.

Though charged with nothing, Assange canceled his departure and voluntarily remained in Sweden for another five weeks to cooperate with the investigation. On August 30, he had an interview with police and answered every question asked of him. But two days later, despite the lack of evidence or testimony from the two women, a special prosecutor, Marianne Ny, was appointed to investigate two lesser allegations of sexual misconduct.

It's unclear whether this happened because Claes Borgström, an ambitious Swedish politician angling to become Minister of Justice, saw an opportunity for publicity, or because the U.S. government had applied pressure behind the scenes. It is clear, however, that both the U.S. and Swedish governments wanted to stop WikiLeaks from publishing the vast treasure trove of diplomatic cables that Manning had uploaded to it. Those cables would later reveal the Swedish intelligence service's unlawful participation in secret CIA renditions and torture of Swedish political refugees from 2001 to 2006.

Unable to pin down Ny about if or when he could make a statement, Assange got the prosecutor's written consent to leave Sweden. On September 27, Assange took an SAS flight from Stockholm's Arlanda airport to Berlin. But one of his bags containing three encrypted laptops with evidence of war crimes and protected legal correspondence was seized by Swedish intelligence and mysteriously disappeared. Though he lodged numerous complaints with the airline, the bag and the laptops were never found.

On October 22, 2010, WikiLeaks published the *Iraq War Logs*, again in conjunction with several major media organizations, including the *New York Times*, the *Guardian, Der Spiegel, Al Jazeera, Le Monde*, London's Bureau of Investigative Journalism, and the Iraq Body Count Project. The Iraq logs consisted of 391,831 U.S. Army field reports from 2004 to 2009—an even bigger leak than the *Afghan War Logs*. Among the most important revelations:

- Out of 109,000 recorded deaths during that period, 66,081 were civilians. And even these numbers are not reliable since U.S. troops often listed dead civilians as enemy combatants—including the two Reuters journalists and the other 10 innocent people slaughtered in the *Collateral Murder* video. Every one of those 12 deaths was an unarmed civilian, yet they were all counted in the logs as "enemy killed in action."
- U.S. troops murdered nearly 700 civilians for approaching too close to checkpoints—including pregnant women and their husbands on the way to the hospital. In addition, private contractors such as Blackwater killed and wounded many other civilians.
- Equally damning, U.S. forces repeatedly handed over Iraqi prisoners to the Iraqi government, knowing that they would be tortured. To transfer prisoners of war in your own custody to another authority known to use torture is a clear violation of the Geneva Conventions.
- More than 1,300 prisoners were tortured and in some cases killed by Iraqi authorities during the administrations of George W. Bush and Barack Obama.

According to the *Guardian,* the logs also reveal that "U.S. authorities failed to investigate hundreds of reports of abuse, torture, rape, and even murder by Iraqi police and soldiers." In fact, the coalition had "a formal policy of ignoring such allegations," unless they involved coalition forces.

Shortly after the release of the *Iraq War Logs*, Len Weinglass and I were finally able to arrange our meeting with Assange. We met him in Marylebone in central London at a studio apartment that belonged to Jennifer Robinson, one of his lawyers who was away at the time.

WikiLeaks had no physical office. It existed only in cyberspace. Nor did Assange have a permanent residence. He was living the same kind of nomadic life that he'd led as a teenager in Australia, moving from city to city, apartment to apartment.

Len struggled as we trudged up to the top floor of the five-floor walkup. Joseph Farrell opened the door, and that is when I got my first in-person look at Julian Assange, who greeted us warmly. Tall and slender, he had longish white hair that reminded me of Andy Warhol. He wore slacks and a plain shirt that Farrell had bought him after the suitcase with all his clothes had been lost on his recent flight from Stockholm.

With Julian was his close adviser Sarah Harrison, a 28-year-old, sandy-haired British journalist who, along with Farrell, had left London's Bureau of Investigative Journalism earlier that year to join WikiLeaks. Julian's British solicitor, Mark Stephens, a frizzy-haired middle-aged man dressed in a striped suit with a broad flashy tie, also joined us.

Perhaps a bit suspicious of American lawyers intruding on his turf, Stephens explained that Julian already had lawyers in Sweden dealing with the allegations there, and he was handling the legal situation in England, along with Jennifer Robinson and the Australia-born barrister Geoffrey Robertson.

"We consider the Swedish allegations a distraction," I said. "We've read the police reports, and we believe the authorities don't have a case. We're here because in our view you are in much more jeopardy in the U.S. Len can explain why."

Julian said nothing and turned to Len.

"WikiLeaks and you personally are facing a battle that is both legal and political," said Len in his quiet, deliberate way. "As we learned in the Pentagon Papers case, the U.S. government doesn't like the truth coming out. And it doesn't like to be humiliated. No matter if it's Nixon or Bush or Obama, Republican or Democrat in the White House. The U.S. government will try to stop you from publishing its ugly secrets. And if they have to destroy you and the First Amendment and the rights of publishers with you, they are willing to do it. We believe they are going to come after WikiLeaks and you, Julian, as the publisher."

"Come after me for what?" asked Julian.

"Espionage. They're going to charge [Chelsea] Manning with treason under the Espionage Act of 1917. We don't think it applies, because Manning's a whistleblower, not a spy. And we don't think it applies to you either because you are a publisher. But they are going to try to force Manning into implicating you as [her] collaborator. That's why it's crucial that WikiLeaks and you personally have an American criminal lawyer to represent you."

Julian listened carefully as we laid out possible scenarios. "The way it could happen," I said, "is that the Justice Department could convene a secret grand jury to investigate possible charges against you. It would probably be in northern Virginia, where everyone on the jury would be a current or retired CIA employee or have worked for some other part of the military-industrial complex. They would be hostile to anyone like you who'd published U.S. government secrets. The grand jury could come up with a sealed indictment, issue a warrant for your arrest, and request extradition."

"What happens if they extradite me?" asked Julian.

Len looked at him and said, "They fly you to where the indictment is issued. Then they put you into some hellhole in solitary, and you get treated like Manning. They put you under what they call special administrative measures, which means you probably would not be allowed communication with anyone. Maybe your lawyer could go in and talk to you, but the lawyer couldn't say anything to the press."

"And it's very, very unlikely that they would give you bail," I added.

"Is it easier to extradite from the U.K. or from Sweden?" asked Sarah Harrison.

"We don't know the answer to that," I replied. "My guess is that you would probably have the most support and the best legal team in a bigger country like the U.K. In a smaller country like Sweden, the U.S. can use its power to pressure the government, so it would be easier to extradite you from there. But we need to consult with a lawyer who specializes in extradition."

Stephens looked skeptical. "You know that Julian has already offered to go to Sweden to answer the special prosecutor's questions," he said.

"I don't think that's wise," Len said, "unless the Swedish government guarantees that Julian will not be extradited to another country because of his publishing work."

"The problem is that Sweden doesn't have bail," I explained. "If they put you in jail in Stockholm and the U.S. pressures the government to extradite you, Sweden might send you immediately to the U.S. and you'd never see the light of day again. It's far less risky to ask the Swedish prosecutor to question you in London."

Julian looked thoughtful, taking it all in. Reserved and controlled, he didn't show much emotion. But it was clear that he understood everything we'd said and seemed to trust us.

We all agreed that for the time being Julian should not go to Sweden. He would stay in the U.K., and we would continue to work together. Len and I volunteered to represent WikiLeaks and Julian pro bono in the U.S. with the support of CCR, and Julian accepted the offer.

Still, after the meeting, both Len and I had the feeling that Mark Stephens wasn't the right lawyer for WikiLeaks. He practiced commercial law and didn't have much experience with political cases or extradition.

Len called his friend of many years, Helena Kennedy, a distinguished British barrister with many years of experience in extradition cases. She confirmed our feelings about Stephens and volunteered to join our legal team as an adviser on extradition.

Soon after we returned to New York, we got the sad news that Len had been diagnosed with pancreatic cancer, from which he died a couple of months later. I had to look for another criminal lawyer in the U.S. Of the three I suggested, Julian selected the highly respected trial lawyer Barry Pollack because he was based in Washington, D.C., where we felt a criminal attorney's presence would be the most helpful.

Meanwhile, in London WikiLeaks announced in late November its publication of the first 220 documents from *Cablegate,* the U.S. State Department classified cables that Manning had uploaded earlier in the year. Sent to the State Department from U.S. diplomatic missions, consulates, and embassies in every country of the world, the entire set of 251,287 cables dated from December 1966 to February 2010 were eventually posted unredacted (aside from the first 220 cables, redacted to protect innocent people) to the WikiLeaks website in September 2011. Published initially in conjunction with five major mainstream newspapers—the *New York Times,* the *Guardian, Der Spiegel, Le Monde* in France, and *El País* in Spain—the cables would later be co-published with 113 news outlets all over the world.

The extent and importance of the *Cablegate* revelations took my breath away. They pulled back the curtain and revealed how American foreign policy functions behind-the-scenes, manipulating events all over the globe. They also provided access to U.S. diplomats' raw, frank, and often embarrassing assessments of foreign leaders. Some of the most stunning revelations:

- In 2009, Secretary of State Hillary Clinton ordered U.S. diplomats to spy on U.N. Secretary General Ban Ki Moon and other

U.N. representatives from China, France, Russia, and the U.K. The information she asked for included DNA, iris scans, fingerprints, and personal passwords. U.S. and British diplomats also eavesdropped on U.N. Secretary General Kofi Annan in the weeks before the U.S.-led invasion of Iraq in 2003.

- The U.S. has been secretly launching missile, bomb, and drone attacks on terrorist targets in Yemen, killing civilians. But to protect the U.S., Yemeni President Ali Abdullah Saleh told Gen. David Petraeus, "We'll continue saying the bombs are ours, not yours."

- Saudi King Abdullah repeatedly urged the U.S. to bomb Iran's nuclear facilities to "cut off the head of the snake." Other leaders from Israel, Jordan, and Bahrain also urged the U.S. to attack Iran.

- The White House and Secretary of State Clinton refused to condemn the June 2009 military coup in Honduras that overthrew elected President Manuel Zelaya, ignoring a cable from the U.S. embassy there that described the coup as "illegal and unconstitutional." Instead of calling for the restoration of Zelaya, the U.S. supported elections orchestrated by the coup's leader, Roberto Micheletti. Opposition leaders and international observers boycotted those elections.

- Employees of a U.S. government contractor in Afghanistan, DynCorp, hired "dancing boys"—a euphemism for child prostitutes—to be used as sex slaves.

- In various cables, Afghan President Hamid Karzai is called "an extremely weak man who did not listen to facts but was instead easily swayed by anyone who came to report even the most bizarre stories or plots against him." Argentine President Cristina Kirchner and her husband Néstor Kirchner, the former president, are described as "paranoid." President Nicolas

Sarkozy of France is described as "thin-skinned" and "authoritarian." Italian Prime Minister Silvio Berlusconi is called "feckless, vain, and ineffective."

- Perhaps most important, the cables said that Tunisian President Zine El Abidine Ben Ali had "lost touch with the Tunisian people" and described "high-level corruption, a sclerotic regime, and deep hatred of... Ben Ali's wife and her family."

These revelations led to the eventual overthrow of the regime in Tunisia. The Tunisian protests spread like wildfire to other countries of the Middle East, resulting in the widespread revolts of the Arab Spring of 2011.

U.S. officials and news media responded to *Cablegate* with more vitriol than ever. Secretary of State Clinton said, "Disclosures like these tear at the fabric of the proper functioning of responsible government." Attorney General Eric Holder announced that the Justice Department was conducting "an active, ongoing criminal investigation into WikiLeaks."

Others were less restrained. Rep. Candice Miller of Michigan called WikiLeaks "a terrorist organization." Former Speaker of the House Newt Gingrich demanded that WikiLeaks be closed down and Assange treated as "an enemy combatant who's engaged in information warfare against the United States." Fox News host Bill O'Reilly even suggested that the U.S. should assassinate Assange with a drone.

To me, it was obvious that WikiLeaks and Assange had hit a raw nerve. For those who ran the American empire, the truth hurt. For the rest of us, it was liberating. With the 2010 release of the *Collateral Murder* video, the *Afghan War Logs*, the *Iraq War Logs*, and *Cablegate,* WikiLeaks went far beyond traditional investigative reporting. It proved that in the new digital world, full transparency was not only possible, but necessary in order to hold governments accountable for their actions.

MOVING THE BAR

On November 30, 2010, two days after the initial release of *Cablegate*, Sweden issued an Interpol "Red Alert Notice" normally used to warn about terrorists. It also issued a European Arrest Warrant seeking Assange's extradition to Sweden. Since he was wanted only for questioning about the sexual misconduct allegations, it seemed clear from the timing and severity of the warrant that the U.S. had successfully pressured the Swedes.

Our legal team discussed the arrest warrant with Assange. In our view, the warrant was invalid since the Swedish prosecutor had filed no charges. Julian decided to turn himself in to British authorities and fight the arrest warrant in British Magistrates' Court.

For 10 days he was held in solitary confinement at Wandsworth Prison. Released on bail of £340,000, Julian spent the next 551 days under house arrest as his case made its way through the courts. British journalist Vaughan Smith offered to let him stay at Ellingham Hall in Norfolk, a couple hours north of London. It was a beautiful but isolated farm that had been in the Smith family for 150 years. Under the terms of his bail, Julian had to wear an electronic anklet and check in with the local police twice a day.

Rather than discrediting him, the arrest only increased WikiLeaks' influence and Julian's personal fame. Assange received *Time* magazine's Readers' Choice Award as "Person of the Year," and in December 2010, funding to the website skyrocketed to $110,000 per day, with an average donation of $5 to $30 from thousands of contributors all over the world.

This prosperity didn't last long. In early December, PayPal refused to process any donations to WikiLeaks. Visa, Mastercard, Bank of America, and Western Union all quickly followed. It became virtually impossible for anyone to donate to WikiLeaks, and its income immediately plummeted by 95 percent.

But none of the financial institutions could point to any illegal activity by WikiLeaks, and none had imposed any restrictions on WikiLeaks' mainstream co-publishers. The financial blockade applied only to WikiLeaks.

The U.N. and O.A.S. Special Rapporteurs on Freedom of Expression issued a joint statement condemning the blockade. A *New York Times* editorial pointed out that "a bank's ability to block payments to a legal entity raises a troubling prospect. A handful of big banks could potentially bar any organization they disliked from the payments system, essentially cutting them off from the world economy."

Eventually, WikiLeaks found ways around the blockade. One of them was to get support from a new group I helped create—the Freedom of the Press Foundation, a non-profit dedicated to protecting public-interest journalism, and whistleblowers, in particular. Donations could be made through the foundation and passed along to WikiLeaks. In addition, WikiLeaks began accepting donations in the alternative online currency Bitcoin, which skyrocketed in value over the next few years. Ironically, this left WikiLeaks in a stronger, more secure financial position than before the financial blockade began.

But in the short term, in late 2010 and early 2011, Assange and WikiLeaks had virtually no money and pressure was mounting from every direction. Just then, Assange's British solicitor Mark Stephens insisted on payment of nearly 400 hours' worth of legal expenses. Since all of the other lawyers were donating their time, this came as a huge shock. To assure payment, Stephens arranged a book deal for Julian worth more than £1.3 million. An intensely private person, Julian did not want to write a tell-all book, but reluctantly went along with it. After contracts were signed, Stephens took nearly half of the advance. Furious, Julian fired Stephens on the spot.

Just around that time the Magistrates' Court ruled against Julian and ordered his extradition to Sweden. If he was going to appeal the ruling, we had to find a new solicitor in a hurry. Helena Kennedy, journalist John Pilger, and I all came up with the same name—Gareth Peirce, who had done such great work on Guantánamo. Gareth agreed to join the team, along with the brilliant barrister Ben Emmerson. In addition, Jennifer Robinson, the young Australian lawyer, decided to quit her job with Stephens and stay on with the WikiLeaks legal team.

Peirce immediately filed an appeal of the magistrate's decision on extradition with the district court. With so much happening, I found myself flying over to London to confer with Julian and the legal team for several days every month. To abide by the terms of his house arrest, Julian would check in with the police in Norfolk in the morning, take the train in to London, meet with us for a couple of hours in the afternoon, and then take the train back to Norfolk to check in with the police before nightfall the same day.

The only time I saw Julian in Norfolk was in July 2011 when WikiLeaks threw a party for his 40th birthday. Julian had become something of a rock star among London's fashion, artistic, and leftist circles, and a who's who of London society, including world-renowned designer Dame Vivienne Westwood and British-Pakistani film producer Jemima Khan, made the trip to Norfolk. It was an outdoor luncheon affair, set in the lovely gardens of Ellingham Hall, an estate that looked like it came straight out of a 19th century British novel—a rambling stone manor house, vast lawns, bucolic farm animals, and hundreds of acres of woods for hunting. The guests drank, ate, and networked, and funds were raised. Julian greeted everyone, and I chatted with him briefly. He seemed in good spirits, but this was one day that no legal work got done.

Julian continued to work from his house-arrest headquarters in Norfolk, releasing files about Guantánamo on the WikiLeaks site in April. The district court denied his appeal, and Peirce took his case to the High Court of Appeal, which also ruled against him. The last appeal, to the U.K. Supreme Court, was argued in February 2012.

By this time, the U.S. government's strategy against Assange had become more apparent. Prosecutors in the Manning case revealed internet chat logs between Manning and an unnamed person at WikiLeaks who they said colluded with Manning by helping the accused traitor engineer a reverse password. Without supporting evidence, prosecutors claimed the unnamed person was Assange. Both Manning and Assange denied it. Nonetheless, it was clear that what Len and I had predicted was happening. The case against Manning was also a case against WikiLeaks and Julian Assange. The two were inextricably linked.

It was a no-brainer for the WikiLeaks/Assange legal team to decide we had to closely monitor every development in the Manning case. What the U.S. government was doing to Manning served as a template for what it could very well do to Assange. On the day of Manning's arraignment, February 23, 2012, Jennifer Robinson and I traveled down to the Army's Fort Meade in Maryland to witness the proceedings.

Though we were attorneys for an interested party, the Army made it hard to get in. They inspected our car and opened the trunk. Once on the base, we waited for hours. And then we walked into an antiseptic courtroom that looked like it belonged in a hospital—eight-foot Celotex ceiling, cheap carpet, bright lights.

The proceeding was supposed to be open to the public, but there was room in the audience for only about eight spectators and another 10 news reporters. Manning walked in, standing ramrod straight in full dress black uniform. Small and slight, with a short haircut and wireframe glasses, Manning sat down next to her attorney David Coombs.

The actual proceeding took about one hour as the government arraigned the 24-year-old Manning for leaking classified military and State Department documents to WikiLeaks. Manning was formally charged with 22 violations of the Uniform Code of Military Justice and the Espionage Act, including aiding the enemy (which carries a possible death sentence), wrongfully causing intelligence to be published on the internet, and theft of public property. The military judge, Col. Denise Lind, asked Manning to plead guilty or not guilty. But with a face that betrayed little emotion, the accused private first class opted to defer prosecution to a later date.

My own view is that there should never have been a prosecution of Manning. She was a whistleblower who found out about war crimes committed by her own government and revealed the evidence of those crimes. I want to see people in the military act out of idealism and conscience. That's how the atrocities at My Lai were exposed. That's what we rely on when governments anywhere act criminally and in secret.

I couldn't get over the irony of it all. On trial was the whistleblower who leaked documents showing the number of civilians killed in Iraq, the *Collateral Murder* video, Reuters journalists being killed, children being shot. To me, the people who should be the defendants were the ones who started the Afghan and Iraq wars, George W. Bush and Dick Cheney, the officials who carried out torture, the people who committed the very crimes that Manning and WikiLeaks exposed. And those who should be observing were the ghosts of the dead Reuters journalists and the ghosts of the children and others killed in Iraq and Afghanistan.

A week after Manning's arraignment, WikiLeaks published an internal e-mail dated January 26, 2011 from the private intelligence firm Strategic Forecasting (Stratfor). Part of a trove of five million e-mails that the hacker group Anonymous obtained from Stratfor's servers, it was written by Stratfor Vice President Fred Burton, a former State Department counter-terrorism expert. It stated clearly: "We have a sealed indictment on Assange. Pls protect." Another of Burton's e-mails was more vivid: "Assange is going to make a nice bride in prison. Screw the terrorist. He'll be eating cat food forever."

The e-mails revealed how far the U.S. government would go to protect its dirty secrets, and how it would use its own secrecy as a weapon. Somehow Stratfor, which has been called a shadow CIA, had information about this sealed indictment that neither WikiLeaks, Assange, nor his lawyers had.

In response, Assange released a statement: "Any student of American history knows that secret justice is no justice at all ... Secret grand juries with secret indictments are apparently [Attorney General] Eric Holder's preferred method of dealing with publishers who hold his administration to account. Eric Holder has betrayed the legacy of Madison and Jefferson. He should drop the case or resign."

Of course, Holder did neither. A week later, the FBI arrested 27-year-old Anonymous hacker Jeremy Hammond and indicted five others in three countries on charges of illegally hacking Stratfor. Imprisoned in Manhattan's Metropolitan Correctional Center and denied bail, Hammond was not allowed to examine the many thousands of documents the prosecution introduced, except in the presence of his lawyers. Since he was not allowed to look at anything online, in effect, this meant he could not participate in preparing for his own defense.

I visited Hammond at MCC. Tall and lanky with long hair and several tattoos, he wore a brown jumpsuit. He struck me as both reserved in his demeanor and deeply committed politically. Clearly he was brilliant—with an IQ of 168—and he described himself as an "anarchist-communist." As I listened to him recounting his 10-year political odyssey through various leftist political causes, eventually leading to his work with Anonymous, I realized that this young man who was approximately my son Jake's age represented a new generation of activists.

When I was his age, I'd been out in the streets demonstrating. But Hammond, Assange, and countless others had found a new way to fight for social change. Hammond was not a traditional whistleblower, revealing secret documents from inside, but a hacker breaking through layers of secrecy from outside to help the public understand what was going on. Though the law might view hackers as different from whistleblowers, in terms of their political mission, I could no longer make that distinction.

Ultimately Hammond decided to plead guilty to one count of violating the Computer Fraud and Abuse Act. I wrote a letter to Judge Loretta Preska asking that he be sentenced to time served because the documents he revealed "for the first time gave the American people a picture of the malevolent part that private intelligence corporations play in surveillance of constitutionally protected activities and activists...

"I raise this to point out the injustice and hypocrisy in prosecuting Mr. Hammond, a person committed to revealing this wrongdoing, while doing nothing to get at those who may have committed the very crimes he brought to light....

"In years of litigating cases involving surveillance, torture, renditions, and war crimes..., we are often met with claims by the government that the lawsuits cannot continue because the matters concern state secrets. Cases are routinely dismissed for this reason and the truth is neither revealed nor is the legality of the conduct litigated....

"It is for this reason that truth tellers like Mr. Hammond have become more and more important in insuring that people know what their government and private intelligence companies are doing in their names."

Ignoring this reasoning, Judge Preska sentenced Hammond to the maximum 10 years in federal prison. As of this writing, he remains imprisoned.

The pre-trial hearings in the Manning court-martial case continued, and I, along with Jennifer Robinson and other CCR attorneys, attended them. The proceedings, which I can describe only as a theater of the absurd, were bogged down by numerous off-the-record conferences held out of sight and hearing of the press and public. Although a couple of dozen members of the public could attend the trial, the court would not permit any transcripts of the proceedings. Nor were the media given access to the government's briefs about the motions being argued. So reporters had to scramble on breaks to compare notes about what had been said.

Perhaps more remarkable was the court's refusal even to provide the press and public with the judge's pre-trial publicity order that detailed what lawyers could and could not reveal about the case. Thus, even the degree to which proceedings had to be kept in secret was a secret, leaving the public and media in a Plato's Cave, able only to glimpse the shadows of reality.

CCR wrote two letters to the court specifically seeking release of the transcripts, filings, and court orders. The Reporters' Committee for Freedom of the Press, representing 47 media organizations including CBS, NBC, ABC, the *New York Times,* and the *Washington Post*, made a similar request. But on April 24, 2012, Judge Lind rejected our requests.

This was a clear violation of the law. The U.S. Supreme Court has insisted that criminal trials must be public, and the Fourth Circuit, where the Manning court-martial was occurring, has ruled that the First Amendment right of access to criminal trials includes the public's right to the documents in such trials. So in response to Judge Lind's ruling, CCR filed a lawsuit, *CCR v. Chief Judge Lind,* seeking a preliminary injunction ordering the judge to grant the public and press access to the government's motion papers, the court's own orders, and transcripts of the proceedings. Our fellow petitioners included media figures Glenn Greenwald, Amy Goodman of *Democracy Now!, The Nation's* Jeremy Scahill, and Julian Assange of WikiLeaks.

Predictably, after a year of litigation, the highest court in the military system, the Court of Appeals for the Armed Forces, ruled 3-to-2 that it lacked the power to hear claims by media petitioners seeking access to courts-martial. And since Congress has narrowly limited appeals from the military courts to the Supreme Court, we could not challenge that ruling.

Circuit Judge Damon Keith famously wrote in *Detroit Free Press v. Ashcroft,* "Democracies die behind closed doors." From the many layers of secrecy around Manning's arrest, imprisonment, and prosecution, it was evident that in this case the doors were tightly shut and democracy was in peril.

MOVING THE BAR

While Manning's pre-trial hearings proceeded in the summer of 2012, Julian Assange waited in Norfolk for his Swedish extradition case to be resolved. On June 14, the U.K. Supreme Court issued its verdict affirming the extradition order to Sweden. (Two years later, Parliament would change the law to require, as we had argued, that to be extradited, a person had to be formally charged in the country seeking extradition. But even that new law was not retroactive and didn't apply to Assange. His other lawyers and I called it "the Julian exception.")

The Supreme Court gave Assange 14 days to appeal to the European Court of Human Rights. It set July 7 as the date by which he had to return to Sweden. However, Swedish prosecutors immediately filed a motion asking that Assange be forced to return immediately. Before the Supreme Court could issue its ruling, Julian decided he couldn't wait any longer.

Taking his destiny into his own hands, he rode his motorcycle to the Ecuadorian embassy in London, entered, and asked for political asylum.

Located in a townhouse, the embassy is hardly lavish. One flight up from the ground entrance, it consists of a few small rooms, all on one floor of a Victorian brick building shared with the embassy of Colombia, and several private apartments. The embassy converted one room and a small bathroom into Julian's private living quarters. In the rear were a kitchenette and the embassy's working offices with desks, computers, and phones, and in the middle was a small conference room with a long table and chairs and heavy drapes covering all the windows.

It was in the conference room that I met with Julian's legal team a few days after he arrived at his new home. This would be the first of many such meetings in this room in the years ahead. Julian's case was like an extremely complicated law school hypothetical. The legal questions it posed were wide-ranging and novel, involving asylum, extradition, various jurisdictions, the U.N., international law, common law, and civil law. The team, consisting of accomplished international lawyers with varying specialties, was always changing. Sometimes as many as 15 lawyers were present, but at its core were Gareth Peirce, Jennifer Robinson, Ben Emmerson, Christophe Marchand who represented Assange before the European Court of Human Rights, Helena Kennedy, Guatemalan human rights lawyer Renata Avila, International Criminal Court lawyer Melinda Taylor, young American lawyer Carey Shenkman, and Swedish lawyers Thomas Olsson and Per Samuelsson. My role was to serve as a hub, coordinating and integrating the advice of all these lawyers and advising Julian on strategy. Julian almost always actively participated in the meetings, asking questions and voicing his concerns and views.

Julian's move to the embassy had come as a shock to all of us. Not even his closest advisers Sarah Harrison or Joseph Farrell knew about it. Julian had acted completely on his own, and now, with a new legal situation and a host of new problems, everything had to be re-evaluated and strategized anew.

"I had to act," Julian explained. "The British were about to turn me over to Sweden."

"Where you would be in prison without bail," I added. "The U.S. would have demanded immediate extradition, and you would have ended up like Manning."

"But why Ecuador?" asked Helena Kennedy.

"I interviewed President Correa a couple weeks ago on my Russian TV show," said Julian, "and he was very sympathetic. I thought I had an excellent chance to get asylum."

Helena shook her head. "Well, you're stuck here now," she said. "If you walk out the front door, you'll be arrested. The British police want you for jumping bail."

"And I imagine there are some pretty unhappy people who put up more than £300,000 in bail who won't be getting it back," added Jen Robinson.

"If I'm granted asylum, can I get out of here and go to Ecuador?" Julian asked.

"In my reading of the law, asylum trumps extradition agreements and bail jumping," I said. "The Ecuadorians could ask the British for a safe passage to get you out of London. But this is a political situation and there's no guarantee the British won't arrest you, even if you're in a diplomatic car. I think that might be illegal, but you'd be taking a big chance."

"So nobody really knows how long I might be here."

"Aren't we getting ahead of ourselves?" said Jen. "First Julian has to get asylum."

"We need someone who speaks Spanish to negotiate with the Ecuadorians," said Julian.

"Preferably someone with an international reputation and experience with European courts," said Helena. "Someone who can organize and direct this messy legal team."

There was silence for a moment. Then Renata said quietly, "Garzón."

Baltasar Garzón, the Spanish lawyer and judge, was known worldwide for prosecuting and imprisoning Chilean dictator Augusto Pinochet in 1998. He was the perfect choice to head Assange's legal team because his own experiences paralleled Julian's. In early 2012, Garzón lost his job as a judge in Spain because he wanted to open up the cases of 140,000 people who had disappeared during the Spanish Civil War in the 1930s. To prevent this, the right-wing Falange party launched a successful campaign to get him suspended from the bench.

Like Assange, Garzón was a truth teller. But he was also an excellent Spanish-speaking lawyer revered all over Latin America, and particularly in left-wing Ecuador. We all agreed. We had found the leader of WikiLeaks' legal team.

A silver-haired, stylish man in his mid-50s, Garzón joined us in July and immediately began negotiating Julian's political asylum with the Ecuadorians. Meanwhile, Julian settled into his 13x15-foot room at the embassy. Drapes covered his only window looking out on a dead-end street. He had a bed, a desk, and a computer. Film director Ken Loach donated a treadmill for exercise, but Julian had no place to cook or to get fresh air or sunshine.

It was far from a healthy long-term environment. Approximately a dozen London police officers patrolled the embassy 24 hours a day, ready to arrest Julian if he ventured outside. Ecuadorian ambassador Ana Albán's office was bugged, and the British Foreign Office threatened a raid on the embassy to take Julian into custody—an act that, if carried out, would be unprecedented in diplomatic history. To protect Julian, the Ecuadorian consul, Fidel Narváez, slept at the embassy while the Correa government considered Julian's asylum request.

As a journalist and publisher of WikiLeaks, Julian Assange had every right to asylum. The law is clear. The exercise of political free speech—including revealing government crimes, misconduct, or corruption—is internationally protected and is grounds for asylum. The U.S. government has recognized this right, having granted asylum to several journalists and whistleblowers, most notably from China.

On August 16, 2012, Foreign Minister Ricardo Patiño announced that Ecuador had granted Assange asylum under the U.N. Refugee Convention of 1951—to which Ecuador, Sweden, the U.K., and the U.S. are all signatories—and that the WikiLeaks publisher was welcome to stay at the embassy for as long as he liked. "We want to make it absolutely clear that we are not a British colony," said Patiño, "and that the times of colonialism are over."

When I heard the news, I was both thrilled and moved. By publishing the U.S. war logs and diplomatic cables, Julian Assange and WikiLeaks had stood up to the great powers of the world. And now the small country of Ecuador had also stood up to the great powers by simply doing what international law required.

From his room in the embassy, Julian continued to work on pending WikiLeaks releases. Faced with worldwide protests, the British government backed down on its threat to raid the embassy. But outside, the metropolitan police remained a constant presence, costing British taxpayers more than £12 million over the next few years.

Garzón was now leading the legal team, seeking a ruling from the European Court of Human Rights that Assange was being arbitrarily and indefinitely detained. Carey Shenkman had taken over some of my legal work, but I still visited Julian every month. I'd stay down the street from the embassy at the Capital Hotel. Each morning I'd go over to Harrods and buy some bagels or croissants and some exotic fruit to bring to Julian. Over breakfast and coffee, we'd discuss world political events, Julian's latest ideas, and any new twists in his legal situation.

By default, I had become WikiLeaks' primary spokesperson in the U.S. To represent my client, I had to monitor developments in the cases of several truth tellers the U.S. government was prosecuting. Perhaps the most heartbreaking of these was the case of internet freedom activist Aaron Swartz, who called me and Margaret Kunstler in late 2012. A prodigy internet activist, Swartz had designed DeadDrop, a way for whistleblowers to submit documents anonymously to journalists through an encrypted connection. And he'd led the fight to protect internet websites by defeating the proposed draconian Stop Online Piracy Act.

A quiet, modest, 27-year-old, Swartz was facing trial on federal charges that could have put him behind bars for 35 years. Acting on his belief that poor people around the world deserved equal access to humanity's collective knowledge, he had downloaded millions of academic articles from servers at the Massachusetts Institute of Technology and made them freely available online. Although the non-profit academic repository JSTOR dropped its civil charges against Swartz, the FBI and the U.S. attorney charged him with multiple felonies.

On the phone, Swartz was hesitant, but Margaret and I suggested that it was important for him to hire attorneys and fight back. In January 2013 he called me again in despair. The government had offered a plea bargain of six months in a minimum-security prison, but he was reluctant to take it because he would be forever labeled a felon. I tried to calm him, but I had a bad feeling when I hung up the phone.

A few days later, Aaron Swartz hanged himself in his Brooklyn apartment. Aaron's death disturbed me profoundly. In its zeal for secrecy, the U.S. government was prosecuting truth tellers, imprisoning them, and now even driving them to suicide. And visible and important cases were yet to come.

The most dangerous of these for WikiLeaks and Julian Assange was the Manning case. In November, I'd traveled to Fort Meade for a pre-trial hearing about the unspeakable treatment Manning had been subjected to since his arrest two and a half years earlier. For the first time, Manning was called to testify in person. What followed was one of the most dramatic courtroom scenes I've ever witnessed.

Though small in stature, Manning sat tall in the witness stand in a dress blue uniform, a tie, and white shirt. The entire courtroom was mesmerized, even the row of officers dressed in formal blue uniforms with epaulets on their shoulders. Press reports led everyone in the courtroom to expect Manning to be weak, fragile, and unable to function. Instead, the young intelligence analyst came across as confident, articulate, intelligent, strong, self-aware, totally credible, and very sympathetic.

In vivid detail Manning described the government's relentless attempt to break her down. For two months she was imprisoned in Kuwait by herself in an animal cage eight by eight feet with a small bed and a toilet. She ate all her meals in the cage and rarely was allowed out. The guards would keep Manning awake all night and let her go to sleep at around noon the next day. "I stopped keeping track," Manning said. "I didn't know whether night was day or day was night. And my world became very, very small.... I thought I was going to die in a cage."

Once Manning got to Quantico, Virginia, the abusive treatment continued under conditions that the U.N. Special Rapporteur, Juan Méndez, described as cruel, inhuman, and degrading. Manning was held in solitary confinement under suicide watch. To illustrate what this meant, Coombs asked Manning to step off the witness stand. And on the floor Coombs drew a chalk outline of the cell with a ruler, six by eight feet. Manning pointed out where the metal rack bed was and where the toilet and the sink were. In front of the cell, Manning testified, there was a mesh screen, but all she could see out of it was a man sitting in the observation booth watching her 24 hours a day.

A bright light shone on Manning all day, every day. When she tried to sleep, if she didn't face the light, guards would come in, wake her up, and turn her around. Once she woke up for reveille at 5 a.m., she was not allowed to lean against a wall or lie down. She could only stand or sit on the bunk with her feet on the ground. Manning stayed in that cell like that for 23½ hours a day—the other half hour she was let out for "exercise." And some of the time Manning was forced to stand naked for hours, supposedly because of a suicide risk, though psychiatrists told the prison administrator that Manning was no more likely to self-harm than any other prisoner.

This torture, reminiscent of the techniques used on Guantánamo detainees, continued for nine months. Manning's lawyer David Coombs said he believed his client was being subjected to these psychological tactics to coerce her into making a statement or false confession implicating my clients, WikiLeaks as an organization and Julian Assange personally.

On February 28, 2013, I again traveled down to Fort Meade. Manning had agreed to plead guilty to 10 of the lesser charges including uploading to WikiLeaks the Iraq and Afghan war logs and *Cablegate* documents and the *Collateral Murder* video—but not to the most serious charges of espionage and aiding the enemy. The judge allowed Manning to read aloud an extraordinary 30-page statement describing her time in the military, what she had done, and how she had come to her decisions.

Manning said her job as an intelligence analyst exposed her to daily log reports of what was happening in the field in both Afghanistan and Iraq. As she read the reports and realized how many innocent people were being killed, she became more and more disturbed and alienated. She thought a serious discussion of counterinsurgency was necessary, that the American people needed to know what was happening in their name and with their tax dollars. She was relieved when she uploaded the documents to WikiLeaks. Manning believed it might lead to a much-needed public discussion and a change in policy.

When Manning first saw the *Collateral Murder* video, it saddened her. "The most alarming aspect of the video," Manning said, "was the seemingly delightful bloodlust they [the soldiers in the helicopter] appeared to have. They dehumanized the individuals they were engaging and seemed to not value human life by referring to them as 'dead bastards' and congratulating each other on the ability to kill in large numbers."

Before uploading anything to WikiLeaks, Manning considered if her whistleblowing might cause harm. Of all the documents she uploaded, "the cables were the only ones I was not absolutely certain couldn't harm the United States," she said. "The more I read the cables, the more I came to the conclusion that this was the type of information that should become public.... I believed that the public release of these cables would not damage the United States."

For me, representing WikiLeaks and Assange, it was extremely important to hear Manning emphasize having acted alone. "The decisions that I made to send documents and information to the website were my own decisions," she said.

Though she communicated with WikiLeaks via online chat, she never knew who exactly was on the other end of the chat. Nor did WikiLeaks know who she was. So despite all the torture the military had subjected her to, Manning refused to implicate anyone at WikiLeaks in her decisions. She said WikiLeaks did not seek to influence or pressure her in any way. It acted just as any other journalistic enterprise would when receiving documents from a whistleblower.

With this statement, Manning had pleaded guilty to charges that could send her to prison for 20 years. She'd done it voluntarily, not as part of a plea bargain. The prosecutor could still go ahead with the more serious charges.

The statement was powerful and moving because it showed the kind of person Manning was. When she saw wrong, she could not sit back and do nothing. She had to act. To me, this maligned, misunderstood 24-year-old Army private had shown that she was a true hero.

Amid ongoing worldwide protests, Manning's court-martial trial began on June 3, 2013 and ended on July 30, 2013. I attended the opening and closing arguments and some of the other sessions. They took place in that same sanitized, small courtroom witnessed by only a handful of spectators and a few reporters.

After previously pleading guilty to 10 counts, Manning now was facing charges on another 12 counts. These included 6 of espionage, which together carried a potential sentence of 136 years in prison, and one of aiding the enemy, which carried a potential sentence of death. The trial was predictable and unsurprising. In both its opening and closing arguments, the prosecution smeared Manning, calling her a "traitor," portraying her as an "anarchist" who sought fame by indiscriminately providing hundreds of thousands of classified documents to WikiLeaks. Of course, this made no sense because all the evidence showed that Manning, rather than seeking the limelight, had actually done everything she could to remain anonymous.

The prosecution's most serious and most outrageous charge against Manning was that she had aided the enemy. The aiding-the-enemy statute applies only to people in the military. It says if you give intelligence directly or indirectly to the enemy, and your intent is for the enemy to have that intelligence and harm the United States, you can be considered to be aiding the enemy. The enemy here, the government claimed, was al-Qaeda.

The prosecution tried to prove that once the Afghanistan and Iraq war logs were released, Osama bin Laden received some of those documents, which were found after his death on his computer in Pakistan. It's true that Manning gave the documents to WikiLeaks and that bin Laden, like anyone else, could download them from the WikiLeaks website. But it was the government's theory that was truly dangerous to the United States. It basically said that a military whistleblower who gives documents to any media, no matter what the whistleblower's intent, is automatically guilty of aiding the enemy—and can be sentenced to death.

It was clear to me that the prosecution was trying not just to convict Manning but to set the stage for a later prosecution of WikiLeaks and Julian Assange. The chief prosecutor claimed that WikiLeaks was not a journalistic enterprise, that it was a group of "information anarchists." And he tried to paint WikiLeaks and Julian Assange as Manning's co-conspirators. I was astonished that in the opening argument alone, the prosecutor mentioned Assange 10 times, WikiLeaks at least 20 times.

The Manning trial was part and parcel of the government's ongoing attempt to clamp down on our free press and to get rid of dissent in the military. Whether the prosecution won or lost, by charging Manning with aiding the enemy, it had created two terrible, chilling effects that could end whistleblowing. First, anybody in the military thinking of leaking documents or talking to the press about, for example, bad body armor or bad food in the military now knew that they would be taking their life in their hands, risking a death penalty charge.

Second, any publisher, whether WikiLeaks or the *New York Times*, now knew that if it published national security information provided by a whistleblower—specifically, if it exposed embarrassing information on criminality and hypocrisy within our own government—it risked charges of aiding the enemy.

Near the end of the trial, the *Washington Post* revealed the extraordinary news that Judge Denise Lind had been given a promotion: she would become a judge on the Army's Criminal Court of Appeals. It reminded me of something similar that happened to the presiding federal judge during Daniel Ellsberg's Pentagon Papers trial on espionage charges. The Nixon administration secretly offered him the job as director of the FBI. When the news leaked, there was a huge uproar, and the promotion never happened. But this time there was barely a whisper in the media about Judge Lind being offered a position on a higher court that Manning would have to appeal to if convicted. Like so much of this sham court-martial, it may have been legal, but it had a distinct odor to it.

In his summation for the defense, Manning's lawyer, David Coombs, made the young private's intent crystal clear. Manning released the documents because she wanted to encourage a public debate on the issues. She had no intention of aiding al-Qaeda or any other enemy of the United States and she certainly had no idea whether bin Laden would read the documents or not. Coombs painted a picture of a sincere young person who wore a dog tag that said "humanist," who wanted to do good for her country and her fellow soldiers, who saw horrible human rights violations and wanted the American public to know about them.

When Judge Lind issued her verdict on July 30, 2013, she found Manning not guilty of the most serious charge of aiding the enemy. But she found Manning guilty of all the other charges, including espionage. Until that moment, there had never been a conviction of a whistleblower for espionage in the entire 100-year history of the espionage statute. She sentenced Manning to 35 years in prison and a dishonorable discharge.

[Editor's Note: In the final days of his second term in the White House, President Barack Obama commuted Manning's sentence. She was finally released from confinement on May 17, 2017, after serving seven years in prison. In March 2019, she was called before a federal grand jury investigating WikiLeaks. She refused to testify and was again held in solitary confinement.]

In early June 2013, shortly after the Manning court-martial trial had begun, I heard shocking news from the other side of the world. A mysterious whistleblower had met in a Hong Kong hotel room with journalists Glenn Greenwald, Laura Poitras, and Ewen MacAskill and given them thousands of classified NSA documents revealing details of the agency's mass surveillance operations.

Beginning June 5, explosive articles began appearing in the *Guardian*, the *Washington Post, Der Spiegel,* and the *New York Times.* The first story revealed that a secret FISA (Foreign Intelligence Surveillance Act) court had ordered the telecommunications giant Verizon to turn over to the NSA all of the metadata it had on phone calls in the United States and elsewhere—how long the calls were, what cell towers they were from, to whom, etc. From that data, the NSA could construct a tree of everybody's contacts and glean a wide range of information about people's connections, both political and personal.

This was an important story because it showed just how pervasive mass surveillance is and how the secret FISA court had misinterpreted its powers under the Foreign Intelligence Act. Many of us, including me, had talked about the surveillance state in the privacy of our living rooms and even in public interviews, but these documents provided concrete proof of what we had only suspected.

The PRISM story hit front pages worldwide the next day, June 6. It revealed that the NSA has direct access to internet data held by corporate cyber giants like Google and Yahoo. Through our computers and phones, the NSA can monitor and store the content of our data—e-mails, texts, internet searches, online purchases, information sent to and from our computers and phones. For example, if I give a speech in support of my clients Julian Assange and WikiLeaks, the NSA can say, "Let's see what we've got on Ratner. Let's see what his doctors know about him. Let's see what he's doing, where he's been, who his friends and political contacts are, what he's bought, what phone calls he's made, what e-mails he's sent." It's a pervasive surveillance system that stores information in NSA files for a very long time, if not forever.

These revelations had two immediate results. First, they proved that James Clapper, the Director of National Intelligence, was a perjurer. On March 12, 2013, Senator Ron Wyden of Oregon had asked Clapper at a congressional hearing whether the NSA collected any type of data at all on hundreds of millions of Americans. Clapper answered, "No, sir. [...] Not wittingly." Clear, 100 percent perjury, and before Congress, no less. The question we have to ask: while the government was busy indicting a record number of whistleblowers, why has Clapper never been indicted for perjury?

Second, the revelations showed that the NSA had illegally been handing over information to the FBI to be used in domestic cases. In criminal cases, one of the first things a defense attorney does is to ask if any of the evidence came from electronic surveillance. In the old days, when prosecutors didn't want to reveal their source, they would occasionally drop the indictment. But now they use evidence from the NSA to then go get a "real" warrant to wiretap a person's phone. Then they use the wiretapped evidence in court because they can show they had a warrant to obtain it. But such tainted evidence is what we call the "fruit of the poisonous tree," an unauthorized use of electronic surveillance. The FBI and prosecutors were never willing to reveal this. And they repeatedly lied to the courts about it.

Each day a new bombshell story landed. And there would be many more to come, including the revelation that the U.S. had spied not only on many of its allies, but on 35 world leaders. These included German

Chancellor Angela Merkel, who protested the surveillance and compared the NSA to the infamous East German intelligence agency Stasi.

Still, no one could identify the source for these stories. On June 9, I was in Colorado listening to Julian Assange's Skype presentation on a big screen in a hall. Julian said, "The surveillance state has gotten so huge, they have to hire thousands of young computer-savvy people, all under 30, to do the work. And among those people, there are going to be some who do not share the politics of a government that is doing this kind of massive surveillance."

Two hours later, I got the news on my computer: Edward Snowden had voluntarily identified himself as the source of the NSA leaks. "I do not want to live in a world where everything I do and say is recorded," he explained. "My sole motive is to inform the public as to that which is done in their name and that which is done against them."

Snowden amazed me because he came forward in the face of the most horrendous government repression of whistleblowers in U.S. history. Despite my reservations about many of his policy views, I had voted for Barack Obama for president in 2008 because I knew his election would be historic and I wanted to say to my children that I had voted for the first Black president of the United States. I'm still glad I did it, but Obama has disappointed me many times since then—particularly on the issue of whistleblowing.

In Obama's first three years in the White House, his Justice Department prosecuted six different cases under the Espionage Act— more than the number of prosecutions brought by all other administrations combined since the Espionage Act was passed in 1917. Despite Obama's claims that he wanted a more open government, his actions revealed the opposite—a growing obsession with secrecy and a willingness to prosecute investigative journalists. People can debate technical violations of the law, but in the end, what the Manning/WikiLeaks/

Assange/Snowden cases were about was simple: the United States government was trying to suppress the truth.

And yet, knowing this, Edward Snowden found the courage to reveal to all of us the nature of the surveillance state we're living in. A near-perfect match for the profile that Julian had outlined, Snowden was a 29-year-old former CIA computer specialist who had worked in Hawaii for NSA contractor Booz Allen Hamilton and had virtually unlimited access to the NSA's classified data.

With a libertarian political perspective very different from my own, Snowden had become gradually disillusioned over several years as he saw the range and power of the surveillance state grow. The last straw was when he watched James Clapper lie to Congress. At that moment, he decided the American people needed to know the truth and he would do what was necessary to get it out to them. He copied thousands of NSA documents and smuggled them out before taking a leave of absence from his job and flying to Hong Kong.

As I watched the events unfold, I had great admiration for Snowden. But neither I nor WikiLeaks had anything to do with him or his revelations—at least not yet. On June 21, the U.S. Justice Department charged Snowden with violating the Espionage Act of 1917 and theft of government property. Trying to stave off extradition, Snowden was stuck in Hong Kong, exploring his options with a trio of local lawyers. Since Snowden had revealed that the Chinese government was among those that U.S. surveillance had targeted, Hong Kong officials were in no hurry to grant American extradition requests.

Meanwhile, unbeknownst to me, Julian Assange was working behind the scenes. He dispatched his trusted WikiLeaks associate Sarah Harrison to Hong Kong to help Snowden find a country willing to provide political asylum. Assange himself arranged with Ecuadorian diplomats for necessary travel documents for Snowden. The plan was for the whistleblower to fly to Moscow, connect to Cuba, and end up in Venezuela or Ecuador.

On June 23, Hong Kong authorities delayed extradition by asking the U.S. for more information about its request. Snowden and Harrison seized the moment and boarded an Aeroflot flight to Moscow. Upon arrival in Moscow, they found out that the U.S. State Department had revoked Snowden's passport. They were not only stuck in Russia, but in the airport itself.

The Snowden affair had become the biggest news story on the planet. Julian decided to hold a telephone press conference to clarify WikiLeaks's role. At the last minute, he asked Jennifer Robinson and me to join him, which we did without any preparation.

Speaking from the Ecuadorian embassy in London, Julian told more than 500 reporters that WikiLeaks had been in contact with Snowden, had paid for his plane ticket, and helped him apply for political asylum. He added that Snowden was healthy, "his spirits are high," and that a WikiLeaks legal team was advising him.

At this point, I had to jump in before he got himself, someone else, or CCR in trouble. "I have to clarify that the Center for Constitutional Rights represents WikiLeaks," I said, "but it does not represent Edward Snowden and is not advising him." In fact, we'd had no contact with Snowden. Nor had Jennifer Robinson or any of WikiLeaks's lawyers.

After the press conference, Jen and I talked on the phone. Requests for interviews were pouring in, and we had to figure out a strategy. Snowden was being publicly condemned as a traitor and no one was coming to his support. Even the Freedom of the Press Foundation told us they were going to have to cut off funding to WikiLeaks because it was aiding and abetting a fugitive. (Later the Foundation changed its mind and added Snowden to its board.)

Jen was young and justifiably terrified, but she was Julian's lawyer, and she was on the scene in London. "Julian has put WikiLeaks out there," I said, "so you just have to go and face the reporters. Tell them Snowden is a fugitive, he has the right to remain silent, but we are not advising him.

He needs to get his own representation, apart from WikiLeaks, and we will help him find appropriate lawyers."

Jen did a fine job, and afterwards we talked. We both agreed Julian was doing the right thing by helping Snowden. But we were frustrated. Julian had acted without consulting us and had said things to the press that might incriminate himself, Sarah Harrison, and possibly others who had aided Snowden.

"He acts out of principle, not self-preservation," said Jen. "Anybody who puts himself first would protect himself, but Julian just doesn't do that."

That was true, but Julian had said things at that press conference that any lawyer would caution him against saying. I said to Jen, "Now it's going to be more difficult for us to get him out of that embassy."

Nonetheless, we both had to admire Julian for supporting Snowden when almost no one else did. Without the daring work done by Julian and Sarah Harrison, there's no doubt that Snowden would be in a U.S. prison today.

The public condemnation of Snowden made clear to me how much had changed since the earliest part of my legal career. In the '70s, the U.S. government also used mass surveillance. Obviously it wasn't on the same scale because the internet and sophisticated computers didn't exist, but the government monitored our phone calls and our mail, and there were informants in our political groups.

Unlike today, however, back then the public was outraged. Congress was outraged. The Church Committee held public hearings about this illegal intrusion into our private and political lives. And Congress passed laws to stop it. But Snowden's revelations proved that those laws were no longer effective. And equally disturbing, opposition to mass surveillance seems to have vanished. The idea that surveillance is being used to stop terrorism has been sold again and again in our mainstream media, despite the fact that the government has provided no evidence that surveillance has prevented even a single incident of terrorism.

My view is that mass surveillance is not really about preventing terrorism, but is much more about social control. It's about stopping an uprising like the ones we had here in the U.S. in the '60s and '70s. It shocks me that Americans are passively allowing this and that all three branches of government have done nothing about it.

Despite mass surveillance, my message for people is the same one that Mother Jones delivered a century ago: organize, organize, organize. Yes, the surveillance state will try to scare you. They will be watching and listening. You won't even know whether your best friend is an informant. Take whatever security precautions you can. But do not be intimidated. Whether you call it the sweep of history or the sweep of revolution, in the end, the surveillance state cannot stop people from moving toward the kind of change that will make their lives better.

Snowden remained in limbo in Moscow, seeking asylum. Sarah Harrison stayed with him. It took months, but eventually Russia granted Snowden asylum and a temporary residence permit until 2020, when he would be eligible to apply for Russian citizenship.

Her job in Moscow done, Harrison moved to Berlin. She was a British citizen and her family lived in London, but the WikiLeaks legal team warned her that it could be unsafe for her to return to the U.K. where national-security journalism was being treated as terrorism.

From Berlin, Sarah wrote an open letter that I found very moving. "In these times of secrecy and abuse of power there is only one solution—transparency....When whistleblowers come forward, we need to fight for them, so others will be encouraged. When they are gagged, we must be their voice. When they are hunted, we must be their shield. When they are locked away, we must free them. Giving us the truth is not a crime. This is our data, our information, our history. We must fight to own it."

She signed it "Sarah Harrison" with the following: "Courage is contagious."

I was very concerned about Harrison. Having helped Snowden, she could all too easily become a pawn in a much bigger legal battle if her situation wasn't handled with care. In 2014, I traveled to Berlin for an international conference on the defense of whistleblowers. While there, I arranged to meet with Harrison, along with Margaret Ratner Kunstler and the British journalist Victoria Brittain. We felt it was in Sarah's best interest to have a lawyer with no connection to WikiLeaks. Victoria found one in England who got her a new passport, and Sarah was eventually able to return to the U.K. without any repercussions.

The whistleblowing conference in Berlin ended on a boat with a birthday party for Wolfgang Kaleck, founder of the European Center for Constitutional and Human Rights. I found myself squirreled away in a corner with several representatives from a group called the Landless Peasants Movement of Brazil (MST). They told me about their struggle to get land back for a million and a half displaced or impoverished farmers. After an hour or so, they started asking me all about Julian Assange, WikiLeaks, Chelsea Manning, and Ed Snowden.

I said, "Why do you, a movement of landless farmers in Brazil, have so much interest in these whistleblowers?"

They said, "All of this work, all of this material from Snowden, from WikiLeaks, from Chelsea Manning, it's all a blow against imperialism."

In a few simple words, those Brazilian farmers crystallized for me the global importance of the truth tellers I'd been defending. Whether you call it imperialism or U.S. hegemony or empire, that is what truth tellers like Manning, Assange, Snowden, and Hammond have been exposing in recent years. They have revealed to us different aspects of how this economic empire functions—secrets that shouldn't be secret, information that the public needs to know. And that is why the government of the United States is coming down so heavily on them.

By mid-2014, Julian Assange and WikiLeaks had been celebrated for their pioneering work with numerous international awards, including the Amnesty International U.K. Media Award, the Martha Gellhorn Prize for Journalism, and the Yoko Ono Lennon Courage Award for the Arts. But the governments of Sweden and the U.K. still refused to recognize the political asylum Ecuador had granted Assange two years before. And as a result, Julian was still confined to one small room in the Ecuadorian embassy in London.

More than 100 lawyers with different specialties had volunteered to represent Julian and WikiLeaks in various venues. I continued to participate in legal decisions and WikiLeaks strategy, but in truth Julian was no longer just a client to me. He had become a personal friend.

I admired his strength, his keen intelligence, and his unflappable courage. But I also saw how confinement was wearing on him. Unable to go outside for fresh air or sunshine, he looked pale, his skin pasty. He couldn't shop for fresh food and didn't have a fully-equipped kitchen, so his diet was limited. Though he exercised on a treadmill, his once rail-thin body seemed softer. He hadn't had access to proper medical care, and though he had thousands of supporters all over the world, visits from his immediate family and closest friends were necessarily limited.

Every time I saw him, the injustice of the situation hit me hard. In Sweden, with no charges filed against him, he was still wanted for questioning. He'd offered to answer any questions in London or via Skype, but the Swedish prosecutor insisted that he must set foot in Sweden. Four years after the initial allegations, the Swedish appeals court refused to rescind the original arrest warrant, but it did reprimand Ny, the prosecutor, for failing to move the investigation forward in a timely fashion. It was a not-so-subtle way to pressure her to go to London to question Julian in the Ecuadorian embassy. Still, the prosecutor seemed in no hurry to comply.

With further appeals to Sweden's highest court dragging on, we decided to bring Julian's case to the attention of the United Nations in two different ways. The first was to appeal to the U.N. Working Group on Arbitrary Detention (WGAD). In our briefs, written primarily by Melinda Taylor and Carey Shenkman, we argued that a person is effectively detained when forced to choose between confinement and running the risk of persecution. That is the precise dilemma Julian faced then.

Both Sweden and the U.K. submitted counter briefs and evidence to the WGAD, which took 16 months to investigate and come to a decision. In February 2016, the WGAD issued its ruling that Sweden and the U.K. had arbitrarily detained Julian Assange since December 7, 2010, including his time in prison, on conditional bail, and in the embassy. The decision was a major victory for Julian and WikiLeaks. The WGAD said Assange should be freed immediately, and in addition he was entitled to compensation from the governments of Sweden and the U.K.

The ruling set an important precedent in international human rights law for refugees and whistleblowers. U.N. High Commissioner for Human Rights Zeid Ra'ad al-Hussein stressed that the ruling was binding under international law and urged Sweden and the U.K. to comply with it. However, prosecutors in the U.K. and Sweden immediately rejected the decision. U.K. Secretary of State for Foreign and Commonwealth Affairs Philip Hammond called it "ridiculous" and said U.K. police would arrest Assange should he leave the Ecuadorian embassy. We had won a favorable decision for our clients, but the relevant authorities chose to defy the law, and we had no way to enforce it.

Pursuing our second initiative to the U.N., CCR submitted a report on the protection of whistleblowers to David Kaye, the U.N. Special Rapporteur on the Protection of the Right to Freedom of Expression. Kaye was conducting a review of national and international whistleblowing laws. He'd asked governments and NGOs with relevant experience to share their views about how to improve protections for journalists, sources, and whistleblowers.

Our report pointed out that the U.S. has in the past offered asylum to whistleblowers from Albania, Armenia, Azerbaijan, Bangladesh, Cameroon, China, Honduras, India, Italy, Philippines, Russia, South Korea, Switzerland, Ukraine, and Uzbekistan. They received protection because their governments persecuted them for their free speech activities.

However, when the whistleblower reveals the U.S. government's own wrongdoings—as in the cases of Manning, Assange, Hammond, and others—American authorities go to extraordinary lengths to stifle, marginalize, suppress, and punish the whistleblower for their actions. Therefore, we stressed, "States have an obligation to protect whistleblowers, a vulnerable group that faces systematic stigmatization as a result of exercising fundamental rights to access and obtain information."

But we made it clear that whistleblowers are not the only vulnerable group. "CCR's experiences representing WikiLeaks and Julian Assange underscore the issue that persecution and censorship of whistleblowers… encompasses human rights monitors and publishers as well. The ultimate effect of these restrictions is an unacceptable chilling on the free flow of information, rights to access information, and freedom of expression."

U.N. Special Rapporteur Kaye issued his final report in late 2015, incorporating many of our recommendations. The report called for national laws assuring the right of access to information in accordance with international human rights standards, protecting the confidentiality of sources and whistleblowers, and also protecting sources and whistleblowers from retaliation. In addition, it recommended expanding protections beyond traditional journalists to publishers, bloggers, citizen journalists, NGOs, authors, and academics.

The report went a long way to setting international standards for the protection of whistleblowers. But one category it failed to mention was hackers who are also whistleblowers. As governments increasingly keep secrets from the public, I have come to recognize the unique contributions of hacker-whistleblowers. Though technically they may be breaking laws, hackers like Jeremy Hammond and Aaron Swartz have given the public vital information that we had no other way of accessing. It is now impossible for me to say, "Protect whistleblowers, journalists, and publishers, but prosecute hackers." In my mind, if they are revealing information that the public has a right to know, they are all truth tellers and need to be protected equally.

By July 2015, Julian had been in custody for five years, three of them confined to the Ecuadorian embassy. That might have broken most people. Not Julian Assange. The work of WikiLeaks continued, and in mid-2015 it published a flurry of new secret documents, including:

- Half a million cables from the Saudi Arabian foreign ministry to its own consulates around the world, exposing the inner workings of an erratic and secretive dictatorship.
- Documents revealing that the NSA had carried out surveillance on high-level officials in France, including the last three presidents, 29 top government officials in Brazil, and 125 top government officials in the German government of Chancellor Angela Merkel.
- A previously secret text of the largest trade deal in history, the corporate-friendly Trade in Services Agreement. The last of a trio of neoliberal trade agreements pushing globalization, TISA would allow giant multinational corporations to skip over borders and undercut local services and businesses by reducing regulations in signatory countries. WikiLeaks had previously revealed texts of the two earlier agreements—the

Trans-Pacific Partnership and the Trans-Atlantic Trade and Investment Pact.

All of these extraordinary revelations were made by WikiLeaks while Julian Assange was still confined in the Ecuadorian embassy in London.

I have asked myself, "Why are truth tellers like Assange, Manning, Snowden, and Hammond so important to me?" The answer is that they have succeeded in doing what CCR and I have been trying to do ever since the so-called war on terror began in the wake of September 11, 2001. For more than a decade, we lawyers at CCR brought at least a dozen lawsuits seeking to expose and end rendition, illegal drone strikes, the wars in Afghanistan and Iraq, and the torture at Guantánamo and other U.S. secret prisons. We tried to hold accountable those responsible for war crimes. But each time the government would go into court and say, "You can't litigate this. National security." Every lawsuit was dismissed. Even in the open-and-shut case of Maher Arar, a Canadian citizen who was taken off a plane at Kennedy Airport, sent to Syria, and tortured, we couldn't get past the Circuit Court. And the one time we did win at the Supreme Court with *Rasul v. Bush* (see Chapter 9) it was impossible to enforce the ruling.

We had reached a dead end. Then, all of a sudden, people like Chelsea Manning, Julian Assange, Edward Snowden, Sarah Harrison, Aaron Swartz, and Jeremy Hammond came out of nowhere. With acts of great courage, they revealed to the world what this country is actually doing. They sparked a much-needed public discussion of the U.S. government's secret, illegal, and inhumane policies. And they brought people into the streets. As a result, we're seeing the unraveling of governments and corporations all over the world.

My experience has taught me that the truth has a way of coming out, even when the most powerful government on earth tries to crush it. Each time a whistleblower, a publisher, or a hacker has been jailed, tortured, or driven to suicide, other truth tellers have come forward. And there will be many more.

(Editor's Note: In April 2019, British police invaded the Ecuadorian embassy in London and forcibly arrested Assange for jumping bail. On May 22, 2019, the U.S. government issued an 18-count indictment against Assange, charging him with violation of the Espionage Act. As of this writing, Assange remains in a British prison in extremely poor health and is fighting extradition to the U.S.)

2
IN THE BEGINNING

I was born during the war. But as someone born in the United States, which has been at war for more than seven decades, this hardly narrows it down. More specifically, I was born in Cleveland, Ohio on June 13, 1943, in the midst of World War II. Even as my parents were joyfully celebrating their first son, millions of other Jews, including many of my relatives, were being murdered in Europe. Two months after my birth, Nazi soldiers destroyed the ghetto in my father's hometown of Białystok, Poland.

I doubt my mother and father were fully aware of the horrors of the war. Reliable information was hard to come by, and their imaginations could not have conjured up such slaughter. Afterwards, no one in our house ever brought up that loaded question—*Did you know?* But the collective trauma had its effects. Growing up, my siblings and I learned to hate everything German: no German cars, no German products of any kind, and certainly no German holidays. By contrast, in reaction to the Holocaust, my parents taught us to love, respect, and revere everything to do with our large Jewish family.

My father Harry had eight siblings. His parents, Moishe and Pesha Ratowzer, owned a small weaving factory—the first in Poland to have electric looms—and the family enjoyed a solid middle-class life in the industrial city of Białystok. But in 1920 the new Communist government nationalized the weaving factory, and the Ratowzer family had to decide whether to stay in Poland or leave for America.

The Ratowzers already had a base in Cleveland, where my father's older siblings Charlie and Freida had been living for more than a decade. My father's brother Charlie—or Kallman, as he was then known—was legendary in our family. He had fled Poland at the age of 13. The story goes that he had either been a courier for anti-czar rebels or had been caught at school standing on a desk singing the Communist anthem, "The Internationale." The Ratowzer family—small businessmen, rabbis, and scholars—were not radical and frowned upon such behavior. In any case, Charlie's teacher advised Moishe and Pesha to get him out of the country.

They sent Charlie to a relative in New York, with whom he didn't get along. He sang on the streets of the Lower East Side for a penny a song, soon made his way to another relative in Cleveland, and eventually joined the U.S. Army, which dispatched him to Panama and Mexico.*

Shortly after leaving the Army in June 1920, Charlie returned to Białystok and knocked on the Ratowzer family's door. One of his sisters answered, but didn't recognize him. He was now a handsome six-foot-tall man of nearly 30, and she had been tiny when he'd left. He asked in Yiddish if her parents were in.

"No one is here," she said, suspicious.

"If you weren't my sister," he replied, "I could fall in love with you."

His parents recognized him immediately, of course, and showered him with kisses, tears, and passionate embraces. Charlie announced he was taking them to the United States. Notwithstanding the pogroms

---

* Charlie was good with numbers, and made enough money playing cards to start what became a family lumber business. This eventually did extremely well, and, still only in his forties, he retired to Miami Beach in the 1930s when his wife needed a change of climate. While there he established another lumber company and built one of the earliest Art Deco hotels in South Beach, named for our hometown—The Clevelander.

and wars that had ravaged that part of Poland, not everyone was eager to leave. My grandparents had an extended network of relatives in Białystok and throughout the Jewish Pale. But in the end, they decided to move the family to America.

My father and his older brother Leonard couldn't leave Poland legally. They were both draft age and subject to military service. So when my father was about 16 (we were never able to establish his birth year), Leonard, Charlie, and he sneaked across the border to Germany, disguised as cattle herders. Once over the border, they hid in haystacks on a farm, waiting for friends to pick them up. But border guards arrived first and stuck pitchforks in the haystacks, injuring Charlie and forcing the others to come out. The three young men were taken into custody, but family lore has it that Charlie bribed a guard and they escaped the next day.

In Germany, the brothers needed to acquire visas from the American consulate to secure passage aboard a ship from Hamburg to the United States. Charlie went to see the consul in Germany, who could see immediately that Leonard's and my father's passports were forged. Charlie was having great difficulty until the consul spotted the Masons ring on his finger: Charlie was a 32nd degree Mason and, evidently, the consul was a Mason as well. He issued the visas, and my father and Leonard took an ocean liner to New York. The passenger manifest for the *Aquitania* listed my father's name as "Oscar Ratowzer," his "race or people" as "Hebrew," and his "calling or occupation" as "worker."

Within a few months, my father's parents and five of his siblings also sailed to America, though my Aunt Fannye's 10-year-old twin brother, Joseph, took ill on the voyage and died shortly after arrival. By the time the whole family finally got to Cleveland, its name had been changed from Ratowzer to Ratner. The siblings shared a house with their parents and gave all money they earned to grandmother Pesha, who would then dole it back out from the kitty as needed.

MOVING THE BAR

As a teenager speaking no English, my father began work as a "water boy" on construction jobs, transporting water in a bucket to pour into a trough for mixing cement. Within a few years, he and several of his siblings saved up enough money to open a creamery, a small deli/convenience store that sold canned goods and milk. The creamery didn't stock fresh items that the larger A&P behind them could sell more cheaply, so when a customer asked for strawberries, my father or one of my uncles would dash out the back door, buy strawberries from A&P, and sell them at the same price.

After the creamery, the brothers started a family lumber business. But my father had a deeply rooted independent streak, and there was an element of competition between him and his siblings. So he decided to go out on his own. In the 1930s, insulation was just beginning to be mass-produced in the United States, and my father wanted to get in on the game. He moved to another state and worked in a factory for a few months to see how it was done. He then returned to Cleveland and established his own company. A fire burnt down his factory and he couldn't afford to rebuild it, but my father kept going with sheer determination and initiative. Whatever it took, he was going to make it.

He bought a truck and started delivering coal. Eventually the coal business developed into a building-supply business—concrete, bricks, mortar, etc. for construction companies. The building-supply business put him in the position of knowing what real estate deals were coming up. Partnering with contractors, he expanded the business, and by the late 1930s he'd become a successful developer of housing complexes, shopping centers, and mini-malls.

Even when he had partners, my father always ran his business by himself, and he liked to do things fast. He told us in his Yiddish accent how he conducted a board meeting. "I stand in front of a mirror and say, 'I vant to do this. How do we vote?' The person in the mirror says 'Yes.' And that's my board meeting."

IN THE BEGINNING

Balding, stocky, and strong, my father had a charismatic personality, taking over any room he entered. He was the last in the family to marry and had a reputation as a man about town—or at least in the Jewish and Italian immigrant parts of town. He had many girlfriends, who were often much taller than he was. At five foot three, he had to stand on a box to kiss them. He also loved to gamble and frequented the Mounds Club, an illegal casino run by the Mafia. My father knew the gangsters well because his building-supply business used truck drivers from the Teamsters, a mob-controlled union.

He spent most of his weekends at a cottage on Lake Erie where he threw many parties. I have photos of him on the beach by the lake, surrounded by bachelor friends, his brothers, and young women. One of these women was Betty. My father approached her and said, "You're too tall for me, but I have a brother Max and he is right." Soon enough, Betty and Max were married.

I have another photo of my father standing beside a horse and embracing two tall women wearing one-piece Esther Williams-style bathing suits. He owned several horses and loved riding, as did several of his siblings. As children in early 1900s Poland, riding had been practically a necessity—not English show-riding, with fancy stables and jumping, but racing through the woods at breakneck speed with no helmets. Once in the United States, my father would buy high-strung racehorses, ride fearlessly, get thrown, break an arm, and get up and ride again.

In 1942, at the beach near his cottage, my father first met my mother. Anne Spott was 22, strikingly pretty, with long black hair. Unlike my father, she came from a very poor family. Her mother Yetta was born in 1877 in Warsaw, and her father Bernard in 1862 in a small town near Krakow, in an impoverished part of the Austrian Empire. They emigrated to America, and in 1918 my mother was born in Cleveland, the second youngest of 12 siblings.

MOVING THE BAR

The Spotts were an Orthodox Jewish family. The home was strictly kosher, and on Sabbath no one cooked or drove or even used light switches. Anne's father worked as a tinner, roofer, and peddler. He thought of himself as a scholar, learned in Judaism. But he also drank and beat his wife and children, and his family considered him a bully.

As a girl, my mother spent hours in libraries. Movies were too expensive, and she read for free. It was a tough life. The family moved from rental house to rental house, lying about the number of kids to convince landlords to rent to them.

My mother attended a vocational high school, learned secretarial skills, and became an exceptionally fast speed-typist. Although accepted into college, she didn't have the $50 tuition, so she didn't go. Instead, she took a job as a legal secretary.

When she met my father, he was 15 years older and under familial pressure to settle down. My mother was getting over her first love. Because the man wasn't Jewish, her family had insisted she end the relationship. My father, on the other hand, represented security. Marrying into the Ratners—even in 1942, when my father was by no means rich— was a big deal in the Jewish immigrant community. The Ratners had all done well for themselves in business, and there were no "bad apples." Very soon after they met, my parents married.

The wedding took place at my Uncle Max's house in Cleveland Heights. Photos and 16 millimeter silent Kodacolor home movies show my mother Anne, beautiful and demure, in a powder-blue dress and padded, tassled jacket. She's standing next to her youngest sister, Ruth, carrying a big bouquet of pink orchids. Only a couple of inches taller than his bride, my father, then 38, beams at her and radiates joy.

Within a year, I was born. My parents named me after my recently deceased paternal grandfather Moishe (anglicized as Michael). My brother Bruce, whose name honored our maternal grandmother Beryl, arrived a year and a half later. And our sister Ellen came next, born in 1951.

IN THE BEGINNING

Throughout his life, my father remained very close to all of his siblings. Although they had their business and he had his, they worked out many deals together. And my father was never far from his family. Every Saturday night, he and his brothers and sisters and their children gathered for big family dinners, and they spent summers together at neighboring cottages on Lake Erie.

My father's building-supply company was just down the road from the Ratner brothers' lumber company. Every day Leonard and Max would pick up my father for lunch at Smith's, a local restaurant. The brothers would immediately start arguing. Usually they quarreled over land or charitable donations. Unlike his brothers, my father wasn't particularly interested in giving to Jewish charities, which often triggered the arguments. Driving with his eyes barely on the road, Max would crane his neck to harangue my father in the back seat.

Yet, the close-knit ties of the Ratners—a sort of internal communism—had enabled my father and his siblings to take their first steps in business in the United States. And that unbreakable solidarity and family loyalty gave us all security.

Politically, my father was liberal, but he was never a radical. One day we were walking in his building-supply yard, between piles of brick, sewer pipe, and concrete block. Suddenly he exclaimed, "We need to make sure the Bolsheviks don't come." No doubt he remembered what had happened to his parents' textile factory back in Poland when the Communist government took over.

He didn't get much involved in politics, but I constantly witnessed my father's humanity and his generosity to others. He had little interest in religion and even less in institutional philanthropy. When he bought his coal truck as a young man, he left buckets of coal for families who couldn't afford to pay. His charity was always personal, individual, and anonymous.

After World War II, thousands of Jewish refugees languished in displaced persons camps with nowhere to go. Of those admitted to the

United States, many came to Cleveland. This was in large part because my father would sign affidavits of support on their behalf. He signed hundreds, more than any other individual. Upon arrival, the immigrants needed a place to live. To help them find housing, my father would go to the newspaper office, pay off the pressmen, and take the apartment listings from the papers before they were delivered. I often found myself trudging up carpeted stairs and along dark hallways with my mother, checking out potential apartments to make sure they were in decent condition.

My father often gave these new immigrants a start in the construction business with never-to-be-repaid loans of building materials and home sites. I remember going with him to one of these jobs. When we arrived, he donned rubber boots—without removing his suit or his trademark fedora—and strode into the muddy ditch. In the trench, laying a concrete block foundation, was a refugee with a concentration camp number tattooed on his arm.

I recall another day when a young concentration camp survivor named Solly came to see my father. One of his arms had been amputated as a result of Nazi torture, and because of this, he couldn't get a job. My father hired Solly on the spot. He swept the floors, did other odd jobs, and was a night watchman in the office. Solly lived to be more than 100, and his mind was clear as a bell to the end.

Occasionally my father and I would drive in his blue-topped 1940s Dodge to a Jewish orphanage called Bellefaire. I remember the kids would rush to the car and surround it. My Dad would roll down the window and hand every kid a Dubble Bubble twist-wrap piece of gum—the one with a cartoon printed on the inside. I didn't realize at the time that these were Jewish children orphaned by the Holocaust or by families too poor to keep them, but I never forgot my father's absolute commitment to immigrants and to the poor.

From an early age, I could see that my father was an important man in the lives of the people he helped. It took longer for me to under stand the class position of my family, and what it meant for me to be a Ratner.

After several buildings burned down in the late 1940s, the Ratner family helped finance a new synagogue in Cleveland Heights—though my father himself probably didn't contribute much. Designed by Eric Mendelsohn, a refugee from Berlin, the synagogue was gorgeous. It featured a fascinating white-bricked, domed ceiling. As big donors, the Ratner clan had 50 dedicated seats along the perimeter, slightly raised so the surrounding glass was at our height. Before Ellen was born, my immediate family had four seats, each with a brass name tag on its mahogany arm. As a Ratner child, I felt special, and perhaps even a bit superior. This was not an attitude my father or mother ever imparted, but came from being a member of a large, well-known, well-off Jewish family in town.

Of course, our riches weren't in the same league as those of the German Jewish aristocracy in Cleveland. Most of that old crowd who had arrived in the 19th century, now attended reform temples, and socialized in Jewish country clubs we could never get into. But the wealth of any Jew in Cleveland was insignificant compared to that of the WASP elites who owned the banks, the ships on the Great Lakes, the steel mills and the mines, ran the City Club (no Jews allowed), and sent their children to private schools (no Jews allowed) and then on to Yale.

Our family history of persecution, emigration, and forging a new life in America remains powerful for me and for most of the family. My Uncle Max spent many years putting together a book containing hundreds of pages of interviews and pictures documenting our history in Białystok and the United States: *The Ratner House, 1881-1998.* This book knits together the themes that formed the fabric of my childhood—a lively Yiddish-Jewish culture; an extremely close, insular, extended family of uncles, aunts, and cousins; education as the supreme value; and going into business, making money, and engaging in philanthropy as the proper and natural path in life.

My early years were spent in our family's modest brick house near my Uncle Max's place in a white-collar neighborhood of Cleveland Heights. We spent our time playing in the yard, roller skating on the sidewalks, and buying ice cream from a truck that drove by every day. My mother took care of Bruce and me, and also helped my father at the office. At home, my father would play with us, throwing us over his shoulders and carrying us up the stairs, repeating "sack of potatoes, sack of potatoes"—his primary food growing up in Poland.

When I was five and a half, we moved to the neighboring suburb of Shaker Heights, an upscale community founded by the Shakers. It boasted public schools that were supposedly among the best in the country. *Nothing* was more important in my family than education. The community was quite restrictive. It didn't have racial or religious covenants prohibiting sales, but you could sell only if the majority of your neighbors or the developer agreed. For that reason, Shaker Heights was, for a while, a neighborhood with few Jews or African-Americans.

My father built a colonial-style house there with surplus materials from his building-supply business. The house itself wasn't special, but the land surrounding it was spectacular: two and a half acres spread around a lake that was shared among half a dozen houses. We had a big, green front lawn with a red brick driveway, and a huge backyard with a gully filled with water flowing from the lake.

In summers we would decamp to another childhood idyll: the cottage my father had built overlooking Lake Erie in Willowick, Ohio, surrounded by several other cottages owned by the extended Ratner family. There Bruce and I were left to our own devices, free to explore and spend our days however we pleased. Usually we played down by the lake, where our family owned a little shack on the beach. Its original owners continued to use it, and they spent hours teaching us how to fish. It was simply paradise.

One summer, when Bruce and I were in camp, my mother arrived unexpectedly. My father had developed peritonitis after an ulcer operation to remove part of his stomach. My mother believed he was dying and had come to collect us so we could see him before he passed. Hospital rules wouldn't allow children into his room, so Bruce and I stood in the parking lot while my father waved down to us from his window.

That time he recovered, and we spent the remainder of the summer with him as he recuperated. But throughout the rest of my childhood, my father had bouts of serious illness.

Shortly after I turned 13, he suffered a major heart attack. I was plagued with anxiety. I felt that he could die at any moment. I comforted myself with the games and magical thinking that come naturally to children: *if I can reach the top of the steps before the bell rings, he will live!* And I would pray to God to keep him alive.

The world that shaped me was very Jewish. We were conservative Jews, and on Friday nights my mother always lit candles for the sabbath. Though my parents were more secular than some, we still kept kosher.

I went to Park Synagogue every Saturday for school, and at least twice a week for other activities. It had a separate educational wing, the Ratner Educational Center, named for one of my uncles. I was always a confident speaker and once won a debate contest there, making the case for a proselytizing Judaism. After my victory, I overheard a kid saying, "Michael won because of his family."

My bar mitzvah took place at Park Synagogue in the shadow of my bar mitzvah teacher's suicide six weeks earlier. The teacher, Mr. Willager, had been quite poor. He lived in a small row house in the Cleveland suburbs and drove a battered old car from the 1930s—in contrast to the four new cars my family owned. When I was working with him on my readings, he invited my family to his daughter's bat mitzvah. It was a very nice outdoor party, with a big tent and a great spread of food. A few days after the party, he committed suicide. I assumed the event had bankrupted him and he saw no way out. I was overwhelmed with guilt that we hadn't offered to help him with the cost.

MOVING THE BAR

Almost all of the organized Jewish activity we participated in supported Zionism. We collected coins in a little blue box for the Jewish National Fund, which purchased land for development in Israel. There were also regular drives to plant trees in the Holy Land. For a few hundred dollars, you could get an entire forest named after you. (I only recently realized that these seedlings often replaced Palestinian olive trees that Israelis had uprooted.)

Even children's books reinforced the impression of a heroic Jewish struggle for survival against genocidal terrorists. *Mickey Marcus*, which our mother read to us when we were little, was an illustrated tale of an American soldier who went to Israel and became a general, leading the good fight against the Arabs. Some years later, I skipped an entire day of school to finish reading Leon Uris's *Exodus*, a thrilling tale of Jews' valiant struggle to establish the state of Israel in the face of cruel and degenerate Arab barbarians.

Fundraising for Israel never ceased in our household. The brother of Israel's first president, Chaim Weizmann, once visited us to secure an investment in Israeli pecan plantations. By the time I was 13, our family had invested in several projects in Israel.

Many relatives from both sides of the family had moved to Israel and made homes there. Some were recent arrivals. Others had lived in Palestine well before the Holocaust. One distant second cousin, Ze'ev Ivianski, had been a member of the Stern Gang, a Jewish militia that fought the Palestinians and the British before the state of Israel was established. The British had jailed this relative, and subsequently he wrote a two-volume history of his militia.

Of course, the Stern Gang, as I was to discover later, was essentially a band of terrorists, responsible for massacres and attacks against Palestinian civilians. When Ivianski was 92, my sister and brother interviewed him at the kibbutz where he lived. He viewed himself as a socialist and expressed no regrets for his actions, including the assassination in 1948 of the Swedish diplomat Folke Bernadotte, a United Nations-appointed mediator who had, ironically, negotiated the release of 31,000 prisoners from German concentration camps during World War II.

In the summer of 1956, just before the Suez Crisis (the Second Arab-Israeli War), I visited Israel for the first time. I was 13 and traveled alone on an El Al flight that lasted 24 hours. It was full of Orthodox Jews praying in the aisles.

My parents had arranged for Israeli families they knew to take care of me. Three couples met me at the airport. The Gorodesckys were a wealthy family from Herzliya, just north of Tel Aviv, where my family owned the Sharon Hotel. The Dashalits were major investors in the hotel. And the Flakovichs, probably the wealthiest of the bunch, owned a textile plant in which my father had invested. My father's investments were never very successful. He wanted to support fledgling businesses in the new state, rather than draw a profit—an approach which made him, and his children, very popular with Israelis.

I left the airport with the Gorodesckys. Although Herzliya was still quite rural, with small houses and no paved streets, the Gorodesckys lived in a fabulous walled estate. They gave me a room all to myself. We ate together at a family dinner every evening, and each morning their nephew would accompany me on the half-mile trek through the desert to get to the beach. The Sharon Hotel overlooked the sea. I stayed there a few nights, holding court with visiting friends and even meeting celebrities like the comedian Danny Kaye.

Next to the hotel stood an old Roman ruin, littered with beautiful fragments of melted glass. My very own dig! I had already developed an interest in archaeology, and it was thrilling to imagine my distant ancestors walking on this same ground where I was walking.

Wild and beautiful, the beach was unspoiled, with a ferocious tide. The hotel had set up a screen on the sand, and at night we'd sit outdoors on wooden benches and watch movies. Relaxing with others on the beach, breathing in the warm, sensuous evening air, listening to lapping waves in what I took to be my family's homeland—it was intoxicating.

Next I traveled to Tel Aviv and stayed with the Flakovichs in a large apartment in a modern stucco building. The Flakovichs took me on an eye-opening three-week road trip across the country, visiting the north, the Galilee, Jerusalem, and the ancient Jewish town of Safed. Swimming in a beautiful river in the north, I reached into the riverbed and pulled out an ancient arrowhead with a geode embedded in it. I was convinced my career as an archaeologist had gotten off to a great start.

Then we flew by DC-3 to Eilat, an almost deserted town sandwiched between Jordan and Egypt at the country's southernmost tip. As I stepped off the plane, a blast of withering heat hit me. It felt like a furnace. There were no hotels or amenities, just a single store selling sodas. But it didn't matter. The Red Sea was glorious, shimmering with coral and teeming with fish.

In Jerusalem, which at that time was divided between Jordan and Israel, I lit a candle at King David's tomb and visited Yad Vashem, a museum commemorating the Holocaust. Situated in an unlit cave, it exhibited soap and lampshades made from the flesh of Jews.

By the time I returned home at the end of the summer, I had fallen in love with the country I thought of as the home of my people. I had my bedroom ceiling painted with the Seven Wonders of the World and a huge map of Israel. I had no idea how my view of Israel would change later in life.

My father always assumed his sons would take over the family business after he was gone. By the time I was six, he began preparing us, taking Bruce and me to the office every Saturday morning. It was a long building, with the shipping department at one end and my father's office at the other. In between were several desks for secretaries and assistants and a huge safe. We'd help out with the accounting by placing carbon-copy sheets in between the invoices before they were typed.

IN THE BEGINNING

As I got older, I would spend my summer vacations there. Sometimes I worked in the office, but I preferred jobs in the yard out back. My brother and I saw the yard as a giant playground—two full acres of concrete stacks, pipes, bricks, metal, cement bags, trucks, and heavy machinery.

My father hated discrimination, but couldn't eradicate it in his own business. The cement-mixer drivers were all white, and the dump-truck drivers, who made much less money, were almost all Black. The yard's foreman belonged to the Teamsters, a corrupt union controlled by the mob. It was also racist. If anyone tried to hire a Black driver for a higher-paid "white" position, the Teamsters would threaten to blow up the truck. As a result, the yard was effectively segregated.

Police would always stop by the yard if they were doing some building or fixing up their houses. My father would give them free or heavily discounted supplies. To the extent that my brother and I ever had trouble with the cops, it would always disappear very quickly.

September 17, 1961 was a beautiful autumn Sunday. It fell between the holy days of Rosh Hashanah and Yom Kippur. That morning, Bruce and I were in our room when we heard a loud thump. My mother called out, and we rushed to my father's room. He was sitting on the edge of his bed, looking ashen and breathing erratically. He had just suffered another heart attack. As we waited with him for the ambulance, my brother and I escaped into fantasy.

"As soon as he's out of the woods," we told each other, "we'll go play squash."

When the ambulance arrived, my mother stood in the hallway near the front door, screaming, "Don't take him! He'll never come back!"

The medics carried my father into the ambulance, and our devoted beagle Cleo jumped in with him. My mother went with my father to the hospital. A cousin drove Bruce, Ellen, and me to Uncle Max's house and dumped us in front of a television. Eventually someone realized this wasn't the right place for us and drove us to Suburban Hospital, which my father had helped found.

By the time I entered his room, he was gone. I said *kaddish*, the Jewish prayer for the dead, and a black emptiness descended.

I remember almost nothing about the funeral, except that more than a thousand people attended. My father was buried in Park Synagogue cemetery, next to his parents and the younger brother who had perished shortly after the trip from Poland. In keeping with the Jewish tradition of sitting *shiva*, we spent the next week at home perched on low stools as an endless stream of people offered their condolences.

But my father's death had profoundly shaken me and presented my family with a dilemma: what to do with Michael? I had been all set to leave the day after Yom Kippur for my freshman year at Brandeis University, near Boston. But almost overnight, everything had changed. The family elders seriously considered keeping me in Cleveland to run my father's businesses while I pursued my education at a local night school. Mercifully, they granted me a reprieve. I could go to Brandeis, and for five years they would run the businesses, as my father had requested.

Just 10 days after the funeral, I got on a prop plane at Cleveland airport with my high school friend Joel Stein and left for college. It was cold and raining, and I was a mess.

Brandeis had been founded right after the Holocaust as a secular, non-sectarian Jewish university. Set in the small town of Waltham, Massachusetts, it had a reputation as an excellent academic institution—a rival to the Ivy League schools. Old red brick buildings dotted the campus, with a few new ones under construction. My roommate Joel and I moved into a shabby dormitory, an ugly, concrete-block structure. We shared a tiny room and a common bathroom with students from five other rooms on the hall.

I was still reeling from my father's death and grateful to have a friend as a roommate. In high school I'd moved among two separate groups: the athletes, who were cool and had girlfriends, and the intellectuals, who boycotted the prom in favor of reading *Lysistrata* in someone's basement. Joel was in the latter group. Funny and extremely bright, he was a gifted writer whose humorous newspaper column "Orts, Dregs, and Lees" made him a minor celebrity in high school.

Joel proved to be a great support to me at Brandeis. He got a night job watching the switchboard, and sometimes I'd stay up with him. One night a telegram came in from Waikiki, Hawaii, where Brandeis' president, Abram Sachar, was entertaining a donor. "Just got million from Gerstenzang," read the telegram. "Please send appropriate biblical quote." We roared with laughter. Leo Gerstenzang, inventor of the Q-tip, wound up with Brandeis's science quadrangle named after him.

Our dorm had a shared living room that had a black-and-white television. One day we all watched as James Meredith, with stoic courage, walked onto campus and became the first Black student ever at the University of Mississippi. We saw images of snarling dogs, angry policemen, fire hoses used against civil rights demonstrators. The world outside was heating up.

Brandeis was known as a progressive school. Most of its professors were liberal anti-communists like Max Lerner, who wrote for magazines like the *New Republic* and *New Leader*. But there were also a few leftist professors who didn't buy into the prevailing Cold War ideology. The most celebrated of these was the German-born sociologist Herbert Marcuse, a prominent theorist of the New Left. Another was Ray Ginger, who'd written brilliant books on the Scopes trial and on the socialist Eugene Debs. Ginger had lost his job at Harvard during the 1950s when he refused to sign an oath that he hadn't been a member of the Communist Party.

Intellectually, Brandeis was an exciting place. But I was sick at heart and lonely. On an old pay phone downstairs from my room I'd call home once or twice a week. My mother came to visit me several times, and I went back to Cleveland for Jewish holidays.

MOVING THE BAR

My deep mourning for my father led me to seek out the familiar. I got some comfort from eating kosher food with the religious students. And every morning before class started, I walked over to temple, put on a prayer shawl, wrapped tefillin on my arms, and recited the prayer for the dead. The Jewish religion requires a minyan of at least ten worshipers—that is, male worshipers—to hold a proper Jewish service. About a dozen orthodox students gathered each morning at the temple, and we'd begin with the prayer thanking God we were not women.

After three months I'd had enough. I stopped going to the temple and standing on the kosher food line. I was still lost.

By the second semester of sophomore year my life really began to fall apart. I was getting more and more depressed and couldn't study. I struggled that second semester and got mostly C's and B's. When I got a D in biology to end the year, I hit a new low.

Nonetheless, in the fall of 1963, I returned to Brandeis for junior year.

One night in late November, I stayed up all night with a group of musicians. I went to sleep as the sun came up. Several hours later, in midday, somebody pushed my shoulder and woke me with the news that President Kennedy had been murdered.

My friends and I were devastated. The liberal leader of our generation was gone. I hadn't agreed with him on some issues, but the young president had symbolized change and the arrival of a new era to replace the conservative 1950s.

School closed down for a while. With nothing better to do, a group of us decided to drive to New York City, where my mother had a new boyfriend. Fifteen years younger than my father, she had scandalized the family by becoming socially active too soon after his death. They had no understanding of her suffering, but I felt for her and wanted her to be happy.

IN THE BEGINNING

The boyfriend's small apartment on 46th Street had almost no light. We stayed there for three or four miserable days, watching the news on television, witnessing Jack Ruby shoot Lee Harvey Oswald, leaving only to get food, and sinking deeper into despair about the world.

By that time, I had become miserable for my own reasons. When everyone else left to go home for Thanksgiving, I remained in the cramped New York apartment by myself. Thanksgiving Day was cold and rainy. I went for a walk and wound up sitting at a counter at Howard Johnson's in down-and-out Times Square, eating turkey and canned gravy. I felt utterly alone.

I didn't go back to Brandeis. I dropped out of school and moved by myself into a dumpy apartment in an old, broken-down house in Cambridge. It had three rooms with plaster peeling off the walls and crooked steps. I stayed in bed for much of the rest of the year, reading Theodore Dreiser's *An American Tragedy*, Lawrence Durrell's four-volume *Alexandria Quartet*, Ernest Hemingway's *A Moveable Feast*, and more.

It was the worst time of my life. I had no sense of purpose. Deeply depressed, I experienced the full weight of my father's death. I did get out a couple of days a week to see a therapist or to have dinner with Bruce and my cousin Mark, both of whom were at Harvard and living nearby in Cambridge. As part of my therapy, I wrote down my dreams and kept a diary. "If I ever look back and call these the best years of my life," one entry read, "may God strike me dead."

It was 1963, the beginning of the buildup for the Vietnam War. Since I was no longer a student, I received a draft notice. My therapist wrote a letter to the draft board, saying I could not have any break in my psychiatric treatment. Even though he'd asked only for a temporary deferment, the draft board in Shaker Heights classified me as 4-F—permanent disability. I never had to worry about the draft again. In fact, out of six Ratner boys in our extended family, none had to go into the army. We all received deferments from the local draft board. The lesson was obvious: young men of privilege would not have to fight this war.

Before deciding to go back to Brandeis in the fall of 1964, I took two summer school classes at Boston University to make sure I was prepared. One was in English literature, the other a writing seminar. I wrote essays about the bridges over the Charles River in Cambridge and studied the poems of John Skelton, poet laureate of England in the 16th century. "Your ugly token, my mind hath broken, from worldly lust, for I have discussed, we are but dust, and die we must" is the only line I remember. I did well. My confidence was coming back, psychologically and academically.

I returned to Brandeis as an English major. I wanted to improve my writing skills and studied everything from medieval lyrics to Chaucer, Proust, James Joyce, and Emily Dickinson. I was in a seminar with Angela Davis, who later became a prominent Black activist, communist, and philosophy professor. We studied Jean Paul Sartre's *Being and Nothingness*. I didn't understand it and dropped the class. I also took advantage of the Brandeis lecture series, where I heard speakers including poet Allen Ginsberg, anarchist writer Paul Goodman, and French artist Marcel Duchamp. Ginsberg was particularly memorable. He came on stage with a shruti, an Indian accordion-style drone instrument, and began chanting "Om" before giving a talk with his lover, Peter Orlovsky. The most powerful speaker, though, was Malcolm X, the tall, brilliant African-American leader who had recently broken with the Nation of Islam. His message was totally new and astonishing to me. In his tough, rapid-fire style, he stressed the origins of American culture in Africa and the need for Black people to stand up for themselves.

The Vietnam War was intensifying. Students held demonstrations and teach-ins on campuses around the country. I chose to write my senior thesis on Vietnam and spent two months in the library doing research.

My thesis argued that the war was primarily an indigenous nationalist struggle with the goal of re-uniting Vietnam. After all sides had agreed to a vote on unification of North and South Vietnam at the Geneva Conference in 1954, the United States prevented it. My professor thought I was wrong. This was a struggle about communism, he believed. If the communists weren't stopped in Vietnam, they would soon be in Australia—the country of his birth. I got a B.

But grades weren't my primary concern. The five-year clock on my reprieve was winding down, and my family was pushing me to return to Cleveland and take over my father's company. Though I felt I was letting my father down, I knew I wasn't interested in the business. I had no particular career aspirations, but I knew I wanted to continue my education. I took the law boards, thinking that perhaps I could study law at night school in Cleveland.

I was astounded when I received an almost perfect score. That meant that, despite my troubled college career, I could apply to Yale, Harvard, and Columbia. I got into Columbia.

I spent the summer in Cleveland and worked with Bruce at my father's office. The more I learned more about my father's business, the less I wanted any part of it. I didn't like the Teamsters and mobsters who sold us supplies for the cement. One of these shady characters came into the office as Bruce and I were sitting at my father's desk. He told us to look out the window into the yard. "You see that pile of slag back there?" he said. The pile was perhaps 60 feet high. "I get 25 cents a ton for that slag." He meant he took a kickback of 25 cents for every ton we bought.

That moment was the turning point for both Bruce and me. We decided not to stay in Cleveland to run the business. When I told my Uncle Max, my father's closest brother, I was going to law school, he tried to talk me out of it. "Just remember this," he said. "Lawyers work for other people." Max was the only one of my father's siblings to go to college. He reminded me that he had also gone to law school. "I practiced law for less than two days." Then he went back into business with the family.

Fortunately, my father had left a letter giving Max, his trustee, specific instructions to hold on to the business for five years. Then, if it was losing money, he was to sell it. The five years had passed. With nobody to take over and turn the company around, the family was forced to sell. The business had deteriorated so much that it could no longer be sold as a single entity. Seventy-five trucks, the building supplies, and the office itself were put up for auction. It was one of the saddest days of my Uncle Max's life.

But I was free.

3
DAYS OF LAW AND RAGE

In September 1966, I enrolled at Columbia University Law School. My mother helped me get settled in Manhattan. For $125 a month we found a wonderful 1920s residence hotel on 103rd and Riverside Drive, a "rough" neighborhood about a 15-minute walk from the law school. My kitchen overlooked the Hudson River, and a wraparound terrace gave me views up past the George Washington Bridge and down to the Statue of Liberty.

Every morning I'd walk up Broadway to the law school building, a 1960s concrete-and-glass monstrosity that everyone called the "toaster." With its sterile fluorescent lights, it was far from how I imagined a venerable Ivy League law school would look. No dark wooden walls, no cozy book-lined nooks and crannies to study in. The only place to socialize was a hallway with a few Formica tables and vending machines offering bad coffee and sickly-sweet Drake's Cakes.

I couldn't know it at the time, but I'd arrived at Columbia at the end of an era. The law school had no female or African-American professors, and in my class, there were fewer than a dozen women and just a handful of African-American students. The courses, covering contracts, civil procedure, and torts, were intended to prepare us for jobs at large corporate law firms. Courses in civil rights or human rights law didn't exist, and learning through clinical practice in the community wasn't an option.

MOVING THE BAR

(Today, Columbia boasts an entire human rights program, both academic and clinical, which I taught in for a number of years.)

I knew only one person in my class. David Berger and I had lived on the same street in Shaker Heights, gone to the same high school, and belonged to the same temple. David had been on the high school wrestling team and lifted weights. I can still see him standing by the lockers in his wrestling shorts, telling me about his plans to go to Israel to compete as a weightlifter in the Maccabiah Games. By the time he got to Columbia he had won a bronze medal in the Games, and shortly before his graduation he won a gold medal. David later competed for Israel in the Munich Olympics in 1972. He was one of 11 hostages kidnapped by the extremist Palestinian group Black September and killed in a German rescue attempt. Then 28 years old, David was reportedly the last to die.

When I learned of David's death, I was still at the beginning of a slow process of doubt and disillusionment with the government of Israel. I have never condoned acts of kidnapping or killing, but over time I came to recognize that the expulsion of the Palestinian population and the imposition of an Israeli state on another people's land have exacted a terrible cost in human lives, both Palestinian and Israeli. David's life was one of those tragic losses.

Law school was intense and competitive. Hundreds of us attended classes held in cavernous lecture halls. The professors expected us to have studied the material thoroughly the night before and could call upon anyone at any time to answer a question. Our response had to stand up to scrutiny from the professor and other students.

It was terrifying. One legendary professor, Harry Jones, looked like a drill sergeant with cropped graying hair and a muscular body. He had a temper to match, screaming in class and on one occasion throwing an eraser at a student who gave a poor answer.

Then, as now, American law schools taught law by studying previous cases. We learned how to read a case and to infer from a judge's determination (or "holding") the likely outcome of new cases. This is harder than it sounds. Cases were long and complex, and often several judges wrote separate opinions about the same case. We became practiced at dissecting legal arguments to determine which facts and principles were decisive in each case and how they might be applied to novel situations.

I loved the process of legal reasoning, not least because I was good at it. Within one year I could read cases better than most and felt I had a grasp of the nuts and bolts of lawyering. But of course I hadn't worked on any real cases or met any actual clients.

My favorite class was contracts. All of the 250 or so cases we examined could be precisely fit together, like an enormous jigsaw puzzle. Each decision appeared to follow directly from those that came before it.

All of this really made sense to me. Law was *logical*. If you understood the relevant precedents, there was always a right answer that could be worked out. A judge's job, it seemed to me then, was straightforward: to understand the law and then apply it to each new set of facts. The notion that other factors might enter into decisions never occurred to me.

When I'd first arrived at Columbia, an old Brandeis acquaintance in the class ahead of mine had given me just one piece of advice: work hard and make law review. Reserved for the top 25 students, law review was the prize everyone wanted. It practically guaranteed a job at one of the best and highest-paying firms upon graduation.

All I did that first year was work. We had classes six days a week. I worked seven, taking off one evening a week at most. At the beginning of the year I had broken up with my wonderful girlfriend, Hollis, in order to focus on studying. I had no social life. During that entire year, I didn't watch a single movie. Despite my earlier interest in the anti-Vietnam War and the civil rights movements, I was disconnected from politics and oblivious of the mounting political tensions around me. As riots swept

American cities, President Johnson escalated the bombing in Southeast Asia, the anti-war movement gathered momentum, and Martin Luther King delivered his famous Riverside Church sermon against the war, all I could see were my looming finals. I have never again worked so hard.

I wanted to do well to prove myself. More importantly, drowning myself in work was a way of shutting out the emotional turmoil that resulted from my decision to go to law school and to separate myself from my father's business, Cleveland, and the Ratner family.

The end-of-year exams, which covered so much difficult material, scared me. With no midterms, the entire grade for a year rested on these five exams. I walked into the contracts exam with 150 others, got out my bluish-green exam book, read the questions, jotted some key points for myself, and began to write. Despite my ability to recite the casebook, the questions were very complicated and represented new applications of material we had learned. I had studied so hard that I almost knew too much. I saw too many subtleties and was really sweating. When it was over, I knew I hadn't flunked, but I was sure I'd missed out on an A. It was a similar story with the exam on legislation. I knew I had gotten through, but that was not enough for me. My sights were fixed on law review.

Several weeks later, my grades arrived in the mail. I had done well—all A's and one B+, in a class called Development of Legal Institutions. Accompanying my grades came an invitation to law review. All my sweat and hard work had paid off. I was thrilled!

The law school posted the grades of the highest-scoring students on the main bulletin board at the entrance to the school. The top five in the first-year class received the title James Kent Scholars. I can still picture that piece of paper with my name printed on it. Despite all the emotional turmoil I'd been through, this was the first time I realized my full academic potential. The achievement gave me lasting confidence in my ability to understand and analyze law. Whenever I'm feeling insecure, I say to myself, "If I could do that, I can do anything."

During that long, hot summer of 1967, Black people in poor urban communities rose up in bloody confrontations with police all around the country. Buffalo, Minneapolis, Detroit, Milwaukee, and Washington all burned. In Detroit alone, during five tumultuous days, 43 people died, 1,100 were injured, 7,200 arrested, and more than 2,000 buildings went up in flames.

Although I was by no means a militant, my sympathies lay with the Black community. I had witnessed racial discrimination my entire life. When I was eight, I'd flown with my family to Florida. As we got off the plane, I was shocked when the Black passengers were herded up to the balcony and the white passengers walked freely into the main terminal. I was equally stunned to see segregated water fountains and bathrooms labelled "Whites Only." But there was a deep racial divide in Cleveland, too. While the poor parts of the city were almost entirely Black, I lived in a white suburb, attended white public schools, and swam at a white country club. The profound inequalities in a country built on a foundation of slavery were inescapable. And the uprisings in the summer of 1967 sent a clear message that many in the Black community would no longer accept an unjust status quo.

It was also the summer of the Six Day War, when the Israeli army occupied the West Bank, the Golan Heights, and Gaza. Here, my sympathies tended towards the Israelis. Back then, I still believed the narrative that the state of Israel was the last refuge of a besieged Jewish minority fighting for its survival.

I returned to New York in August to begin work on the law review. Our staff had access to a dedicated suite of offices with expensive furniture and big windows. We were like an elite officer corps within the school. The professors treated me with new respect, and suddenly many of the country's most important and prestigious law firms wanted me. Even a clerkship on the Supreme Court was within reach.

Law review required at least 20 hours a week on top of demanding classes. It, too, was competitive, as we all chased appointment to one of five or six top positions. Our first job was to make sure that all submitted and edited articles had perfect legal citations—and I mean *perfect*: not a space, bracket, capital, or italicization out of place. We had to learn an arcane method of referencing whose labyrinthine rules were collected in a volume called the "Blue Book." It was painstaking and often boring work. Each of us also had to write an article for publication in the law review during the year.

During those first weeks on law review I had a striking political realization that, in retrospect, seems utterly naïve. The third-year students in charge gave a talk in which they informed us that judges did not always reach the correct conclusion, that their reasoning could be poor, and that in our own articles we were supposed to critique their decisions.

I was stunned. *Critique the judges?* This defied everything I had learned in my first year. Wasn't law logical? Didn't holdings fit together like a jigsaw? Was it not obvious that judges could get it wrong, and not only by misreading precedents? *Brown v. Board of Education*, the 1954 school desegregation case, had reversed years of judicial decisions finding segregated schools constitutional. If the Constitution had a fixed meaning, how could this have occurred? Here I was, in my second year of law school, on law review, at the top of the class, without the faintest clue about how the real world of judging operated.

Of course the political context and a judge's beliefs and life experience could affect the outcome. During my first year at Columbia, however, we had been given the firm impression that law was more or less immutable. Today, this is a view of law I find absurd, except as it touches core human rights principles, like prohibitions on torture and slavery. Yet it's a view many still hold. During the July 2014 Supreme Court confirmation hearings of Judge Sonia Sotomayor, for example, senators on both sides of the aisle took turns to insist upon adherence to law—as if the "law" were engraved in stone and waiting to be discovered, fully-formed, like the 10 Commandments. Looking for a judging robot, the senators forced Judge Sotomayor, the first Latina woman to be nominated, to state repeatedly that empathy and a judge's background had no place in rendering legal decisions.

That fall of 1967, the law review editors decided to devote an issue to what the white press called the "urban riots." Since I was sympathetic to the uprisings, I jumped at the opportunity to contribute. My article was supposed to examine the circumstances when it would be lawful for the president to send the U.S. military (or a federalized National Guard) into cities to assist or supplant local police in suppressing unrest and restoring order. The constitutional question was extremely complex, requiring analysis of the Constitution's guarantee to each state of a "republican form of government" and protection against "domestic violence"—clauses intended, in part, to permit federal intervention in case a rebellion of the poor threatened or seized control of a state.

It was also complex politically. I opposed using the military to suppress the uprisings, for the same reason I today oppose military patrols on our streets: at least the police have some training in constitutional rights, while soldiers often shoot first and ask questions later. On the other hand, I supported using federal troops to end Jim Crow in the South.

This paradox posed a problem. How could I interpret the law to prohibit the use of federal troops in situations where I opposed intervention, without prohibiting the use of federal troops in situations where I supported intervention? My goal was simply to write an explication of the law. But the law could be read narrowly or expansively. Which reading would do more to protect fundamental rights, particularly those of minorities and the poor? Did I want the federal government to meet a very high burden before resorting to troops, or a lower one? Would I have thought differently about this question during Reconstruction? I had no answers, and writing the article proved difficult.

I worked hard on the research all through September and October, making more than 50 pages of handwritten notes on the precedents. But my notes seemed a mish-mash, and I had no idea whether I would be able to organize them into a coherent article. Other law review members had already completed rough drafts of their articles, yet I felt overwhelmed. I remembered that same feeling from my third year at Brandeis when I'd spent hours reading and amassing notes on a paper without ever being able to structure them or bring the effort to completion. That was the year I had dropped out.

Several weeks after I started work on law review, the law school's new semester had begun. My brother entered the first-year class and took an apartment adjacent to mine. Bruce had graduated *cum laude* from Harvard, but his grades and work fell far below his potential. Before our father died, Bruce never got a grade below A, served as class president, and showed true brilliance at math and science. After my father's death, he'd started coasting academically and developed a wild streak, getting in trouble for erratic driving. In retrospect, he was depressed, and this affected his work at Harvard. Now we were both at Columbia, and I loved having him with me. We had always been close, and our father's death brought us even closer.

One of Bruce's apartment mates was another first-year law student named Gus Reichbach. Stocky, with curly dirty-blond hair, Gus came from a working class Communist Jewish family in Brooklyn. He was a fast-talker, razor-sharp, and quick on his feet. Gus had met my brother while standing in line to register for law school and had asked if he could "crash" at Bruce's apartment. My big-hearted brother said yes, and had a guest for the first semester. When Bruce's girlfriend Julie visited, Gus stayed on a couch in my apartment.

Like Gus, a number of Bruce's classmates were leftists who hailed from Communist families. One of these was Margie Leinsdorf, whom I would later marry.

I would later drift into the activist crowd, but at this point I was too busy with law review and classes. My politics were liberal, certainly not leftist. I fundraised for Israel in the wake of the 1967 war without a second thought. And when it was time to apply for jobs, I assumed I would go straight to a big commercial firm.

Yet I was struggling. The law review article had me paralyzed with writer's block, and I was weeks behind with classes. I found it impossible to focus and couldn't bring myself to open a textbook. For nearly a year, I had pushed everything besides work out of my mind, keeping a fanatical schedule. But the emotional fall-out from the break with my home, my girlfriend, and my family couldn't be ignored forever. Finally, in November 1967, I took a leave from law school, just as I had at Brandeis four years earlier.

The law school was fine with it. After all, I was one of their stars, and my overworked burnout was something they'd seen before. Although I couldn't face another year at school, I wanted to work at a law job of some sort, preferably in the field of civil rights. I had an interview, and the NAACP Legal Defense Fund, now called LDF, hired me.

The LDF operated at the cutting edge of civil rights law, primarily on behalf of African-Americans. Thurgood Marshall, who argued the famous *Brown v. Board of Education* case in 1954, had led the organization for many years. Marshall eventually left to become Solicitor General and then a Supreme Court justice. But the LDF continued its aggressive, pioneering efforts to dismantle Jim Crow in the South, as well as de facto segregation in the North.

LDF lawyers traveled everywhere, litigating against segregation and discrimination in schools, public waiting rooms, hotels, restaurants, jobs, and housing. They had won the case prohibiting Arkansas Governor Orval Faubus from interfering with the integration of Little Rock High School and represented James Meredith in his battle for admission to the University of Mississippi. I had watched both historic events on television and had been very moved.

MOVING THE BAR

In 1963 alone, the LDF won cases desegregating public parks, hospitals, and restaurants. That same year LDF lawyers defended Martin Luther King for demonstrating in violation of an injunction in Birmingham, Alabama—the protest that led to his famous "Letter from Birmingham City Jail." They were part of King's legal team and worked on his Poor People's Campaign. While the civil rights movement fought pervasive racism with protests and civil disobedience, LDF fought it with lawsuits. The two strategies, courts and streets, complemented and fed off each other. And there I was, working at the center of it all. I couldn't have been more excited.

The LDF's office was next to the Coliseum at 59th Street and Broadway, a short subway ride from my apartment. Back then we had no computers or copying machines. We did legal research primarily from large casebooks. Although LDF had a pretty good library, I often went up to Columbia to use its bigger library. I wrote all my work by hand in those days, and secretaries typed it.

Jack Greenberg, Thurgood Marshall's successor, headed LDF. He and his board picked the cases, and Jack argued almost every Supreme Court case. This did not sit well with his staff of mostly white, ambitious, young, Ivy League-educated lawyers in search of their own opportunities to shine. But I always found Jack friendly and helpful.

The atmosphere at LDF was informal. Doors were always open and the staff discussed everything. The associate director, a Black lawyer named James Nabritt III, befriended me. Son of the president of Howard University, Jim had studied at Yale and spent most of his legal career at LDF. I often hung out in his office discussing cases. He didn't have the presence of a legal powerhouse, and Jack Greenberg didn't seem to esteem him highly. But Jim was a masterful brief writer. And a year after I started at LDF he argued *Shuttlesworth v. Birmingham* before the Supreme Court, winning an important victory. The court threw out civil rights leader Reverend Fred Shuttlesworth's conviction for parading without a permit.

I shared a windowless office with Anthony Amsterdam, a professor at the University of Pennsylvania law school. I never became close with Tony, who was reserved and quiet in the office, but what a thrill it was to be in his presence. One of the most brilliant, knowledgeable, and accomplished attorneys in the country, he had gained both fame and notoriety by leading the legal campaign to abolish the death penalty. Tony's strategy was to delay and delay as many death penalty cases as possible, using every legal argument he could contrive. Principally he argued that the death penalty had a disproportionate impact on Black people and was imposed so capriciously that it violated the Constitution. He hoped that eventually, when thousands of people languished on death row, the Supreme Court would intervene and abolish it.

Tony would go on in 1972 to argue *Furman v. Georgia*, the most important death penalty case ever decided by the Supreme Court. He won it 5–4, and the justices wrote nine separate opinions. Two justices found the death penalty inherently unconstitutional. Three others found that race was a factor in its imposition or that its imposition was arbitrary. In effect, that struck down the death penalty and opened the door for state statutes to be rewritten. This happened quickly, and hundreds of lives were saved. But by 1976, with the execution of Gary Gilmore in Utah, the death penalty in the United States had resumed.

Most often I did research for small projects at LDF, but a few cases stood out for me. *Sniadach v. Family Finance Corp.* was a Supreme Court case about a practice called "pre-judgment garnishment." Creditors and collection agencies would collect small debts, often fraudulently, by "garnishing"—that is, taking some part (often half) of the debtors' wages directly from their employers. The debtors involved were often poor. But the nasty part was that this garnishment could be done before any court had ruled that a debt was even owed. This practice impoverished thousands of people. The LDF challenged it on the basis of the Fifth Amendment, which prohibits the taking of property without due legal process.

MOVING THE BAR

A very smart young graduate of Yale Law School, Philip Schrag, handled the case. Short, curly-haired, and fast-talking, he was interested in cases that involved economic well-being. Although garnishment disproportionately targeted Black people, *Sniadach* was not directly a race-related case. I didn't know whether LDF had made a conscious decision to go into the area of what was then termed "poverty law," or whether it just allowed Phil to pursue his interests. But the case reflected the spirit of the times, when the issue of poverty captured a lot of headlines.

Phil assigned me to research which states permitted pre-judgment garnishing, and under what circumstances. Today, preparing a memo on this topic would take two or three days. In 1967, with no computers, it took me a month. I recall how proud I was that a shortened version of my research paper appeared in the LDF's brief to the Supreme Court. LDF won the case, and pre-judgment garnishment, which the court decision called "a most inhuman doctrine," disappeared forever.

My next case with Phil was more personal. The Truth in Lending Act of 1968 required disclosure of the key terms in consumer credit transactions, particularly the rates of interest. Several months after the passage of this law, I received my own credit card statement. I noticed that it didn't include the interest rate I would be charged if I failed to pay the balance in full. What's more, this non-disclosed interest would be applied retroactively to the time the charges were incurred. I was sure this had to be a violation of the law. I showed my credit card statement and my research to Phil, and so began the case of *Ratner v. Chemical Bank*.

Phil filed it as a class action, which meant we would be representing anyone who had received a similar bill. This turned out to be 130,000 people. We estimated potential damages at somewhere between $100 and $1,000 per person. Therefore, we sued for damages of between $13 million and $130 million, certainly enough to teach the banks to respect the new law. And if we were successful, the attorney's fees, potentially in the millions, would do wonders for our work at LDF.

Phil filed the case in a federal court in lower Manhattan, the Southern District of New York. The court, located just a few blocks from Wall Street, often issued decisions that protected banks and other financial institutions. But Phil and I were happy that the case was randomly assigned to Judge Marvin Frankel, a relatively liberal Columbia law professor who had been on the bench only four years. Sure enough, in June 1971 we won the case without a trial. Judge Frankel ruled that the law was clear and Chemical Bank was in violation. Rejecting all of Chemical Bank's defenses, he found that it had "carefully, deliberately—intentionally—omitted the disclosures in question."

But the bad news followed eight months later. Judge Frankel would not permit the case to proceed as a class action. Chemical Bank had been found guilty of intentionally violating the law, but was let off with $26,000 in damages—$1,000 to me, $25,000 in legal fees. This was a disaster, and not just because LDF would receive much smaller attorney fees. We felt that Judge Frankel had effectively issued corporations a license to break the law at consumers' expense. Commentators called his decision unprecedented, and its ghost still haunts class action law.

Ratner v. Chemical Bank later came up in my 1971 interview with the Bar Character Committee, which was then made up of conservative older white men from major law firms. The committee's job was to assess whether those of us who had passed the bar exam had the moral fitness to practice law. I wasn't too concerned. I had no arrests on record, had not written anything inflammatory, and was by then clerking for a federal judge.

I arrived for my interview at the most ornate marble courthouse in New York, replete with glittering chandeliers, wood-carved ceilings, and oil paintings of whiskered judges. My interviewer greeted me without a smile. Very straight-looking in an expensive suit and vest, he was a prominent attorney at the big business law firm White & Case. He asked a few routine background questions, which I answered.

Then, suddenly he asked, in a somewhat hostile tone, "Do you think it's a good idea for young lawyers to sue major banks?"

I was almost lost for words, but I came up with some kind of even-tempered, non-committal response. We moved on, and I was admitted to the bar. I later found out that White & Case represented a major bank.

My aggressive pursuit of Chemical Bank in that credit-card case foreshadowed my approach to the law going forward. When I saw a serious legal violation that interested me, I pursued it swiftly and relentlessly, rarely hesitating even if the case was not the strongest on the law. I almost always believed it was better to act than not to act.

But the law had its limits. It was 1968, and the world seemed to be coming apart. Despite my political inactivity the previous year, I was now closely following developments in the Vietnam War, which had polarized America. New York Senator Bobby Kennedy had announced he would challenge Lyndon Johnson for the Democratic nomination for president. This was a sign of Johnson's unpopularity and weakness. He was responsible for the deaths of thousands, and the war had seriously damaged his reputation. But I had no trust in Kennedy either. In 1964, the first election I was eligible to vote, I'd cast my ballot for Johnson against Barry Goldwater. I'd believed Johnson, the peace candidate, would end the war. Instead, he escalated it massively. I did not vote for many years after that.

I had begun to see the Vietnam War as a struggle for national liberation and wanted the guerrillas of the Viet Cong to win. The war dominated the news. One unforgettable photo showed a South Vietnamese officer executing a very slight, dark-haired young man, allegedly a member of the Viet Cong. The young man grimaces as the bullet enters his skull. I still have the Associated Press photograph hanging on the wall behind my desk. Next to it is James Griffith's photo showing the murdered man's mother. She's holding a Vietnamese newspaper with the execution photo and, in the other hand, a medal awarded posthumously to her son by the Vietnamese.

DAYS OF LAW AND RAGE

It was in this context in early 1968 that the LDF asked me to clerk for a lawyer who was researching the possibility of a school desegregation lawsuit in Baltimore. The suit would attempt to merge the school systems of two counties, one almost all Black, the other almost all white. My job would be factual research concerning the racial make-up of the various schools and what an integrated system would look like.

On a cold, wet winter evening, I boarded the train to Baltimore. I was nervous both because of the importance of the assignment and because it meant working with a private lawyer I did not know. I arrived at the 1930s railroad station, which had seen better days. The grimy columns holding up its high-ceilinged waiting rooms sagged with disrepair. A grizzled man in his late forties, wearing a fedora, met me. He was formal rather than warm and told me I would be staying at a cheap motel rather than with him, which suited me fine.

It was a lonely job. I visited local government offices to collect school statistics and met mostly with Black residents who might be the plaintiffs in a lawsuit. But I had no friends in Baltimore. I worked and ate alone, and spent my evenings in my motel room reading or watching TV.

On the evening of April 4, 1968, a news flash shattered this grim monotony. Martin Luther King Jr. had been murdered in Memphis, where he was supporting Black sanitation workers who were paid lower wages than their white counterparts and had decided to strike. I was already in a minor depression, having dropped out of school to live in a motel, doing work that barely engaged me. King's murder nearly paralyzed me.

Uprisings broke out in scores of Black communities across the United States. Baltimore's was among the biggest and most violent. I was living in a Black neighborhood with a curfew in force most of the day. I didn't leave my room for two days. I subsisted on motel coffee, crackers, and chocolate. I could see tanks and armored carriers patrolling outside, as thousands of National Guard and federal troops flooded the streets. I felt trapped and profoundly alone. After several more days I finally escaped Baltimore and didn't look back.

MOVING THE BAR

When I returned to New York, the mood in the LDF office was somber but determined. Before his death, King and his organization, the Southern Christian Leadership Conference (SCLC), had been pushing for the passage of an Economic Bill of Rights and anti-poverty legislation. He had planned a massive Poor People's Campaign, featuring a large tent encampment outside of Washington D.C. SCLC decided to continue this work, and LDF was busy securing the legal permits and doing background work. I was assigned to assist Haywood Burns, a young, smart, engaging Black lawyer with whom I became close friends. Haywood would later have an important career, which included defending Angela Davis and the inmates involved in the Attica prison rebellion. He became dean of the City University of New York Law School before he died tragically in an auto accident in South Africa in 1996.

Shortly after I returned from Baltimore, Columbia students had begun to demonstrate against the university's connections to the Vietnam War and its plan to build a gymnasium in Harlem's Morningside Park. Over several days, the standoff escalated into tense confrontation, and I got caught up in it.

On April 30, 1968 I passed through the wrought-iron gates at 116th Street and Broadway and entered the campus. Students milled about in the main courtyard. Some wore crew cuts and dressed in khakis and loafers as they had in prep school, but others sported long hair and Che berets or psychedelic tie-dye T-shirts. They listened to fiery speeches and browsed at card tables stacked with radical pamphlets, buttons, and posters. I soaked up the festive atmosphere.

A week before, protesting students had taken over five buildings, including Columbia's huge, domed, Romanesque centerpiece, Low Library, where the university's president, Grayson Kirk, had his office. Classes had been cancelled, and now hundreds of protesters were occupying the buildings around the clock, snoozing on marble floors in sleeping bags, hanging out of windows, eating whatever food supporters handed up to them from outside.

The students had made two key demands: that Columbia cancel its contracts with federal agencies involved in the Vietnam War, and that it stop building a gymnasium in a public park in neighboring Morningside Heights. The gym was to have two separate entrances, one for Columbia students and the other for the predominantly Black residents of West Harlem. At a time when "Whites Only" and "Blacks Only" signs were still being removed from schools, bathrooms, and lunch counters across the country, the university had enraged students and residents alike with its plan for the gym.

No members of my law school class were involved in the occupation. This was partly because my class was relatively conservative, but it also reflected the fact that law students faced special risks. Between each of us and our careers stood the Bar Character Committee. Occupying buildings or getting arrested could end our chances of admission to the bar.

To my amazement, however, Eleanor Stein and Gus Reichbach had joined the occupation, risking everything. My politics were progressive and I was sympathetic to the students' demands and their tactics, but for me, not having been in school for several months, the occupation came out of the blue. To join now felt like jumping off a cliff. It was a leap that I was not prepared to make—at least not yet.

As the sun set on April 30, the skies darkened and the mood began to change. The campus became oddly quiet. The "Majority Coalition," students who opposed the occupation, disappeared. Rumors began to spread. Someone said to me, "Columbia is calling in the cops."

I was shocked and angry, and the situation was frightening. Whenever the police came in—though at elite universities they generally had not—violence was almost inevitable. I knew mass arrests were possible. And my mind kept playing images of bloody police attacks against demonstrators. Only two months before, white police had fired on a crowd of protesters at South Carolina State College at Orangeburg, killing three Black students and wounding 27.

My visits to Columbia the previous week had been a pleasant distraction from my personal problems. But now the rapidly escalating situation forced me to confront myself at a basic level. A moral choice stared me in the face. I could fade into the outskirts of the crowd, slink back to my apartment, and avoid any commitment. Or I could join the protesters.

I hesitated a moment. Then I walked up the steps toward Low Library. I approached a line of protesters blocking a key entrance to protect the occupying students inside. I knew no one on that line. But a young man held out his arm. I reached out and linked my right arm to his. On my left side, a young woman held out her arm. I linked my other arm to hers.

I was scared. I had never done anything like this before. As the hour grew late, the number of students thinned. About 20 of us stayed, arm-in-arm, in front of the right-side entrance to Low Library.

Suddenly, around 2 a.m., they appeared: waves upon waves of cops flooding through the main gates, more than a thousand of them, some in uniform, some in plain clothes. As the police marched toward us in military formation, we tightened our chain of arms and began to sing "We Shall Overcome."

But it was over in seconds. Armed with billy clubs, the cops stormed our puny barrier and started swinging. A muscular cop in plain clothes picked me up like a matchstick, carried me a few feet, threw me on the ground, and gave me a couple of hard whacks with his stick. I lay stunned.

When I was able to look up, I saw violent chaos all around me. Terrified students from other occupied buildings tried to run away, but enraged police wielding nightsticks chased them down and smashed their skulls. Blood stained the ground everywhere I looked. I picked myself up and staggered toward the gate at Broadway, seeking a way out.

But even at the gate there were more cops beating students. It was totally one-sided. I saw no one fight back against the police. In one night, 150 injured students ended up in the hospital. More than 700 were arrested and taken into custody. Somehow I escaped. Bloody, bruised and sore, I walked down Broadway. My heart beat fast, and my mind raced.

In the end, the police violence backfired on the university administration. Furious students led a strike that effectively shut down Columbia for the rest of the school year. President Grayson Kirk did not even attend the graduation ceremony and resigned before the fall semester. The brutality had radicalized hundreds if not thousands of students—as it had me.

I still had a job at LDF, but it was no longer my priority. All I remember of the rest of that spring and summer of 1968 is hanging out at Columbia with Margie, Eleanor Stein, and other radicals from the law school and university. I also got to meet some of the left-wing lawyers who wound up representing many of the students who had been arrested during the protests. These lawyers would become my role models, colleagues, and friends throughout my entire legal career.

Columbia filed disciplinary charges against the students. In response, the radical lawyers filed a federal lawsuit against the university that would later be an inspiration for my work at the Center for Constitutional Rights. The lawsuit, *Grossner v. Trustees of Columbia University*, sought an injunction against the disciplinary charges on the grounds that the "sit-in," as it was called in the papers, was peaceful, no illegal acts had been committed, and the university had failed to seriously consider student demands. The suit also charged that students had been assaulted, and asserted that the university's administrative structure was "essentially unchanged since 1754" and "affords no participatory power in the faculty or student body in the determination of policies and programs of the University."

The suit claimed that the university failed to implement the recommendation of a Joint Committee—of faculty, administrators, and students—that all trespass charges be dropped. The Joint Committee had found that the students did not deserve the maximum punishment that would be given in an "ordinary atmosphere" because the situation was not "ordinary"; that those engaged in the "sit-in" had acted out of "deep commitment, not personal animus, convinced that the university was not responsive to legitimate demands," and that the university might share responsibility for what occurred.

This extraordinary political-legal lawsuit changed the way I viewed the law. While some of its legal claims were valid, many others lacked merit and were instead political points about Columbia's wrongs and its authoritarian structures. The suit's emphasis on student participation in university decision-making reflected the radical principle of participatory democracy, as set out in the Students for a Democratic Society's Port Huron Statement of 1962. One of the lawsuit's main purposes was to continue publicizing the students' demands and to legitimate the sit-in. The lawyers were willing to craft the suit around political demands, even if these arguments had little chance of legal success. They understood that their clients' political struggle must remain front and center.

About a dozen lawyers worked on the case. Most were from the Center for Constitutional Rights (CCR) and the National Lawyers Guild (NLG). Founded in 1966 by lawyers who'd worked in the Southern civil rights movement, CCR had a mission to protect those trying to bring about progressive social change. Three of CCR's four founders—William Kunstler, Arthur Kinoy, and Morton Stavis—were involved in the Columbia case, along with two of its younger attorneys.

The NLG was a much older bar association, established in 1937 as a liberal alternative to the conservative American Bar Association, which did not admit Black people. The NLG had supported President Franklin Roosevelt's New Deal programs, and at one point included among its membership the likes of Thurgood Marshall and prominent liberals. But the Guild came under attack during the McCarthy period. The House

Committee on Un-American Activities branded it the "legal bulwark of the Communist Party." Although the Guild eventually overturned that designation in court, the damage was done. By the time of the Columbia sit-in, its membership had dwindled to about 400.

Among the NLG lawyers working on the case were Mary Kaufman, Jonathan and David Lubell, and William Schaap. Collectively, they represented the NLG's historical trajectory. Kaufman, an original member of the NLG and an avowed Communist who had been a Nuremberg prosecutor, was a great veteran political lawyer. The Lubells were twin brothers in their mid-30s who had both graduated from Harvard Law School in the 1950s. As law students, they had declined to answer questions about their membership in the Communist Party. As a result, the Harvard law review had rejected them and, for many years, the New York Bar refused to admit them. Most students of their generation had been too afraid to join an organization declared subversive by the government. The Lubells were among a handful of NLG lawyers in that age group. Bill Schaap, just a few years older than me, represented the influx into the Guild of lawyers from the New Left.

Skilled as these lawyers were, they did not win the case. Judge Frankel (the same judge from my Chemical Bank case) ruled against the students, some of whom were suspended. Still, the lawyers had kept attention on the occupation, which turned out to have its desired effect. The university did not build the gym in Morningside Park, and it stopped much of its work with the Pentagon.

In June 1968, moments after winning the California primary, Bobby Kennedy was assassinated. It seemed as though the world had gone mad. The endless Vietnam War, the assassinations of King and Kennedy, the urban rebellions, and police brutality experienced first-hand at Columbia—all of these events disabused me of any previously held belief that the United States and its officials stood for or did good in the world. If I'd had any doubts about whether Dr. King was right to describe the U.S.

as "the greatest purveyor of violence in the world today," by June 1968 they had been decisively dispelled.

I returned to law school at Columbia in the late summer of 1968, a bit earlier than other students. I rejoined the law review, but left after a few weeks to give myself time for political activism. My politics were becoming more radical, and I went to many anti-war protests in Washington and New York. But I was not yet at the point of joining the thousands of anti-war protesters who besieged the Democratic Convention in Chicago that August in the "Days of Rage." On television, I watched as the Chicago police beat demonstrators. I talked about the events in Chicago with Margie, who was as shocked as I was. I had not had a girlfriend for two years. I was lonely, but it felt good to share my feelings. Margie had recently gotten divorced, and we were becoming closer.

When the academic year began, it was clear that the occupation and the political climate of 1968 had transformed the law school. A new governance structure had been put in place, and the students elected me to represent them on the faculty appointments committee. I was a compromise choice—an academic star liberal enough for the students without being too overtly radical for the administration.

Margie, Gus, Eleanor, and I also helped establish a law-school chapter of the NLG—the first at Columbia since the 1950s. We set up a registration table at lunchtime, just inside the main entrance. Within a few hours we had signed up more than a hundred dues-paying members.

For the next two years, the academic side of law school didn't figure significantly in my life. I never went back to working the way I had the first year, though I still got excellent grades and graduated at the top of my class. But my focus had turned to political activity.

Protests and picketing continued at the law school and Columbia through spring 1969. Students condemned the university's complicity with the Pentagon and its refusal to reinstate those suspended for participating in the April 1968 occupation. Eleanor, one of the Students for a

Democratic Society (SDS) leaders, told the *New York Times*, "We've effectively shut down the college and cut down attendance at the university by half." She warned that unless Columbia met its demands by the end of the spring vacation, SDS would "take further action."

Although I took part in the picketing, I played a more central role in the legal defense of Gus Reichbach, one of the protest organizers. The university had singled him out for serious disciplinary charges that could have resulted in his expulsion. Gus was supposed to stand "trial" before a panel of two or three professors and one student. The student, Ken Kimerling, turned out to be sympathetic to SDS. (Ken, who is still a friend, later pursued a progressive career as a lawyer with the Puerto Rican Legal Defense and Education Fund and then with the Asian American Legal Defense and Education Fund.)

Eleanor, Margie, and I formed Gus's defense team, assisted by attorney Gerald Lefcourt from the NLG. Lefcourt had co-founded The Law Commune, a radical firm whose brash young lawyers defended many activists and draft resisters. Gerry himself became one of the finest criminal defense lawyers in the city, representing, among others, Yippie activist Abbie Hoffman and the Black Panthers.

We were not yet lawyers and did not know much law, but truthfully, there wasn't much in the law that could help Gus. In the earlier *Grossner* decision, Judge Frankel had already established that because Columbia was a private university, most constitutional protections did not apply. Our 12-page brief to the "judges" defended the students' actions and demands and sought to have the charges dismissed on the grounds that the entire "trial" procedure violated due process. We were happy with it, but in Lefcourt's view, we had made no decent legal arguments. Still, after we guilt-tripped him, he remained on the team.

While we worked on the brief, we also mobilized the students. We had to convince the administration and the "judges" that Gus had massive student support and that if he were punished there would be a high cost to the university. Eleanor and I designed a simple quarter-sized button, with black capital lettering across a white background reading: "FREE GUS." We made hundreds and distributed them throughout the university. Along with SDS, we organized many protests, where hundreds of students gathered around the sundial at the center of campus.

The trial took place in the largest room of the law school. At the front stood a podium with four chairs and a wooden table, behind which sat the "judges." They all had stacks of papers in front of them and looked extremely serious. Eleanor, her husband Jonah, Margie, Gus, and I walked in together. Gus wore an eye-catching number—my black velvet vest, covered with red roses. Students jammed the room, mostly scruffy SDS types who were in no mood for a trial.

A stodgy old white guy presented the administration's opening statement. It was impossible to understand because catcalls, screaming, and spitballs from the increasingly raucous crowd kept interrupting it.

Then it was Gus's turn. He began by turning his back on the judges and facing the crowd. It was an electric moment. The first of his family to go to law school, Gus was facing expulsion and a possible end to his career, but he remained courageous and unbowed. Gus understood that his fate would be determined more by the mobilized students than by the university. The cheering crowd repeatedly interrupted Gus's speech, which culminated to thunderous applause and screaming.

When the administration resumed its droning, Eleanor turned and whispered in my ear, "Do you think we've had enough?"

"Yes, end it," I said.

Eleanor turned to Jonah and said, "That's it, end it."

There followed one of the greatest scenes ever to grace the law school. Jonah vaulted over the wall in front of the podium and onto the judges' table. He proceeded to kick all of the judges' papers off the table and onto the floor.

Pandemonium ensued. The audience pelted the podium with tennis balls and soft objects. The judges fled. This trial was over.

Determined to make an example of Gus, the university organized a second trial which only law students would be permitted to attend. Eleanor, Margie, Mark Rudd—the main SDS leader on campus—other SDS activists, and I met a couple of days beforehand to hatch a plan. The university had already chained all of the doors to the auditorium where the second trial would be held. Mark volunteered to go into the building the day before and hide in the bathroom with a wire cutter. On the day of the trial, SDS would create a distraction by protesting at one set of doors, while Mark would cut the chains on another. A second throng of SDS students would then stream in.

On the day of the trial, it was quiet when we walked into the auditorium. The judges sat on stage, before a silent audience of a few hundred law students. A couple of minutes in, loud chanting began outside: "Free Gus!" "Open the trial!" "End the war!" Within minutes, a mass of screaming students had surged onto the stage behind the judges. Our plan had worked perfectly. The second trial was finished.

The university stubbornly held a third trial, this time open only to faculty. But we had already won. The university knew that any severe punishment of Gus would provoke a full-scale student rebellion. Gus walked away a hero, his law school career intact. (Later, his admission to the bar was held up for more than a year because of his activism and his co-authorship, with Kathy Boudin, Brian Glick, and Eleanor Raskin, of *The Bust Book: What to Do Until the Lawyer Comes.* He eventually became a prominent, very liberal judge in New York City.)

The lessons from Gus's Columbia experience were obvious. The professors and the administration were out of touch with what was happening in the world. As the Vietnam War raged, all they could think about were their precious rules of decorum—and their government defense contracts. For Columbia, 1968 was business as usual—until militant student actions made that impossible. It became clear to me that trials are not just won in the courts, but through sustained activism.

In spring of 1969, Margie and I moved in together. Though leftists, her parents objected to our living together outside marriage. So we tied the knot in June at a wedding attended by only a dozen immediate relatives.

I was happy. Margie and I honeymooned on St. John's in the Virgin Islands, where Margie taught me how to snorkel. We then visited my Cleveland family who—despite their rift with my mother—threw a nice party for a hundred or so Ratner relatives to meet Margie.

But the upheaval of our times continued. Over that summer, the United States landed the first person on the moon. At Chappaquiddick, Ted Kennedy had the car accident that killed Mary Jo Kopechne, and in California, the Manson Family murdered Sharon Tate and four others. I remember these events well, though the Stonewall riots in Greenwich Village that launched the gay rights movement completely passed me by. I was aware of the Woodstock festival, but Margie and I did not go. Nor did we attend the Chicago SDS convention in early June, when the SDS split. Some of my friends, including Eleanor Stein, joined the new faction that eventually became the Weathermen.

Margie and I were living a bourgeois life. But our sympathies were with the most militant students, especially the Weathermen. If we did not directly participate, this reflected our personalities more than our beliefs. It was clear to us that the Vietnam War was so devastating and wrong that mass demonstrations had to be supplemented with civil disobedience and a refusal to allow business to continue as usual.

I have almost no memory of the classes I took during my final year at law school. They were the least of my concerns. I went to numerous demonstrations that year, including the National Moratorium in Washington, where I was tear-gassed for the first time and found myself choking and collapsed on the ground. Soon after, the gruesome images from the My Lai massacre in Vietnam were published, and in early 1970 the U.S. government expanded the war into Cambodia, triggering huge protests everywhere, including at Columbia. At Kent State in Ohio, the National Guard murdered four student anti-war protesters, and less than two weeks later at Jackson State in Mississippi, police killed two students and wounded 12. It felt as though the country's young people were in open revolt. At the same time, the FBI escalated its COINTELPRO operations, engaging in systematic surveillance and repression of progressive groups.

The Chicago Eight trial, in which Abbie Hoffman, Bobby Seale, Jerry Rubin, and others were accused of conspiracy to riot at the 1968 Democratic Convention, dragged on from late 1969 into 1970. It was a transparent attempt to destroy the leadership of the anti-war movement. Bill Kunstler became a national figure for his defense of the protesters. Every day the defendants and their witnesses, including radical poet Allen Ginsberg, challenged their aged foil Judge Julius Hoffman and made front-page news with their antics. At the end of the trial, Judge Hoffman sentenced Bill to more than four years in prison for contempt of court—the longest such sentence ever imposed on a lawyer.

I didn't know Bill then, but I will never forget his appearance at the NLG dinner in New York a few days after the sentencing. He had just gotten out of jail on bail. Proud of his actions during the trial, he thrust his fist in the air. At the time, such courageous defiance was unimaginable to me. This was a lawyer facing extended prison time and possible disbarment. Yet he showed not a trace of fear or regret.

Meanwhile, Eleanor had stopped going to classes, pouring all her energy into activities with the Weathermen. I always loved seeing her. One day in October 1969 she described to me the "Days of Rage," a confrontation between Weathermen and Chicago police after the radicals had smashed windows and trashed cars in keeping with their slogan "Bring the War Home." She showed me a photograph of the Weathermen preparing to march. Bill Ayers, whom I did not then know, stood in the front line. Many wore helmets and some carried baseball bats. Today as I look at that photo, they all seem very young.

In December 1969, after Chicago police murdered Fred Hampton, the charismatic young leader of the Chicago Black Panthers, I met with Eleanor. She really wanted me to come with her to the Flint War Council where the future of SDS was going to be decided. I was not even close to going.

A few weeks later the Flint War Council dissolved SDS, and the Weathermen decided to go underground to carry out bombings and other military activities against the war. Thrown out of law school, Eleanor left New York.

That was the last Margie and I heard from her until the next spring when we received a phone call from someone who spoke only a few words: "Eleanor was not in the townhouse."

The anonymous caller was referring to the townhouse on West 11th Street in Greenwich Village that exploded on March 6, 1970. Some of the Weathermen had been building an anti-personnel bomb intended to be detonated at a U.S. military base. Instead, the bomb had gone off in the townhouse, killing three people and leaving two survivors. Eleanor was not present or involved. But others we knew were, including Kathy Boudin, one of the survivors. The townhouse belonged to the wealthy parents of Cathy Wilkerson, the other survivor.

It is remarkable how quickly the Weathermen moved from militant protest to the Days of Rage to bombing property to anti-personnel bombings. It all happened in the space of a few months, and the West 11th Street explosion put an end to what some leftists from that generation deride as "townhouse politics"—a term that refers to well-off kids playing with bombs in their parents' homes.

I didn't believe in every action the Weathermen engaged in, and I never have countenanced killing people. Nor do I believe that violence alone, outside of the context of a strong grassroots movement, can change policy in a progressive way. But I had no problem with symbolic bombings in which no one was injured. And though I would not engage in such acts myself, I understood why friends and clients of mine said, of another bombing, "We didn't do it, but we dug it."

I still argue with some of my friends about violence. A friend in an anti-Vietnam War group said: "We were out on the streets every day, handing out leaflets, organizing marches and demonstrations. The movement was growing. Bombing alienated ordinary people and set back the movement."

I disagree. The leaflets and marches were important and showed the depth of the movement. But they didn't end the war. I believe that change comes when policy makers are made uncomfortable and daily life is disrupted. Today, I look back on the Weathermen and other bombers as having been helpful to build the movement and stop the war.

And yet, by temperament I was more or less a pacifist. I couldn't resolve the contradiction between my political views and my personality.

As we approached graduation, Margie and I began planning for life after law school. Margie wanted to defend the poorest of the poor. She took a job as a criminal defense lawyer at Legal Aid. I decided to clerk for a federal judge, which is what many of the top students did for one or two years after law school.

Although I had quit law review, I had worked at the LDF, and some of the more liberal professors respected me. Walter Gellhorn, a renowned Columbia professor, suggested I clerk for Judge Irving Kaufman on the Second Circuit Court of Appeals. It was a prestigious job that might have led to a Supreme Court clerkship. But I had read Judge Kaufman's decision in the "atom spy" case of Julius and Ethel Rosenberg, parents of two young children. He meted out the death penalty with language that still rings in my ears:

I consider your crime worse than murder... I believe your conduct in putting into the hands of the Russians the A-bomb
years before our best scientists predicted Russia would perfect
the bomb has already caused, in my opinion, the Communist
aggression in Korea, with the resultant casualties exceeding
50,000 and who knows but that millions of more innocent people may pay the price of your treason.

Kaufman had presided over a trial filled with constitutional errors and
bereft of any solid evidence that a "secret" to the bomb had been passed
to the Russians. Though the Rosenbergs were convicted of conspiracy,
not espionage, Kaufman sentenced them to death after prosecutors
insisted this would coerce the Rosenbergs to confess. They did not. They
died in the electric chair on June 19, 1953.

Remarkably, because of the caring parents and community that
adopted them, the Rosenbergs' children led productive and interesting
lives. I eventually became close to Robbie Meeropol, the younger of the
two. His daughter Rachel, Julius and Ethel Rosenberg's granddaughter,
now works with me as an attorney at CCR.

Judge Kaufman was as Jewish as the Rosenbergs. I have no doubt
that he intended his severe rhetoric and the death sentence to demonstrate that not all Jews were Bolsheviks, that Jews, too, could be patriotic.
There was no way I could work for him.

Instead, I applied to clerk for Thurgood Marshall on the Supreme
Court—a long shot—and for two other federal judges. Judge Frankel,
who had presided over *Ratner v. Chemical Bank*, offered me a prestigious clerkship—his clerks often went on to clerk for Justice Marshall.
However, federal district court Judge Constance Baker Motley also
offered me a clerkship. At the time, she was the only Black woman federal
judge in the United States.

It was hard to decide. Judge Frankel was very smart, but often made decisions I disagreed with—he had a narrow view of the law. I agreed with Motley's decisions far more, and I admired her intelligence and courage. She had worked at LDF, argued numerous cases in the Supreme Court, and was among the most liberal judges in the country. I decided to accept the job with Judge Motley.

Law school ended with a bang and a whimper. The bang was the April 1970 U.S. invasion of Cambodia. Students all around the country went on strike. Columbia suspended many classes and gave students the option to skip finals and accept a pass. Some students still took the exams, but other leftists and I refused to participate.

The whimper was the graduation ceremony. My brother, Margie, and I were all receiving our law degrees. It was a big deal, especially for my mother. But none of us attended the ceremony. For my mother's sake, it's a decision I still regret.

4
WORKING FOR THE JUDGE

Our work began that fall of 1970. Margie's legal aid office was in the decrepit old Manhattan Criminal Courthouse at 100 Centre Street. That building told you almost everything you needed to know about how the authorities treated urban crime. It was dirty—dirty windows, dirty marble walls, and dirty floors. The elevators, jammed with Black and Puerto Rican defendants and their families, often broke down. The courtrooms, presided over by mostly white male judges, were dark and depressing. In one of them, a letter had fallen off the "In God We Trust" motto on the wall. It read "In God we rust." Dickens was alive and well at 100 Centre Street.

Walking a few blocks from Margie's office to the federal courthouse at Foley Square where I worked was like going from an impoverished neighborhood to a wealthy white enclave. Designed like a massive, columned Greco-Roman temple, the limestone courthouse was built on a six-story foundation that covered almost an entire block. On top of it rose an imposing 30-story tower. The temple design sent a message of power—that law comes from on high and that judges simply carry out immutable principles, resting on a sacred foundation. Of course, this is poppycock. Laws are made by people and reflect the class, biases, and politics of those who write and enforce them.

This intimidating building housed the district court where federal cases, both civil and criminal, were litigated. These included most of the major Wall Street financial cases, embezzlement cases from federal agencies, bank robberies, major Mafia and drug cases, and a few civil rights and constitutional-law cases. In addition to the district court, the Second Circuit Court of Appeals, probably the second most important appeals court in the country, was located in the same building.

Every day for a year, dressed in a jacket and tie, I would take a subway downtown and walk up the steep steps to the courthouse entrance. In contrast to the dingy Manhattan criminal courthouse, the federal courthouse boasted a lobby with a 30-foot-high ceiling, polished white marble floors, and gleaming, bronze-encased elevators.

As one of the newer members of the court, Judge Motley worked in isolated chambers on the 29th floor. Her secretary, Roberta Thomas, sat in a small antechamber, where she typed all the opinions, making duplicates on carbon paper. I shared a small room with the other clerk, Lynn Huntley. Our desks were crammed in, back to back, but the views were spectacular—you could see the East River, the New York harbor, all of Brooklyn, parts of Queens, and beyond. And all of the walls were painted dark pink.

"When I picked the color, the other judges were a bit shocked," Judge Motley told me, laughing. "They said no judge had pink chambers."

Judge Motley was about 50 years old, tall, and very dignified in her well-made, sober dresses from Lord and Taylor. She was serious almost all the time, but when she found something funny, she would throw her head back and roar with laughter. "Michael, did you hear that?" she would say. Often, "that" was an unprepared lawyer who had made a foolish argument or tried to pull the wool over her eyes.

Like Judge Motley and Roberta, the other clerk, Lynn, was Black. Like me, she had graduated from Columbia Law School. She was liberal, less radical than I, and much more wedded to the law.

Our job as clerks was mainly to research and draft opinions that Judge Motley would review, edit, rewrite, and issue. We also attended oral arguments and trials. One of us would accompany the judge to court and be ready to run to the library to do some quick research or to bring her a law book. Judge Motley, whom we simply referred to as "the judge," did not give us a lot of direction. Sometimes legal papers would pile up in our office, and Lynn and I would look through them and draft opinions without any direction. Mostly, though, we would go into her office, briefly discuss the case, and she would tell us what she wanted the result to be and how we should construct our opinions.

One day in early spring of my first year there, Lynn and I were working in the chambers until almost six. A lawyer came in with legal papers on behalf of his client, a pregnant prisoner awaiting trial in the Women's House of Detention, then located in the heart of Greenwich Village. (Later replaced by a beautiful garden, the prison once housed a number of well-known prisoners, including Angela Davis.)

"My client, Afeni Shakur, is having a difficult pregnancy," the lawyer said. "She wants to see her own doctor, and the prison warden won't let her. Her health and the baby's health are in danger. She needs to see a doctor immediately."

The lawyer handed us a few papers and asked for a hearing that evening.

"Wait outside while we review this and talk to the judge," I said.

We knew that Afeni Shakur was one of 21 Black Panthers who had been charged with more than 100 counts of conspiracy to bomb New York City landmarks—including the New York Botanical Garden in the Bronx. No explosions had actually occurred, and the idea of a plot to bomb a garden seemed absurd. Many of us on the left thought the Panther 21 case was a political prosecution intended to destroy the Black Panther Party (BPP) in New York. (Years later, FBI documents released under the Freedom of Information Act revealed that the Panther 21 prosecutions, like the murder charges against Bobby Seale and Ericka Huggins in New Haven and the murder of Fred Hampton in Chicago, were carried out as part of the FBI's Counter-Intelligence Program.)

Lynn was not enthusiastic about Afeni Shakur's request for a hearing. "There is no constitutional right at stake," she argued. "This case belongs in state court."

Normally, only one clerk presented a case to the judge and went to the courtroom with her. If Lynn were the accompanying clerk, she would argue that federal intervention was not warranted.

"I think there is a due-process right to decent medical treatment in prison," I told Lynn, "and Afeni is not getting that."

"The judge won't buy that argument, Michael," Lynn answered. "But if you're so sure, then you take the case to her."

I went into the judge's office and explained the situation.

"Michael," Judge Motley said calmly, "call the attorney for the prison and have him, the warden, and Afeni come to court this evening."

A few hours later we gathered in the district court's largest "ceremonial courtroom." With high ceilings and dark wooden benches that could hold a few hundred people, it was used for special occasions such as the swearing in of new citizens and for emergency cases. Back then, each judge spent at least two three-week sessions adjudicating emergency cases, which were not randomly assigned as were the normal cases. Instead, anyone filing an emergency case would get the judge who happened to be on duty. This system encouraged blatant judge shopping. Clearly, Afeni's lawyers had waited until Judge Motley, the most liberal judge on the court, was on emergency duty.

Only the litigants, Judge Motley, the stenographer, and I were in the courtroom. Afeni, a small, intense 20-year-old woman with a bulging belly, was far along in her pregnancy.

Her attorney began. "Given Afeni's critical health situation," he argued, "a request to see her own doctor is reasonable."

"The prison doctors are competent and professional, your honor," responded the prison's attorney. "Moreover, this case doesn't belong in federal court, and there are all kinds of security issues."

Judge Motley asked the warden, a tough-looking Black woman, to take the stand.

"How can you deny this woman the right to see her own doctor?" the judge asked.

The warden could not provide a good reason.

Dismissing the claimed security problems, Judge Motley focused on the essential humanitarian issue. The hearing was over almost before it began. From the bench Judge Motley ruled that Afeni's doctor could treat her in prison.

On May 13, 1971, Afeni and the other Panther 21 defendants were acquitted of all charges. Although the trial had taken nearly a year, the jury deliberated for only 45 minutes. I went to the victory party that evening at the law commune at 640 Broadway. Many of the Panther lawyers were from the commune, including Gerry Lefcourt, who had helped us with Gus Reichbach's Columbia trial. The party was an exhilarating, scruffy affair, full of long-haired, bearded, radical lawyers. Although the case was a major victory for New York's Black Panthers, the leadership had been imprisoned for two years and during that time the party had become a shadow of its former self.

One month and three days after the Panther 21 acquittal, Afeni Shakur gave birth. Named for the Peruvian revolutionary Tupac Amaru, Afeni's son became one of the most famous rap stars in the world—Tupac Shakur.

I never met Tupac, although I had the chance. Sometime in the early '80s as I walked into CCR, the receptionist, Alberto, who played and loved music, called to me through the glass window. "Hey, Michael, you want to go hear Afeni's son, Tupac?"

I replied with almost no interest, "What are you talking about?"

Alberto explained, "He's playing at a party tonight, and we can go."

Tupac was an unknown teenager at the time. The last thing I wanted to do was hear a young kid rapping—a hasty decision I would later regret.

In 1996, at the age of 25, Tupac Shakur was murdered in Las Vegas by an unidentified drive-by shooter. But his profound influence on rap music lives on to this day.

As in Afeni's case, Judge Motley often ruled with a combination of the law, her heart, and her life experience—especially her own experience of racism. One day when I had some rare spare time, I discovered a pile of moth-eaten petitions on a shelf near my desk and started to read them. Most were from desperate prisoners who had exhausted their state court appeals and were asking the federal court to set aside their convictions because of a constitutional error. Often the convicted prisoners had filed the handwritten petitions themselves without a lawyer, and the return address was a prison. But almost none of the hundreds of petitions were ever heard in federal court, and only a minuscule number of prisoners were given a new trial or released. So judges and clerks literally put the petitions on the back shelf, where they often sat for more than a year before anyone reviewed them. (Over the years, Congress has so severely limited a state prisoner's recourse to the federal courts that today it almost does not exist.)

I picked up one of the languishing petitions actually filed by a lawyer.[2] The petitioner, a Black man, had been convicted of robbery in a New York state court and was serving a long sentence. One of the many claims stuck out: the prosecutor had used racially prejudicial language in his examination of a witness and in his summation, but the judge had failed to exclude the language from the jury's consideration. The petition claimed the language was so harmful that the jury could not reach

---

2   Lynn Huntley, the other clerk, tells the same story with different details about which of us read the original petition and some of the offensive language.

an unbiased verdict. I searched the transcript and found the passage in question. The prosecutor had examined an eyewitness:

Q. "Can you describe the defendant's hair?"
A. "Yes, it was short, curly and black."
Q. "Did the hair on the defendant remind you of anything?"
A. "Yes, the fur on an animal."

The defendant's attorney objected to the comparison of the defendant's hair—and by implication the defendant himself—with that of an animal. The judge overruled the objection.

I then read the prosecutor's summation. "The eyewitness was sure of the defendant's identity," the prosecutor told the jury. "She said he had hair like that of an animal. Look at the defendant's hair. Is his hair not like that of an animal?"

The blatant racism stunned me. I walked into Judge Motley's, explained the case, and showed her the transcript.

The judge called Roberta in, sat back in her chair, and proceeded to read the prejudicial passages aloud, shaking her head and laughing. Then she said, "We're going to reverse the conviction. Just let the Second Circuit [the appeals court] tell me this wasn't racist."

This time the Second Circuit upheld her decision.

But the appeals court very often reversed her decisions, and her courthouse critics gossiped that Judge Motley was "not that smart"—referring to a woman who had argued ten cases in the Supreme Court and won nine of them. No appeals court judge had a record close to that. "Not that smart" simply meant that the conservative, business-oriented appeals court did not agree with decisions she had based, at least in part, on elementary fairness or equal treatment before the law.

I have often thought about this question of who is "smart." Somehow, conventional legal pundits consider Supreme Court Chief Justice John

Roberts "very smart." He can upend court precedent by narrowly reading earlier decisions that established fundamental protections. He can find all the ambiguities in those cases and can color key facts in his own way. He can reach a decision that appears logical, but is simply a scholastic exercise masquerading as a judicial opinion. However, when a woman and/or Black judge reads cases to establish rights broadly and inject fairness into a decision, the legal pundits label that judge "not smart."

Judge Motley was the first Black woman admitted to the almost entirely exclusive white male club of the federal bench. Many of the judges in both the district and appeals courts had worked at major law firms representing large corporations in the financial district where they protected their own. Of the dozen or so appeals court judges, none was a woman and none was Black. Thurgood Marshall had briefly sat on the court on his way to the Supreme Court, but he was the lone exception.

Initially, political pundits had expected Judge Motley to be appointed to the federal appeals court. But as she wrote in her autobiography, "[T]here was so much opposition on the court and among Wall Street lawyers to my appointment....that [President Lyndon] Johnson was forced to withdraw my name."

Judge Motley was never appointed to the higher court. "[T]hey found fault with my liberal views... and my belief in sending stock manipulators to jail," she wrote. Judge Motley often sentenced white-collar criminals, who were almost exclusively white, to very severe sentences. "Most of the judges in this court treat white-collar crimes with a slap on the wrist despite their seriousness," she explained to me. "Yet those same judges give nearly life sentences to Black drug dealers." White drug dealers often got lighter sentences because the judges believed they were dealing "recreational" drugs, as opposed to "hard" drugs.

The judge's efforts to overcome this different treatment of white and Black defendants did not mean she was lenient with Black ones. Once when she had to sentence a Black businessman from Harlem, she told me,

"Michael, just wait until you see what happens. The front row of the court will be crowded with all the important people who run Harlem. They will sit there trying to intimidate me so I give a lighter sentence." Of course, she did not bend to the intimidation.

Judge Motley rarely, if ever, lunched with other judges in the special judicial dining room. As a result, Lynn, Roberta, or I had to bring her lunch from the cafeteria—a task I didn't enjoy. I'd been trained to do legal research and draft opinions, not deliver lunch. In retrospect, however, I understand the judge's reluctance to dine with her colleagues. I think she felt uncomfortable in a situation where she appeared not wanted.

On rare occasions, Judge Motley took Lynn and me out to one of the local restaurants for lunch. She told us wonderful stories. One of the funniest was how she got appointed as a district court judge in 1966. She had already served as the first Black borough president of Manhattan and hoped to be the first Black woman federal district court judge.

The official story written by historians is that Senator Robert Kennedy of New York courageously pushed for her and that President Johnson nominated her, despite opposition from Southern senators and federal judges. At lunch Judge Motley told us a different story.

"I was in the New York state senate," she said. "Bobby was a U.S. senator and wanted his own person as majority leader of the state senate. I wouldn't vote for his choice. When it came time for my nomination to the court, Bobby opposed it—but not publicly. Probably to spite Bobby, Johnson nominated me for the court."

Holding her hand to her ear as if it were a telephone, she described the call from Johnson, "Hello Connie, this is the president," she said in perfect imitation of Johnson's Texas drawl. "I just want to congratulate you on your confirmation. I have Bobby Kennedy next to me. He wants to be one of the first to congratulate you." The judge, almost beside herself with laughter, then imitated Kennedy's Boston accent: "Connie, it's just wonderful to have you as a federal judge, congratulations."

Already known for his support of civil rights, Kennedy had no choice but to vote for her nomination. President Johnson had purposely put him in an awkward position, and had given Judge Motley a good laugh as well.

I was sitting in my office one day when Bill Kunstler and Morton Stavis, two of the founders of the Center for Constitutional Rights, rushed in looking for Judge Motley. I didn't know either one, but noticed they were both aggressive, forceful, and loud. Morty, large, heavy-set, and determined, did most of the talking. I could barely get a word in and felt intimidated.

Morty explained that their colleague, the lawyer Arthur Kinoy, had been subpoenaed to a grand jury to testify about the whereabouts of his daughter Joanne Kinoy. The government claimed she knew the whereabouts of some people in the Weather Underground. "Arthur refused to testify," Morty said, "but then his daughter appeared in court and the government served her with a subpoena to testify. So now we need Judge Motley to hear a motion to quash the subpoena against Joanne Kinoy— and we need the hearing immediately."

I already knew about the case and about Arthur Kinoy, a law professor at Rutgers and another founder of CCR. Physically he was hardly imposing—about five foot four, thin, and small of frame—but radiated brilliance and intensity. Always on the front line of what he called "the people's struggles," he began every speech with "Sisters and brothers." Arthur had argued and won *Dombrowski v. Pfister*, a landmark Supreme Court case that challenged Louisiana's attacks on the civil rights movement. He was a pre-eminent activist lawyer who had represented witnesses before the House Un-American Activities Committee, where he had been roughed up and physically removed by marshals. He was also active in the Southern civil rights movement and a key lawyer in the appeal of the Chicago Eight anti-war activists.

Initially, Judge Frankel had heard the case against Arthur and his daughter—the same judge who'd decided the Columbia occupation cases and *Ratner v. Chemical Bank*. Kinoy had asserted a parent-child privilege, saying he should not have to testify because it could impair his relationship with his daughter. It was a novel argument. There was no such privilege, as there was with the marital privilege that protected spouses from being compelled to testify against each other. But this was the kind of aggressive defense that I learned was a hallmark of the litigators at CCR.

Frankel ordered Kinoy to testify—something Kinoy would never do. Morty, Bill, and Arthur believed the subpoena to Arthur was a political move to embarrass and possibly imprison him. It may have also related to his role as the primary appeals lawyer for the Chicago Eight. Morty thought the Nixon administration was determined to jail them all.

But at this point Joanne Kinoy appeared, obviating the need for Arthur to testify. The prosecutor asked Joanne to "give testimony and provide other information as defined with respect to the whereabouts, places of residence, activities, acquaintances, habits and customs of two named individuals." It seemed like a prosecutorial fishing expedition. The individuals in question had gone underground. I doubt that Joanne had any idea of their whereabouts.

At the time, the Nixon administration wanted to blunt the force of the anti-war movement. Under the direction of a notorious prosecutor, Guy Goodwin, the Justice Department was using the grand jury as a weapon to attack and jail political activists. The grand jury was supposed to determine whether there was sufficient evidence to charge someone with a crime. It was not supposed to be an intelligence-gathering mechanism. However, that is how it was clearly being used against Arthur Kinoy, Joanne, and others. So far, the courts were not willing to stop this illegal practice.

Anyone subpoenaed to a grand jury had a Fifth Amendment right against self-incrimination. To get around it, the Justice Department would often ask a court to give activist witnesses immunity—a guarantee that the witness cannot be prosecuted for crimes relating to his or her testimony. Because this supposedly removed any Fifth Amendment protection against self-incrimination, the witness could be forced to testify about other activists, demonstrations, and organizing work. If the witness still refused to talk, a judge could send the witness to jail until he or she was willing to testify. This could be months, sometimes stretching into years.

Activists, however, developed a strategy of refusing to talk to the grand jury even if they received immunity. Some went to jail. Those who talked to a grand jury about their friends and political activities were considered rats, like those who named names during the days of the McCarthy anti-Communist witch hunts.

Now that Arthur's testimony was no longer needed to find Joanne, the attention was on her. Joanne asserted her Fifth Amendment right against self-incrimination. The Justice Department promptly went to Judge Frankel, who gave Joanne immunity. It was very unlikely she would testify, and jail loomed.

However, as Morty explained to me, they were now fighting the subpoena with an additional claim. The federal immunity statute had been recently amended so that the immunity now given to witnesses, called "use" immunity, was much narrower than traditional "transactional" immunity. "Use immunity doesn't protect Joanne's right against self-incrimination," Morty said. "It's unconstitutional, and therefore she can't be forced to testify."

I told Morty and Bill I would talk to Judge Motley and get back to them. My heart was pounding. The most prominent leftist lawyers in the country had brought us an important political case. Resistance to the subpoena was really a challenge to Nixon's Vietnam War. I desperately wanted Judge Motley to throw out the subpoena and relieve Joanne from testifying. I did not want to draft a decision that might send Arthur's daughter to jail. While I did not personally know any of the lawyers or Joanne, they were my heroes and an important part of the movement that was taking on Nixon and the war.

After reading the briefs and the cases, I realized that Morty and Bill had a very good argument. The immunity given to witnesses *had* been narrowed. Prior to this new law, the witness could not be prosecuted for a crime related to his testimony, even if independent evidence were used. For example, if I were involved in a robbery and testified to the grand jury, under the old law I could not have been prosecuted for the robbery. Under the new law, while nothing I said could be used against me, if there was independent evidence of my participation in the robbery, I could still be prosecuted.

The constitutional issue before Judge Motley was whether the new and narrower "use" immunity fully protected Joanne's Fifth Amendment right against self-incrimination. The Supreme Court had never dealt with this new statute, but had ruled 70 years before, in 1892, that the older, broader immunity statute fully protected Fifth Amendment rights. Could it be said that the narrower statute did so?

I read all the relevant cases and worked with the judge for many hours in the evening and on weekends in her sprawling, dark apartment on West End Avenue. At first skeptical of Joanne's argument, Judge Motley worked her way through the thicket of contradictory prior opinions. As we talked, her opinion gradually changed.

For the first time, Judge Motley did not ask me to draft any part of the opinion or even a memo. She wrote the entire lengthy, complex decision herself. She found that the narrower immunity offered to Joanne "plainly does not protect a witness against all of the perils which are manifestly within the orbit of the privilege and that it is not consistent with our constitutional notions of fair play." Since the Supreme Court had not explicitly overruled its prior 1892 decision that provided for full Fifth Amendment protection, Judge Motley felt she was "without power to do so."

MOVING THE BAR

I breathed a sigh of relief. Pending appeal, Joanne was out from under.

Amazingly, the government did not appeal, probably for two reasons. First, the Supreme Court still had a liberal majority, and it may well have agreed with Judge Motley. Second, the new use immunity law was passed to help stop organized crime, but Joanne was a political activist, not a Mafia chieftain. A liberal court and a sympathetic defendant didn't look promising for the government.

Two years later, however, the composition of the Supreme Court had changed. In a California case, *Kastigar v. United States*, a couple of non-political witnesses refused to testify to a grand jury, arguing that the use immunity they'd been given did not protect them from self-incrimination. The district and appeals courts ruled in favor of the government. The witnesses appealed. This time, the more conservative Supreme Court ruled against the witnesses and upheld the constitutionality of use immunity.

As much as I liked working for Judge Motley, current events were pushing me further to the left. During the year I clerked for Judge Motley, Lieutenant William Calley was convicted of killing 22 unarmed civilians at the My Lai massacre in Vietnam, and the Weather Underground bombed the Capitol to protest the war. Though I never would have engaged in any bombings, I thought bringing the war home was necessary and supported the huge civil disobedience demonstrations that began on Mayday, 1971.

On June 13, 1971—my 27th birthday—the *New York Times* published the first installment of the Pentagon Papers. In the courthouse where I worked (but not before Judge Motley), the government argued its case to stop the publication of this top-secret Defense Department study of U.S. military involvement in Vietnam starting in the 1940s. By mid-June both the district court and the court of appeals enjoined publication. Then the Supreme Court reversed, allowing the *Times* to publish.

I wanted to be part of all this. While I had the greatest respect and even love for the judge, I knew I couldn't be a traditional civil rights lawyer who depended primarily on the courts to make social change.

Yet I began to see the very personal risks of being an activist lawyer. At the time, Margie and I were living in a garden apartment on the Upper West Side. Our small rocky back yard was separated from our neighbor's by a six-foot wooden fence. In the spring of 1971, our neighbor began to chat with us. He said he owned Alice's Restaurant in New York, named after the famous Arlo Guthrie song. We became friendlier, and our neighbor invited us over for a drink. He said he did a lot of hunting and showed us his rifles.

A few days after our visit, an assistant United States attorney who was prosecuting a criminal case in front of Judge Motley dropped into my office. He was one of the few assistant U.S. attorneys I could stomach. Most of them were arrogant, Ivy League elitists. This one, though, was a charming, down-to-earth, red-haired guy.

"Hey Michael," he said, "one of my clients is a friend of yours." I had no idea what he was talking about. His only client was the United States government, and his job was prosecuting alleged criminals. "He's a neighbor of yours, owns Alice's Restaurant."

"Yes, I know him," I said. "But how do you know him?"

"He's one of my drug informants," he explained. "We caught him in a drug deal. To get a lighter sentence, he sets up drug deals and helps us bust the dealers."

To say I was astounded would be an understatement. Margie and I had a really close call. The informant could easily have offered us a joint. We could have taken a hit from it and been pulled into a messy situation, especially since I was working for a federal judge.

The neighbor obviously was reporting every contact he had to the prosecutor. As a favor to us, the prosecutor was protecting us from our neighbor, warning us to stay away.

I never liked informants. I liked them even less after this—and I hadn't begun to see the breadth of the informant networks the government would use against activists over the next decade.

While I was happy enough in my job with Judge Motley, Margie found her job at legal aid depressing. As a beginning criminal lawyer, she represented people accused of the pettiest street crimes—soft drugs, purse snatchings, car break-ins. Almost all of her clients were Black or Puerto Rican, young, and very poor. These defendants were often jailed pending trial for weeks, even months, because they couldn't raise bail. Margie came home each night thinking about the young men left in jail for lack of a few dollars. Soon most of her salary was going to her clients' bail. The work took an enormous emotional toll on her. Within a year or so, she quit.

Margie and I were having our own troubles. From the outside we were a perfect couple, two lefty Columbia law graduates living in heady political times in the heart of New York City. But that was not enough. I was somewhat oppressive and overbearing, and Margie felt constrained by her job and our relationship. Toward the spring of 1971, we separated. I was devastated. But after discussing our problems, we got back together, trying to make it work.

My one-year clerkship with Judge Motley was about to end. I could have applied for another clerkship at an appeals court and conceivably later at the Supreme Court. But I wanted to get active in the movement. I spent hours pondering what to do.

"Where can I do the most good for the left?" I asked.

After hearing me repeat this for the tenth time, Margie said, "Enough already. You are not that important. Just get a job."

She was right. I applied for three jobs. One was at the most important leftist law firm in New York: Rabinowitz, Boudin, & Standard. Leonard Boudin and Victor Rabinowitz had played chess with Che Guevara and represented revolutionary Cuba. They were among the best-known and smartest constitutional lawyers in New York. All the firm's lawyers interviewed me. One of them, Kristin Booth Glen, a feisty, beautiful young woman wearing a belt made of fake bullets, particularly impressed me.

I next interviewed with the Center for Constitutional Rights. The offices were in a run-down loft above a paint store, just around the corner from the porn shops in the seedy Times Square neighborhood. CCR was run as a collective, and all the lawyers and legal workers interviewed me, including the big shots—Bill Kunstler, Morty Stavis, and Arthur Kinoy who'd met me during the Joanne Kinoy case. I told them I wanted to work at the Center because I wanted to represent the movement.

My third interview was for a teaching job in the constitutional law clinic at Rutgers Law School. I had never practiced law, so I wondered how I could teach at a clinic. Still, the interview proved very interesting because it was conducted by a professor on the appointments commit-tee—Ruth Bader Ginsburg, who would later become a Supreme Court justice and an iconic pioneer of women's rights law. After the interview, she took the bus back to Manhattan with me and tried to convince me to come to Rutgers. Persuasive as she was, I didn't really want to teach. I wanted to be a radical lawyer and an activist.

CCR and Rabinowitz, Boudin & Standard each had only one job opening. I knew I was highly qualified, but another really good candi-date, Rhonda Schoenbrod (later Rhonda Copelon) had also applied for both jobs. She had gone to Yale Law School and, like me, had clerked for a federal judge. While Rhonda's politics weren't then as far left as mine, she was a strong, smart, progressive feminist, with the makings of an outstanding lawyer.

To our great surprise, both of us were offered both jobs. Both of us turned down Rabinowitz and accepted jobs at CCR. It was a sign of the times that we both jumped at the chance to work at an aggressive, risk-taking, and overtly political collective.

At the end of the summer of 1971, it was time for me to leave the clerkship with Judge Motley. I felt I'd learned as much as I needed to about the federal courts. And I was impatient with what I saw then as Judge Motley's liberal, limited politics. She believed in social progress primarily through the legal system. Echoing the new left, I believed that change comes from the streets. I was eager to get out into the radical world around me.

I continued to meet Judge Motley for a friendly annual lunch, and for a few years I went to her Christmas party. Occasionally she asked me to take a pro bono case for someone who couldn't afford an attorney. The cases were always dead losers. But I could not say no to the judge.

As time went on, I felt the gap between our politics had grown. At one lunch, after the judge had gone with a delegation to South Africa in the apartheid years, she spoke to me about what she had seen.

"Michael, it's just like the South used to be," she said, "and it will change."

I was disturbed that she hadn't joined the anti-apartheid boycott and had gone to South Africa at all, thus legitimizing the regime. And I was sure that she was wrong about the comparison to the South.

This was one reason I stopped seeing her for lunch or going to her Christmas parties. By the mid-1970s her calls stopped coming.

Today I think, "How could I have been so intolerant?" A remarkable, strong, and courageous woman who had often placed herself in dangerous situations, Constance Baker Motley was wonderfully stubborn about critical social issues, especially race. Her ancestors had been enslaved on the tiny Caribbean island of Nevis. Her family was poor, and only because of a well-off white man's charity could she go to college. She had none of the advantages I'd enjoyed growing up. I cannot believe what a fool I was to cut off the friendship when there was still so much to learn from her.

For many years I had no contact with Judge Motley. Then one day in 2004 a board member at the Center said he wanted to recommend me for the Columbia Law School's Medal for Excellence, its most prestigious award. He wrote to Judge Motley, who had gone to Columbia, to ask her to support me for the award. I wasn't sure how she would respond.

Judge Motley sent back a note on the letterhead of the United States District Court: "Michael Ratner was, in retrospect, the ablest law clerk I have had in my tenure on the bench. After leaving his clerkship here, as you know, Michael devoted himself to public service, making significant contributions to the development of our constitutional law."

I got the Medal for Excellence. At the fancy awards lunch at the Waldorf Astoria in New York City, I finally saw Judge Motley. Both delighted to be together again, we gave each other a long, silent, warm embrace.

Judge Motley died on September 28, 2004. After her death, I read the judge's autobiography. One sentence in the preface struck me and made me see how badly I had misjudged her politics:

"Sexism, like racism, goes with us into the next century, but I see class warfare as overshadowing both. What to do about those of all racial and ethnic groups left behind by our latest economic revolution will challenge us all."

5

IN THE CENTER OF THE SEVENTIES

In early September 1971, on a crisp fall morning in New York City, I walked up the dingy stairs to the badly lit second-floor loft of the Center for Constitutional Rights.

CCR was a small, low-budget, ambitiously radical organization. My office was not really an office. Like everyone else, I had a desk and a telephone. The loft was chopped up by dividers surrounding our desks. If I stood up, I saw over the wall. If I took a step on the chipped linoleum floor, I was in the open space where legal workers sat behind typewriters. Most of us handwrote our work on long yellow legal pads. Legal workers typed it up in triplicate, with carbon paper, making corrections with white-out. If we wanted multiple copies, the document would be typed on a stencil, put on a roller, and mimeographed—page by messy, smelly page.

Our office was run as a collective and remained so for many years. During this period, collectives, legal and otherwise, were popping up all over the country. At CCR all of us made the same low pay, whether we were attorneys, legal workers, or administrative personnel. (The founders and other older cooperating attorneys were not paid. They had their own law firms or were professors.) As a law clerk, I'd made $12,500 a year. As a CCR attorney, I made under $10,000. At weekly meetings of the collective, all of us decided which cases to take and how to do the work.

MOVING THE BAR

On September 9, within two days of my arrival at CCR, an uprising erupted in an upstate New York prison I had barely heard of: Attica. A maximum-security prison, Attica housed more than 2,000 inmates, 85 percent of them Black and Puerto Rican. It was located 400 miles from New York City in an all-white community, and all the prison guards were white.

The prison administration had ignored the inmates' ongoing grievances about racial discrimination and physical and mental abuse. Feeling there was no way to make their voices heard, many of the inmates took control of "D" Block. They seized a few guards as hostages, released others, and issued a list of 28 unanswered demands that had been sent to the prison warden earlier that summer. The list included adequate medical treatment, drug rehabilitation programs, religious freedom, and an end to censorship of reading materials.

Almost immediately, the inmates asked Bill Kunstler to join a small citizens' committee to help negotiate the demands and put an end to the uprising. Bill went up to the prison and into "D" yard. The media painted the inmates as dangerous killers, and we at CCR were all worried about Bill's safety. I don't think Bill was nervous, but he worried about what the state might do to quell the uprising.

The negotiations stretched on for a few days. Although the prison warden and state officials agreed to many of the demands, they were not willing to grant amnesty to prisoners for their part in the uprising. The prisoners asked for Governor Nelson Rockefeller to come to Attica. They thought only he could guarantee the implementation of their demands and grant the amnesty that would end the uprising. But Rockefeller refused.

Instead, on the morning of September 13, hundreds of armed New York state troopers, state police, sheriffs, national guardsmen, and corrections officers launched a massive assault on the prison. It began with tear gas and a hail of bullets shot into "D" yard. Sharpshooters picked off many of the alleged leaders. Inmates had no time to surrender. The assault was over in a couple of hours.

Margie and I woke up in our Riverside Drive apartment hearing a radio report that 32 inmates and nine hostages had been killed. Within an hour or so of the assault, Walter E. Dunbar, the Commissioner of Correctional Services, alleged that inmates had killed most of the hostages. Their throats had been cut and some had been castrated, Dunbar claimed.

"I don't believe anything he's saying," Margie said.

Eventually, once autopsies were completed, the stories of inmate atrocities proved to be lies—lies fabricated to justify the assault, to turn people against the legitimate demands of the prisoners, and to protect Governor Rockefeller. The nine guards had actually been murdered by the state in its indiscriminate lethal assault.[3] The lesson for me could not have been more clear. Racism and class underlay the tragedy of Attica. Blacks and Puerto Ricans were expendable, but so were white working-class guards.

After retaking the prison, the guards engaged in a four-day orgy of brutality against the prisoners. They beat injured prisoners—some on

---

3   One of my favorite Judy Collins songs, "The Hostage," written by Tom Paxton, is in the voice of a hostage at Attica who tells a fellow guard not to worry, that the state won't allow the guards to be killed. When the assault begins and he's hit with bullets, he compares his plight to what would have been the fate of Governor Rockefeller had he been a hostage:

> They come in yelling curses, like they were caught in the River Rhine
> Shot down every God damned thing they saw.
> And while I lay there wounded, I took another one in my spine,
> Poor Jim Kelly took another one in his jaw.
> They say we had our throats cut, by a band of desperate men,
> Say they saved as many of us as they could.
> Well the governor he should know it, but I think I'll say it again
> That the governor cut my throat and he cut it good.
> Let them take the governor, hold him for a couple of days.
> See who goes in shooting to set him free.
> Hell they'd open every jail in the country, they'd send them on their way
> They'd never do to him what the governor done to me.

stretchers—with sticks, belts, bats, or other weapons. They forced others to strip and run naked through gauntlets of guards armed with clubs. They dragged some prisoners on the ground and marked others with an X on their backs. They spat on prisoners and burned them with matches. And they used sticks to poke still others in the genitals and arms.

CCR and the National Lawyers Guild immediately sent lawyers up to the prison both to protect prisoners and to gather evidence for lawsuits against Rockefeller, the prison warden, and others involved in the massacre and ongoing abuse. I was part of that fact-finding team.

I had never been in a prison, never dealt with prisoners, and never had to relate to those who had been abused and tortured. I was nervous, but Morty Stavis gave me my marching orders. "Michael, just go spend a week up there in the hospital ward," he said. "Take your time, and take notes on everything that's said. Your purpose is to find out about the assault by the state, what happened afterwards, and how people were injured," he said.

Morty warned me not to ask about the initial prisoner takeover of "D" yard or go into facts that would be relevant to criminal charges against various inmates. My visit was not as a criminal defense attorney, but as an attorney intending to protect the prisoners from state violence and to determine who in the state could be sued on their behalf.

So with a few other young lawyers, I flew to Buffalo and rented a car. As we approached Attica, the state prison loomed up behind an imposing, medieval-looking turreted wall, surrounded by broad fields. It was like something out of a fairy tale, but in the worst way imaginable—one of those mythical, inescapable places where evil flourishes.

We waited a long time to get in. It took the better part of a morning to get through various searches, permissions, and delays. Finally, guards escorted us to the prison hospital, a single big room with more than 30 beds. Wounded prisoners were lying in the beds, handcuffed to the metal frames. Even though all but one of our group was white, the inmates were willing to talk with us because of Bill Kunstler. They loved Bill, and they saw us as part of his team.

I was in shock seeing these crippled Black and Puerto Rican men in that hospital ward. And my shock deepened as they recounted stories of near escapes, bullet wounds, and the notorious gauntlet where guards forced prisoners to run over broken glass and beat them with clubs. After a week, I returned to CCR. With legal aid , the National Lawyers Guild, and others, CCR would soon file an important lawsuit to protect the prisoners from further abuse.

But the state attorney general had also launched a criminal investigation—not of the state's massive assault, murders and beatings, but of the inmates. That investigation resulted in 62 indictments of prisoners on serious charges including assault and murder.

We were outraged. We did not think the inmates should be charged, especially when there was no effort to investigate and charge state officials for their actions before, during, and after the uprising. I believed those officials, including the governor, should be charged with murder.

The problem we faced is that the decision to investigate and prosecute, with a very narrow exception, is solely up to the state or federal prosecutor—and it is almost impossible to compel them to act. We were watching the unfolding of a great injustice. There was to be no accountability for outright slaughter.

Morty, Arthur, and I felt something had to be done, even if a case trying to compel prosecutions would likely lose. Arthur believed in audacious legal actions, particularly if they had grassroots political support. He considered such legal actions to be important parts of political struggle. He frequently talked about a case I had never heard of, *COFO v. Rainey,* that he, Morty, and Bill had filed in 1964 in Mississippi after the disappearances of Michael Schwerner, James Chaney, and Andrew Goodman, three young civil rights workers who had come to Mississippi to register voters. Mississippi officials were doing nothing to find them, investigate their disappearance or later their deaths, or to protect civil rights workers. Under a Reconstruction law from the 1860s, a coalition of civil rights groups in Mississippi (COFO) sued the sheriff in charge of the county jail where the men had last been seen. That law allowed federal commissioners to take over arrests and prosecutions if state and local police were not enforcing the law. The case had mixed success legally, but it succeeded politically. As Arthur said, "It turned, even for a moment, those attacked into accusers" and helped organize the entire community.

Arthur spoke rapidly and gesticulated with his hands. "Michael, think *COFO v. Rainey*," he said. "We brought together all the groups, and we put the power structure in Mississippi on the defensive. We need to do that here."

COFO, and its concept of political struggle, was a guiding refrain that would echo through my work and CCR's for decades. Take the offensive, use the law, work with the grassroots. Change the dynamics of struggle.

Of course, Attica was not Mississippi. There was not a strong grassroots movement in New York to go after Governor Rockefeller. While that did not mean the case should not be brought, it did limit its political possibilities.

I set to work drafting my first federal complaint. For more than a month, I worked hard, learning everything I could about Attica. My first draft, throwing in every fact I'd uncovered, was awful. Morty worked with me hour after hour to tighten up my hodgepodge and make me understand that this complaint was intended for the public as well as the court.

About three months after the killings, we filed our case, *Inmates of Attica Correctional Facility v. Nelson A. Rockefeller*, on behalf of individual and murdered inmates against a variety of state officials. In its first paragraph it charged the officials with murder, manslaughter, assault, and other crimes. In 25 pages the complaint detailed the treatment of the inmates before, during, and after the uprising. We asked the court to order the state to submit a plan for the prosecution of state officials. And, under the same Reconstruction-era statutes used in *COFO*, we also demanded the federal prosecution of state officials for civil rights violations.

In response, state and federal officials asked that the case be dismissed, claiming there was no recognized right to compel prosecution of state officials. The next phase of the case was to make an appearance before the judge.

I wasn't sure if the appearance was just a calendar call for the judge to determine what should happen next, but I prepared for days as if it were an oral argument. It was to be my first appearance in court as a lawyer. When I entered the courtroom, I was very nervous. Scores of other lawyers were waiting to have their cases heard. To calm myself, I just kept practicing what I was going to say.

After a few hours I heard the clerk call, "*Inmates of Attica v. Rockefeller.* Will counsel approach the bench?" I walked toward the raised bench, behind which the judge was sitting, wearing a black robe. Judge Lloyd F. MacMahon, a conservative Republican appointed by President Dwight Eisenhower, had been randomly assigned to the case. It was not a lucky draw for us. Judge MacMahon was stern and did not smile. I felt about two inches high. He asked me only one question, "What's this case about?"

I started to explain, "Your Honor, this case is about the state's failure to investigate the role of officials in the Attica killings and beatings. Plaintiffs want to compel the state and federal governments to investi...."

The judge cut me off. "I have had cases like this before," he intoned. "There is no right to compel an investigation or prosecution. Case dismissed."

He did not bother to hear from my opponent—or to write an opinion.

It was an embarrassing moment for me. All that work and I never even got to present my argument. No one from my office was there, and we had not notified the press, so the dismissal got no attention.

Later, CCR appealed. I'd left the Center by then, and a colleague argued the case. This time the three-judge court wrote an opinion which repeated our allegations at length. Citing its prior injunction against the state regarding the beatings, the court acknowledged that inmates in certain instances may have the right to bring a case of this sort. However, the court concluded "that the extraordinary relief sought [compelling prosecution] cannot be granted in the situation here presented."

We were disappointed, but the court had left a theoretical opening for the future. Such a ruling is typical of courts, particularly those that claim to have a conscience. While denying relief to the plaintiffs, these judges do not slam the door shut on all such suits. But the theoretical "situation" when the judges would actually enforce the law never arises. If Attica was not that situation, what would be?

Attica was my first lesson in understanding the need to be "as radical as reality itself." The quotation is attributed to Vladimir Lenin and probably goes back to Karl Marx. I never understood what it meant until Attica. The "reality" of Attica was that those state officials who murdered scores were not even investigated, while inmates with legitimate demands were prosecuted. A "radical" response to that reality was to do everything in our power, including filing lawsuits, to exonerate the inmates and hold Rockefeller and other state officials accountable for the murders and beatings. And although far more lethal than the force unleashed on us at Columbia, the assault at Attica likewise taught me that some authorities will resort to violence to quell even those legitimate demands they are unwilling to meet.

Over the next few years, a number of inmates involved in the Attica rebellion completed their original sentences and were freed. Margie and I invited one man to our upstate New York cabin. I was in the backyard using a small chainsaw to cut branches for firewood when he asked if he could try it. I handed him the saw, showed him the trigger, and he set to work. He placed the saw against a branch and depressed the trigger—except he depressed it all the way. The saw roared and flew out of his hand. I explained that the trigger needed a light touch.

"I'm sorry," he said. "I've never used a power tool in my whole life. I was in a juvenile home since I was nine, out for a short while, and in prison until now."

I still think about that incident—the circumstances that put him in prison and the utter failure of the state to teach him any skill, even using the most basic power tools, from which he might have earned a living.

I also think about some of the inmates for whom CCR filed wrongful death claims against the state. Those claims took 27 years to settle, if they were settled at all. In my files is the death certificate for one of those inmates, Allen Durham, whose mother had asked me to represent him. He was 20 years old and serving a ten-year sentence when the state murdered him. The certificate says he died on September 13, 1971 at 10 a.m. in a "prison riot." The cause of death was reported as internal hemorrhaging resulting from gunshot wounds to the back, kidney, spine, and extremities. All the shots came from behind.

Much of CCR's work was on cases that the founders—Arthur Kinoy, Bill Kunstler, Morty Stavis—and their associates were involved in. They had connections to left movements everywhere. Morty spent the most time at CCR and taught the younger lawyers. Most of what I learned was from him. Bill Kunstler had recently been convicted of contempt of court in the Chicago Eight case and was facing significant jail time. Morty and Arthur Kinoy were the key lawyers on the appeals of those cases. I wasn't part of that team, but other young lawyers were, and that work consumed a large part of CCR resources.

Peter Weiss, an "almost" founder, was also around CCR a lot. While he was not an activist left lawyer, Peter brought to CCR something no one else did—an interest in international law, particularly its human rights protections. International law was not enforced in U.S. courts.

Peter wanted to establish enforceable human rights precedents. Most of us were not so interested in what we considered an abstraction. We were radical civil rights lawyers. All our victories were based on the U.S. Constitution, and we felt we represented the "movement."

After reading a draft of one of my lawsuits concerning the war powers of the president, Peter would often call me and say, "Michael, you need to add the international law claim."

"Peter, I don't know anything about international law," I'd reply. "What's the claim?"

And he proceeded to tell me. "The war violated the U.N. Charter. War can only be authorized in self-defense or by the Security Council."

I barely knew what he was talking about. That was not taught in the law schools of the time. "Peter, if you draft it," I said, "I will put it in."

I did add his claims, faithfully. But when it came time to brief the issue and argue it, I would barely present it to the court. I could not have been more mistaken. Long before it was fashionable, Peter's insistence on including human rights claims in almost every case we litigated was prescient and provided the basis for many of our big cases in the decades ahead.

But in the 1970s, CCR continued to represent the tail end of the militant Southern civil rights movement. Just before I arrived at CCR, Bill Kunstler argued what may have been the last major Supreme Court case resulting from this movement.

Palmer v. Thompson challenged a Mississippi town's decision to close its municipal swimming pool rather than integrate it. Wasn't this a form of discrimination? I thought so, but the decision came down 5-4 against us.

I was shocked. My lawyer friend Bill Goodman, whose dad Ernie was involved in the case, later explained the loss: "Michael, until *Palmer* we never lost a major case in the South. But this was 1971, and the days of militant demonstrations in the South were over. There was no pressure on the court, and they could get away with a bad decision. Had the court made a similar decision a few years earlier, there would have been rioting in the streets."

Though *Palmer* was a devastating loss, other progressive young lawyers and I learned an important lesson. Without pressure from social movements, it's harder to win in court.

The long-term effects of the *Palmer* decision were brought home to me years later, in 2005. My sister Ellen was involved in a charitable project to construct a swimming pool in Pass Christian, a town on the Mississippi Delta that had been devastated by Hurricane Katrina. Apparently, it was the first integrated pool in southern Mississippi since *Palmer.*

Along with those civil rights cases, and the appeal of Kunstler's and the Chicago Eight's convictions, CCR's young lawyers had a lot to do. We went to demonstrations and negotiated with police. We represented those in the anti-war movement who had been jailed, spied on, and beaten up. We defended soldiers court-martialed for resistance to the Vietnam War. We represented members of the Young Lords, Black Panthers, and citizens brought before grand juries investigating the rash of anti-war bombings and the leaks of the Pentagon Papers.

Some of our work was controversial, even for CCR. Although the number of female lawyers in the U.S. was still small, and the founders were all men, a majority of CCR's staff attorneys were women. There were four women, one other man, and me. These women pushed CCR into taking on pioneering cases on behalf of women's rights. Some of CCR's founding generation did not see abortion or reproductive rights as civil rights issues. But the women prevailed, and CCR became a leader in litigating women's right to abortion.

Most cases challenging the ban on abortion had been brought on behalf of physicians, who claimed it interfered with their medical choices and with the doctor-patient relationship. Newer cases brought by CCR and others put the issue where it belonged: the right of a woman to control her own body and make her own decisions about abortion and reproductive issues. In 1973, in *Roe v. Wade* (a case not brought by CCR) the argument for that right prevailed in the Supreme Court.

An interesting aspect of CCR in those early days was the way young and inexperienced attorneys like me were pushed to get into court and argue major cases. My first high-profile case involved Edwin A. Goodman, the general manager of the progressive non-profit radio station WBAI and also a scion of the family that owned Bergdorf Goodman, the luxury department store on Manhattan's Fifth Avenue. Goodman was refusing to comply with a New York district attorney's request for information about a prison rebellion.

In early October 1971, just a few weeks after Attica, prisoners at the Manhattan House of Detention for Men, known as the Tombs, had revolted. They were protesting intolerable living conditions: 1,450 men sardined into cells built to accommodate 875. During the rebellion, WBAI had recorded and broadcast phone calls from inmates.

The district attorney indicted the alleged leaders of the rebellion, and in February 1972 issued a subpoena to WBAI for the taped recordings of inmates' calls, particularly those that had not been broadcast.

Goodman and WBAI came to CCR for representation. Goodman believed that the subpoena interfered with WBAI's right to report the news. We told Ed that while we thought he had a decent legal claim, we might well lose. If he then refused to turn over the tapes, he could be held in contempt and even jailed. Ed had no doubt that an important principle was at stake. He was willing to go all the way.

Rhonda Copelon and I worked on the case along with an older civil liberties attorney, Jeremiah Gutman. We filed papers in the New York state lower court claiming that the subpoena for the tapes violated Goodman's and the WBAI staff's rights as news-gatherers and reporters. Today, many states have shield laws that provide some protections to journalists. There was no such law of reporters' privilege in New York at the time, and we knew we had an uphill battle.

Our first court appearance was in front of Judge Gerald Culkin, widely known as "the watermelon judge." In a 1968 hearing on a notorious murder case where four black defendants had requested Bill Kunstler as one of their lawyers, the judge had mocked the defendants' race and intelligence by saying: "Those boys wouldn't know a good lawyer from a good watermelon."

The initial hearing on the Goodman-WBAI case took place on February 28 in a dingy courtroom at 100 Centre Street. It was brief, and not many reporters showed up. On March 2, the judge issued a decision denying our claims, and ordered a hearing to enforce the subpoena the very next day.

We again appeared in court—this time with many more reporters present. Judge Culkin asked Ed Goodman if he and WBAI were going to turn over the tapes. Ed answered, "It is our intention not to produce these materials until such time as we have exhausted our legal remedies." We wanted a chance to test the legality of the subpoena in the higher courts.

The "watermelon judge" ordered Ed Goodman to do 30 days in the civil jail "or until such time as he [produces] the tapes." The theory of such a sentence is that the person jailed holds the keys to the jail. He can open it when he complies with the subpoena. We asked the judge to stay the sentence on appeal and grant bail. The judge refused, and the guards immediately took Ed Goodman to jail.

The next morning, Saturday, March 4, we applied to get Ed out of jail while his appeal was pending. The Appellate Division, First Department, was located in one of the most ornate courthouses in New York, a three-story, Beaux Arts limestone building at the corner of 25th and Madison. Murals covered its interior walls, and glittering chandeliers hung from the ceiling. Most likely because of the reputation of the Goodman family, we found a single judge, James McNally, willing to hear the case that morning.

McNally, born in 1896, had no liberal credentials and was known for his campaign to have the motto "In God We Trust" inscribed on the wall behind every judge in New York. The white-haired judge let us into his dark, wood-paneled chambers and listened to our argument. Although Ed was not a danger to the community, McNally refused our request to free him. The judge said the full court would hear the case on Tuesday.

This was Rhonda's and my first litigation, and we were not going to give up. We appealed to New York state's highest court. It also turned us down without argument. But we had another idea based on the writ of habeas corpus, the foundational legal guarantee against unlawful jailing, which dates back to the Magna Carta in 1215. It literally means "may we (the court) have your body" and it's addressed to the jailer holding the body of the prisoner. Habeas corpus gives prisoners convicted in state courts a second chance in federal courts, if a federal constitutional issue is involved. But the limitation of habeas corpus is that the state courts must have already heard the case.

In our view, Ed Goodman had exhausted his remedies in state court. It was Saturday afternoon. We knew the federal court in Manhattan had an emergency judge. We called and were connected to Judge Frankel— the same judge who had ruled against Kinoy in the grand jury case and who had given me a mixed ruling in *Ratner v. Chemical Bank*. By this time we knew each other well.

Judge Frankel asked, "Where is Mr. Goodman now?"

"In prison," I replied. "We went to the appellate state court and the court of appeals and they scheduled the case for Tuesday. Mr. Goodman will remain in prison until then, if not longer. There is nowhere else we can go."

Without even hearing from the district attorney, Judge Frankel issued an order: "I am going to hear this case Sunday at 10 a.m. at the Larchmont Town Hall. Papers should be filed with the clerk in the federal court in New York and brought to Larchmont."

IN THE CENTER OF THE SEVENTIES

We were all amazed. Why hear the case in Larchmont, far from the downtown Manhattan federal courthouse? It had to be for drama. Larchmont was near where Judge Frankel lived, and this was a chance for him to get local publicity and exhibit his skills in an informal setting.

On Sunday morning, we drove up to Larchmont and entered the town hall, a white-columned building off a beautiful town square. It was packed and noisy. Judge Frankel pressed the lawyers for the district attorney: "Is there any state court Mr. Goodman can go to before Tuesday? No? Then have not his lawyers tried everything?"

The DA's lawyers argued that a few days' delay in a hearing should not allow someone to bypass state courts and go straight into federal court.

But Judge Frankel was not convinced, especially because this case involved the First Amendment, free press, and the "journalist's privilege," all issues then under consideration by the Supreme Court. Those rights, he reasoned, are precious and require the fullest protection. Jailing someone like Goodman, even for a few days, could cut the heart out of the right to free speech and press.

After a raucous hearing, Judge Frankel issued the writ of habeas corpus on a single sheet of paper. It was a simple order directed to H. William Kehl, the sheriff of New York County, who was in charge of the jail where Goodman was incarcerated.

Our co-counsel Jerry Gutman, Rhonda, and I took the order and drove straight to the jail in Manhattan. Within minutes Goodman was released and on his way home. We rejoiced, but the DA immediately appealed the order, asking that Goodman be returned to jail until the outcome of the appeal.

The U.S. Court of Appeals for the Second Circuit scheduled the argument for Thursday, March 9. Our team decided I should argue the case, although it was obvious that our co-counsel Jerry would have been a wiser choice.

I had gotten almost no sleep the night before the hearing, which took place in the federal courthouse at Foley Square. The ceiling in the ceremonial courtroom on the 18th floor must have been 30 feet high, and the judges' podium seemed about ten feet above my head. The courtroom was jammed. Three judges heard the case, including the chief judge, Henry Friendly, one of the most respected appellate judges in the country—who had a reputation for directing withering questions to counsel.

I am still mortified by how much I fumbled as I presented my argument, my first in a federal appellate court. I was ill-prepared and really had no idea how to answer the court's questions. At one point, my co-counsel Jerry Gutman had to stand up and bail me out.

Goodman remained out of jail until the decision came down five days later. As expected, the court reversed Judge Frankel's release order. However, it said it would hold the order dismissing the case for 48 hours. During this time we returned to state court, and the judges continued the release. So Goodman did not go back to jail.

The issues we raised in the Goodman case persuaded New York state to pass a journalists' shield law. Other states followed. Still, the issue remains contentious, and journalists continue to face subpoenas for documents or testimony.

The Goodman case taught me a lot. Our legal strategy was audacious. We worked days, nights, and weekends. Following my embarrassment in argument, from then on I always over-prepared and tried to walk into court knowing everything about a case that I could. Though I had argued poorly and we lost the case, we had kept our client out of jail. For me as a young lawyer, the litigation was a vivid example of how progressive lawyers could fight and succeed—even when losing.

In 1973, I left CCR for a year to teach at New York University Law School. But I continued to litigate cases with CCR and on my own. With my good friend Richard Levy, an outstanding attorney, I worked on several cases in support of Puerto Rican *independentistas*. I had become involved because of my anti-imperialist politics and my belief that Puerto Rico was an exploited colony, seized by the United States after the Spanish–American War in 1898. Today Puerto Rico is called a commonwealth, but it remains under U.S. control.

Colonialism had devastated the island. Multi-national pharmaceutical companies and other businesses had received substantial tax breaks to open plants in Puerto Rico, which ultimately led to Puerto Ricans' complete dependence on mainland U.S. business. Farming, in what was once a rich agricultural country, virtually disappeared. Women were routinely sterilized. And 70 percent of the island's three million residents depended economically on money transfers from the United States.

In the early 1970s the Puerto Rican independence movement had a strong presence both on the island and in the United States—especially in New York, home to approximately one million Puerto Ricans. I got to know many young Puerto Ricans who belonged to the Puerto Rican Socialist Party (PSP), which appealed to many young activists.

The PSP was not a narrow ideological party like so many others that claimed to represent the only true version of the thinking of Marx, Lenin, Stalin, or Mao. That kind of ideological perfectionism was not for me. Some factions of the Puerto Rican independence movement, like the Armed Forces of National Liberation (FALN), included violence among their tactics, but the PSP did not. It was a militant socialist party with a wide working-class and progressive base committed to fighting for Puerto Rican independence. It did not engage in endless ideological debates, and there was room in the party for different views.

The PSP referred my first *independentista* clients to me—poor Puerto Rican young men who refused to be drafted into the U.S. military. Richard and I did not charge a fee to represent them. I recall one stocky, young PSP militant with jet-black hair coming into the office. José Velazquez had received a draft notice that contained a clerical error, which ultimately would become the key issue in the case. José said to me, "I consider myself an *independentista* living in a colonized country, and I won't go in their army."

On behalf of José, Richard and I made all of the technical arguments available based upon the complex law governing the draft. But we also studied the history of Puerto Rico, the treaty by which it was "transferred" to the United States, and its current situation, and fashioned political arguments in the guise of legal claims. If a Puerto Rican living in Puerto Rico could not vote in a U.S. election and thereby influence policy, how could he/she be subject to that policy? Drafting people who had no representation violated the Constitution. We argued: "No supreme sacrifice without the supreme right."

We were pretty sure none of our arguments would prevail. On the other hand, articulating them with legal dressing in court was a way to bring to light a history the United States government had chosen to bury. The courtrooms where these cases were heard were often filled with supporters of the clients we represented—young, courageous activists willing to go to jail for their ideals. Often we would find technical errors the draft boards had made, and we got our clients released. Other times a good judge would be sympathetic to our clients, and no jail time was ordered.

In the José Velazquez case, federal Judge Lawrence Pierce, a Republican African-American appointed by Ronald Reagan, dismissed the criminal case on a technicality in the draft laws. But our political arguments probably made that particular judge more sympathetic to the defendant. The government appealed. In our brief we argued that the government's appeal ran afoul of the Constitution's double jeopardy prohibition: once the trial judge had dismissed the indictment, the government could neither appeal nor try our client again.

Somehow I never saw the letter setting the argument date for the Velazquez appeal. One beautiful fall morning I was sitting in my NYU office just off Washington Square in the heart of Greenwich Village. I was getting ready to teach my next class when a law school secretary burst in and said, "Call the Second Circuit immediately. The court wants you there now for the Velazquez argument. They are waiting on the bench."

I felt as if a spear had gone through me. Normally, arguments are set a month or more in advance, giving plenty of time to prepare by reading the briefs, going to moot courts, and outlining a presentation. Breaking my rules about preparation after my embarrassment in the Goodman case, I had done none of this.

I jumped into a cab. I did not even have the briefs with me. I had written them two months before and could not recall the important legal details I would need to give a successful argument. Within a few minutes I would be in that ceremonial courtroom facing some of the smartest, most important judges in the country. I was terrified.

Since we had won in the lower court, the government argued first. Then I had 15 minutes to present my case. Two of the three judges were conservative and pro-government, a liberal lawyer's nightmare. Luckily for me, the third judge was on my side—Irving Kaufman, the "liberal" judge who had ordered the execution of the Rosenbergs. As the conservative judges peppered me with hostile questions to which I had no answers, Judge Kaufman would answer for me. "That is a very wooden way to look at the issue," he scolded one of the others.

Two months later the decision came down. We lost the appeal, with Judge Kaufman writing the dissent. He excoriated the other judges: "We have begun a process of eroding the absolute protections of a Constitutional command: 'nor shall any person be subject for the same offence to be twice put in jeopardy of life or limb.' That principle, 'one of the oldest ideas in western civilization,' is justly founded upon 'fear and abhorrence of governmental power to try people twice for the same conduct.'"

Rather than appeal to the Supreme Court, I asked that all the judges on the appeals court hear the case, but it made no difference. At the same time, the Supreme Court had chosen to review a similar case and it agreed with the majority opinion that the double jeopardy clause had not been violated.

José Velazquez went back before the trial judge. He was convicted, but the judge imposed no jail time.

The Velazquez draft case was just a small part of my work supporting the independence of Puerto Rico. For much of the 1970s I worked closely with a smart, hardworking Puerto Rican lawyer, José Antonio "Abi" Lugo, a member of the PSP who worked for a time at CCR. Dark-skinned, wiry, and intense, Abi had many girlfriends, smoked marijuana, and was a great dancer. He became one of my best friends, but I could never keep up with his partying.

The most interesting Puerto Rican cases Abi and I worked on together concerned Vieques, an island off Puerto Rico that the United States used as a naval base and bombing range. The base occupied a substantial part of the island, and the munitions that detonated on the land and in the water destroyed not just the land and reefs, but made fishing impossible for much of the year. The local fishermen had an economic interest in stopping the bombing, but the base itself was also a symbol of the colonial status of Puerto Rico for people far beyond Vieques.

In the late 1970s, Puerto Rican activists organized to stop the bombing and demand the closure of the military base. CCR and I got involved when we were asked to represent the Vieques Fishermen's Association, headed by Carlos Zenón.

My trips to the beautiful island were extraordinary. There were no real hotels and only a few bars that served food. The dunes, the ocean, the palm trees, and the weather were dream-like—and the expansive, pristine beaches were empty. "Magical" would be an understatement to describe Vieques—except for the bombing.

At the time of my visits, the National Lawyers Guild had an office in San Juan. One of the NLG lawyers was Judith "Judy" Berkan, a U.S. citizen who stayed in Puerto Rico to continue legal and political work. Judy had striking black hair and spoke rapidly with a slight accent she'd picked up in Puerto Rico.

A tough, risk-taking lawyer, Judy was part of the team representing the Vieques protesters, an ecumenical group that included several priests. In May 1979, hundreds of protesters using small rubber boats landed on the beach at Vieques, and walked up a few yards onto land that they believed belonged to the naval base. Twenty-one people were arrested, including Judy Berkan and other legal observers.

I attended their trials in the federal courthouse in San Juan. It was surreal. Although the judge, prosecutors, lawyers, most witnesses, jurors, and spectators all spoke Spanish, the trials were conducted in English. If a witness testified in Spanish, the testimony would be translated into English, though everyone was listening in Spanish. At off-the-record conferences with the judge everyone spoke Spanish. The English requirement was a charade—except that juries were chosen only from a pool of fluent English speakers, the educated upper class. Sitting in that courtroom, beneath the U.S. flag, I understood the power of the occupier.

The trial judge, Juan Torruella, was known as the most conservative, least competent judge in the First Circuit, the judicial district covering parts of the Northeast and Puerto Rico. Rumor had it that he carried a gun under his robes. Torruella was not an *independentista,* and it was clear he would not be sympathetic to the 21 people arrested on Vieques.

Like many *independentistas* in previous cases, the activists didn't recognize the authority of the occupying colonial court and refused to participate in their trials. All were convicted and sentenced to the maximum six months—a ridiculously severe sentence for a misdemeanor trespass. The judge and U.S. military authorities wanted to send the message that independence movement activists were not to go near the military base.

Continuing their non-cooperation, the activists chose not to appeal, and were sent to federal prisons in the United States. One of them, Ángel Rodríguez Cristóbal, was "found hanging" in his cell in Tallahassee, Florida, apparently with cuts and bruises on his body. He was 31 years old and had two children. This would not be the last time that our clients died under suspicious circumstances with the U.S. authorities claiming "suicide."

Judy Berkan's arrest was particularly disturbing because she had been a legal observer at the demonstrations, not a protester. The government claimed she was trespassing on the military base. Its key witness said the border of the military base began at the high-water mark in the sand and that Judy was arrested on the dry sand above that mark.

On this basis, Judge Torruella convicted Judy of trespassing and sentenced her to six months in jail. She received bail pending appeal. The problem for Judy was that conviction and jail time could mean her disbarment.

By this time I felt more confident in my skills as an appeals lawyer, and so did Judy. She asked me, along with Puerto Rican lawyer Harry Anduze, to handle her appeal to the federal appeals court in Boston that had jurisdiction over Puerto Rico.

After studying the transcript, old maps of the naval base, and the original property deeds from Spain, I confirmed that the land of the base began at the high-water mark. But what was the definition of high-water mark? It struck me that the line between the wet sand and the dry would vary depending on the tides and the season of the year—e.g., in the northeast of the U.S., tides could vary from summer to winter by more than 18 feet.

I couldn't introduce new evidence in the appeals court. But if I could find a precedent that defined the term "high-water mark," the court could look at that. After extensive research, I finally found one Supreme Court case that defined "high-water mark" as an average of the highest winter tides that occurred over a period of 18 years. It was an imaginary line on the beach. Its precise location could be determined only by 18 years of measurements and a surveyor. This meant that the prosecution's key witness could not identify the actual high-water mark and thus could not place Judy or the 20 other defendants on the property of the naval base.

In February, I travelled to Puerto Rico to argue before the appeals court. I was confident I had a winning argument, but when I walked into the small, packed courtroom I got very nervous. Of the three judges, two were fairly conservative. The third was Stephen Breyer, a liberal eventually appointed to the Supreme Court.

I went right to the key point: "Judy Berkan was convicted of trespass, but the government never proved that she was above the high-water mark where the base began." Then I described the legal definition of the "high-water mark" and made fun of the wet sand/dry sand distinction.

The government admitted I was right about the high-water mark. However, it now argued that the military base included *all* of the beach and its surrounding waters, which the United States obtained from the Spanish in 1899. That was a very complex legal and factual question, about which the court seemed skeptical— especially since the government had not raised this argument at trial.

Three months later, the decision came down. We won! Judy's conviction and that of the three others who'd joined in the appeal were reversed.

A pure legal issue decided this case. But I think we won for a couple of other reasons as well. First, the court was reluctant to jail a respected white attorney. Second, the charge was trespassing, not murder. The more serious the charge—and the less the litigants resembled the class, race, and ethnic background of the judges—the more likely a court would bend over to ignore the law, or give lip service to it while denying relief. For example, my efforts to compel an investigation and prosecution of those responsible for the Attica killings failed. The prisoners killed were

African-American and Latino. The killers were white. The court upheld the principle of compelling investigations, but refused to say the principle applied in the Attica cases. Of course, a jury can sometimes make a big difference in the outcome of a case. But even with a jury, the closer the class and race of the defendant match that of the jurors, the better for the defense.

Margie and I had been married in 1969. By the fall of 1972 our marriage was starting to come apart. I cannot really say why, except that I was young, a bit immature, and self-involved. I'm sure Margie had her own issues as well.

One day I was standing with Margie on the corner of 103rd and Broadway in front of a greasy spoon called the Red Flame. We were looking at a *New York Times* article about the U.S. Virgin Islands. On September 6th, eight people had been shot to death at the luxurious Rockefeller-owned Fountain Valley Golf Course in St. Croix. Authorities claimed the motive was robbery. Five local Black men had been arrested. Bill Kunstler, along with local counsel, had offered to represent them.

While this was a brutal killing, Margie and I viewed it in the context of increasing racial violence in the U.S. The FBI's brutal murder of Fred Hampton, the 21-year-old Black Panther assassinated in his bed in Chicago, and the unjustified police killings of Black people all over America had triggered a violent reaction from armed Black militant groups. Some were fighting back—including a group calling itself the Black Liberation Army, which had allegedly killed a number of police officers.

The news stories suggested an overt political motive for the murders on St. Croix: militant Black people hoped to drive white people off the island and gain independence from the United States. Over the next month, more killings of white people followed, and ABC described the situation as a "small scale Mau Mau rebellion." By October 1972, a

New York Times headline screamed, "Three More Slain in Virgin Islands; White Death Toll Up to 18."

But it wasn't that simple. Four white tourists had been killed, but so had three white workers and one immigrant Black worker. Still, we said to ourselves, the young men accused of the murders shared the growing anger of the time about racism. The killings occurred on a Rockefeller golf course, a reminder of how the islands had been exploited. And by traditional legal standards, there was a solid reason for us to represent these young men: even unpopular clients are entitled to a vigorous defense.

The chances that they could receive a fair trial were close to nil. Of the approximately 40,000 people on St. Croix, 80 percent or more were Black. Economically, the island depended heavily on tourism from the United States. But after the killings, tourism had dropped dramatically. To salvage what remained of the island's idyllic reputation, St. Croix's court was going to make an example of these defendants.

As Margie and I discussed the situation of the men who became known as the Fountain Valley Five, she said, "Michael, I would love to work on those cases. I'll talk to Bill and maybe I can go down to the next hearing in St. Croix."

"Great," I said, although it would mean some separation. I didn't think about the growing relationship between Margie and Bill.

During the winter of 1972 and the spring of 1973 Margie began to work with Bill, and I accompanied her to St. Croix several times. After the killings, authorities had rounded up more than 100 Black suspects, and some had allegedly confessed. Because Margie and Bill had serious questions about whether these confessions may have resulted from torture, I helped them examine the transcripts of those confessions. I also helped work on jury selection to try to assure fair representation of Black and women jurors.

While we were preparing the case, we stayed with a Black lawyer high on a hill in the middle of a rainforest. It was a fancy house with

360-degree views all the way to the sea. Big, ferocious dogs guarded the house at night when strange noises echoed through the forest.

There were raucous parties with pigs barbecued over an open pit, lots of rum, and loud music. I recall one calypso song in particular—probably because of its odd lyrics and my increasingly troubled relationship with Margie. I can still remember the chorus of "The Big Bamboo":

> *She want the big bamboo, always long*
> *The big bamboo grows so bold and strong*
> *The big bamboo stands so straight and tall*
> *The big bamboo pleases one and all*

In the several months before the start of the Fountain Valley Five trial, our personal lives began to change dramatically. While teaching at NYU Law School, I'd gotten to know a smart, strikingly beautiful blond lawyer, Kristin Booth Glen, who also taught a course there. Though Kris was married with two young kids, we had an occasional lunch with drinks and an intense flirtation for a few months.

In the spring of 1973 the University of Havana Law School invited a group of lawyers, mostly from the National Lawyers Guild, on a two-week trip to Cuba. The U.S. trade embargo had banned travel to Cuba and prohibited U.S. citizens from spending money there. For this reason the Cubans offered to pay for our entire trip.

At the time, I was representing the Venceremos Brigade, North Americans who unlawfully travelled to Cuba to help cut sugar cane or do construction work. The U.S. government had constantly harassed and placed informants within the groups, and made the brigade members' re-entry to the United States difficult and scary. When the government threatened to prosecute the *brigadistas* for breaking the embargo, I helped defend them.

IN THE CENTER OF THE SEVENTIES

Kris and I decided to go on the trip. Margie declined, saying she had to work in St. Croix. But more likely, for both of us, the separation was a chance to explore our relationships with potential new lovers.

Although Cuba was only 90 miles from the Florida coast, there were no direct flights or connections. So our group had to travel to Mexico City, then connect to Havana on a Cubana plane. At the Mexico City airport, we spent hours waiting to board our flight to Havana while someone, probably a CIA or FBI photographer, took pictures.[4] Finally, we climbed into a DC-3, a two-engine propeller plane, for the two-hour flight. Our group of nine were the only passengers. The flight attendants served us lots of Cuban rum and wonderful Cuban cigars.

On the bulkheads on both sides of the aisle were engraved metal plaques. The one on the left had a map of Chile marking the route for Fidel Castro's 1971 trip to visit one of our heroes, the new Socialist president of Chile, Salvador Allende. On the right side of the aisle was a map of Vietnam, Cambodia, and Laos that highlighted the Ho Chi Minh trail, the supply route the Vietnamese were then using to fight the American military. We soon realized that our plane had flown on both these historic trips. The plaques commemorated victories. Allende had won in Chile and the Vietnamese were beating back U.S. aggression in their country. I could not help but think that U.S. imperialism was on the decline, that self-determination and socialism were on the rise. It was a heady, optimistic time.

We were pretty smashed when we got off the plane and stepped into a warm and embracing Havana night. All of us were thrilled to be

---

4 An FBI document dated July 26, 1973, released under the Freedom of Information Act, confirms the surveillance and presumably names those of us travelling. Almost the entire two pages of the document are blanked out. However, I now know the date of the trip. My name is number nine and the only one on my document: "......a group of nine United States citizens traveling as a party were passengers aboard the Cubana Airlines flight of June 15, 1973, from Mexico City, Mexico to Havana, Cuba......(9) Michael David Ratner, age 30, born in Cleveland, Ohio, married, an attorney, resident at 299 Riverside Drive, New York City."

in revolutionary Cuba and excited to see socialism in action. The Cuban revolution, victorious in January 1959, was our dream back then of what a society could be.

We boarded a small bus with two guides and a translator. They took us to a gorgeous, two-story restaurant that looked like a Roman or Greek ruin. Located in a large park, Las Ruinas had been built on the site of an old sugar mill. We walked up the marble stairs to the dining room that featured 20-foot-high ceilings and stained-glass windows designed by the famous artist René Portocarrero. A pianist played quietly in the background. Dinner was served on the best china. It was all as romantic as I could imagine.

We asked our guide what such a fancy place was doing in the middle of a socialist revolution. "There are no rich people in Cuba anymore," he said. "Working class people can come to this restaurant and afford it, at least a few times a year."

Our next stop was a hotel whose name said it all: The Hotel Havana Libre, formerly called the Havana Hilton. Completed only a year or two before the revolution, it had a gaudy, 1950s marble interior reminiscent of Miami Beach hotels. For a few months after Fidel's victory it had served as his headquarters. Now, like all American hotels, it was nationalized, and its casino was closed. International visitors stayed there, but so did Cuban cane cutters, women's groups, and workers.

The Libre lobby in 1973 was a wonderful place to sit and watch revolutionaries and anti-imperialists from all over the world coming and going. We met Black Panthers who had fled the United States, soldiers in uniform from Vietnam, Chileans fighting to keep their socialist government, and many former guerrillas who had fought in the revolution with Fidel or alongside Che Guevara before he was killed in Bolivia in 1967. We saw ourselves as part of this worldwide struggle for socialism and equality—and though it may seem naïve today, we believed we were winning.

IN THE CENTER OF THE SEVENTIES

Within a day of our arrival, I received an urgent call from my brother and sister. My mother, who was only 53, had been diagnosed with an aggressive cancer and was going to have emergency surgery the next day. U.S. citizens could not return via Mexico because of pressure from the U.S. government. I would have to fly to Spain and then back to New York, crossing the Atlantic Ocean twice in three days in order to get to a country 90 miles away. There was just no way for me to get back in time for my mother's operation. Painful as it was for me, I decided to stay in Cuba and see her when I returned.

In Havana, we had many discussions with workers at the hotel, on the street, and in factories. A doorman at the hotel told us his job paid enough to live on, and the differential between his wages and those of a professor or an executive of a company was not great. The doorman's living expenses, like everyone's, were not high. Rents were set at 5 percent of income. The charge for electricity was minimal, and health care was free. The government encouraged him and other workers to continue school and go to college, which was free. Even if he remained a doorman, his wages would increase with more schooling.

The revolution made education an important priority. One of its first and most successful programs had been a nationwide literacy campaign, in which young city people spent a year traveling around the country-side teaching adults and children to read and write. Cuba's literacy rate became one of the highest in the hemisphere.

New schools were sprouting up everywhere. They were attractive, two- or three-story concrete slab buildings, brightly painted, with wall-to-wall windows facing courtyards. We spent a day at a school in a rural area where there had never been a school before. What most interested me was that this school combined academic learning with agricultural work. Every Cuban student of a certain age, whether in Havana or in the countryside, was required to live and work on a farm for six weeks a year. In this school the students picked oranges. Perhaps it was a way to get necessary work done, but it was also a way to develop Che's "New Man"—an educated person who understood the importance of manual labor.

Before the revolution, seasonal employees planted and cut sugar cane, a major export. However, when cane season ended, tens of thousands of them had no employment and became impoverished. Now, unemployment had nearly disappeared. There weren't luxuries, yet almost everyone could live a decent life.

But the embargo had hit Cuba hard. With spare parts unavailable, cars were literally taped together. By 1973, Havana had begun to look shabby. Paint and building materials, both hard to come by, were used for schools and housing outside the capital.

One unintended effect of the embargo was that it forced Cuba to rely on the Soviet Union, which became its major trading partner. It was hardly a perfect fit. Cuban socialism needed to develop its own structures. The country had a joyous energy that was not present in the Soviet Union.

Our group visited one steaming-hot factory where workers turned sugarcane into sugar. I can still recall the pungent aroma of the sweet molasses. Workers ran the factory, although the government in Havana set its production schedule. The workers told us they didn't believe in the "capitalist concept of competition." The word they used instead was "emulation." The worker or factory that did the best on a monthly basis was placed on the top of a chart. Everyone else's goal was to emulate what that worker or factory had done, not to compete with or beat them. This approach came from Che Guevara. It was part of his concept of a cooperative and non-materialistic "New Man."

Workers in the factory also helped build much-needed infrastructure. "Every month, a few of us volunteer to form micro-brigades to build housing," one worker told us. "Six or seven of us leave the factory for about two months. Our jobs are covered by others in the factory. This is happening all over Cuba."

Those left in the factory had to work harder, and those on the micro-brigades would be away from family and friends for long periods. They did it because in the early '70s, Cuban workers were infused with a selfless spirit. The revolution was giving them a real chance for a better life.

Everywhere we went I saw signs of change. Our hotel had a fancy beauty parlor on the lobby floor. A woman there told me that before the revolution, working-class and poor women could never have gone to a beauty parlor. Now they had a diverse group of Cuban women of all races sitting together under hair dryers, beneath a poster with the image of Che and the words "Award of the Heroic Guerrilla." The beauty parlor had been honored for how well it was managed and for meeting its goals.

We were all impressed with the revolution, but we were also naïve. We expected to see a full-scale socialist society without any contradictions. So we were shocked to see that Cuba still had a national beauty contest, which for us represented the objectification of women. "Fidel abolished it," a guide told us, "but then the people wanted it back." We debated this with each other. Some in our group argued that people needed to move slowly to accept the changes a socialist egalitarian society would bring. Some more or less excused the sexism. Others did not.

As children of the '60s in the United States, we had a very different cultural perspective from that of the Cubans. For example, at one point we visited a swimming pool in the countryside. As we put on our swimsuits, one of the women in our group decided to go topless. After all, she thought, this was a liberated socialist country. To put it mildly, that did not sit well with our hosts. Nor did any discussion about gay rights.

We all learned later of the repression of gay people in Cuba. In the mid-'80s, I went to Cuba with my sister Ellen. She is not a wilting flower about gay rights—or anything else. Ellen wanted to talk to everyone about gay rights. When we visited *Juventud Rebelde* (Rebel Youth), the state-run newspaper for young people, my sister got into a heated argument with the editor.

"I was born gay," Ellen said. "I knew I was gay as a 12-year-old girl. It's genetic."

"No, homosexuality is caused by social conditions, and it's not normal," the editor responded. "Before the revolution there was a culture of drugs, prostitution, and poverty that was responsible for people becoming gay. Under the revolution those conditions are gone. Homosexuals are part of a decadent society that is no longer Cuba."

Part of the repression of gay people in Cuba resulted from the leadership's misguided beliefs expressed by that editor. But part was just patriarchal machismo, and part was deep-seated prejudice. Repression of gay people lingers on in Cuba today, but I'm glad it is on its way out.

We spent several of our days at the University of Havana Law School discussing Cuban law before and after the revolution. It was on this beautiful campus, with its classic Greek-Roman-style buildings, that Fidel first became a student leader. And it was this campus that the dictator Fulgencio Batista closed in the 1950s because of student protests.

After the revolution, many of the previous laws were abolished. Businesses could no longer be privately owned, so there was no need for the property law taught in most U.S. law schools. There was even a period when some revolutionaries argued that Cuba should abolish law altogether.

I had a long discussion with the law school's dean about politics in Latin America. "You know that Cuba has been suspended from the Organization of American States," he said.

"Yes, the U.S. government pushed for that," I replied.

"We need to find governments in Latin America who support us in trade and diplomacy."

"Are there any?" I asked.

"Of course, there is Chile," he said. "I can't stress enough how important Salvador Allende's victory was—an open Marxist winning the presidential election. But Allende is not alone. The Tupamaros are fighting in Uruguay, and Peru has a progressive military government. The tide of socialism is rising throughout Latin America, and Cuba supports all revolutionary movements in the region."

It was an exciting conversation, and I had high hopes. But three months after this conversation, on September 11, 1973, a bloody U.S.-supported coup overthrew Chile's lawfully elected president, Salvador Allende. General Augusto Pinochet seized power. For the next decade, the dictator led Operation Condor—a program to kidnap and kill thousands of leftists—effectively destroying any hope that socialism would spread in Latin America in the near future.

I learned an important lesson. The United States has a tremendous military, economic, and political ability to roll back revolutions and get rid of any government attempting to escape its orbit. I saw this again in the 1980s in Central America and in the 1990s in Haiti. Only after the attacks of September 11, 2001—when the United States was so preoccupied with the "war on terror" in the Middle East and Central Asia—were some of the countries in Latin America able to establish governments that benefitted their people.

Near the end of our trip we had some free time in Havana. Kris and I had fun eating and drinking at La Bodeguita del Medio, a small bar/restaurant in Old Havana where the mojito was supposedly invented. Over the years, patrons—including notables like Salvador Allende—had covered the bar's aging plaster walls with graffiti. Novelist Ernest Hemingway had written: "My mojito in La Bodeguita, my daiquiri in La Floridita [another Havana bar.]" Getting drunk on mojitos at La Bodeguita with a new lover was wonderful. It was difficult to imagine a more romantic and exciting place than revolutionary Cuba.

MOVING THE BAR

Our trip at an end, we flew back to the United States by way of Madrid. The dictator General Francisco Franco still ruled Spain, and his heavily armed soldiers patrolling the airport provided a stark contrast to the friendly, open atmosphere we'd experienced in Cuba. We took our last photograph together and got on a flight to New York City.

I took a cab straight from the airport to my mother's Manhattan apartment. As I write this, I am still upset. She had recently married a very nice man and had been living a good life. She was home from the hospital, but a massive tumor had been removed from her intestine. The primary cancer was probably ovarian.

I also had to deal with my deteriorating relationship with Margie. She and Bill Kunstler were now romantically involved, though Bill was still living with his wife. And I had to consider whether a future with Kris might work out, though Kris was still with her husband. None of it was easy.

Despite our complicated personal issues, Margie, Bill, and I continued to work together on the St. Croix murder cases as they came up for trial in the late summer of 1973. St. Croix was a U.S. possession, and federal law ruled the territory. The federal courtroom was out of another century, with a high ceiling and only big wooden overhead fans to bring relief from the oppressive heat and humidity.

St. Croix's federal judge, Warren Young, was white. He'd been a corporate lawyer, and it was obvious this was not going to be a friendly court to the defendants. But Bill Kunstler was a major celebrity in St. Croix, and the case was the major event of the year, so during the trial there were crowds both outside and inside the courtroom.

At the end of the trial, the jury deliberated for many days, seemingly unable to agree. After a week or so they delivered a unanimous verdict: the five defendants were convicted of eight murders, and each received eight life sentences.

But the lengthy deliberation raised serious questions. When Bill later interviewed jurors, they told a remarkable story. As usual, the jury was sequestered. They went from the jury room to dinner and their hotel under the watchful eyes of court officers. They could not speak to others or read about the case. But some jurors told Bill that court officers had warned them that the FBI was investigating the jurors and their relatives, and unless they came up with a guilty verdict, the investigations would continue.

The jurors' story, if true, meant that the verdict would need to be set aside since the jurors had been unlawfully influenced and intimidated. Multiple jurors independently confirmed this story. One even told Bill that the FBI had visited his house during deliberations. It seemed obvious that there were grounds for a mistrial. But the judge refused Bill's request to hold a hearing on the issue, and the verdict stood.

I appealed to the federal appeals court in Philadelphia, confident that the verdict would be reversed, or at least a new hearing granted in which jurors could testify about the deliberation process. We won the appeal for a hearing. But it was to take place in the same federal court in St. Croix, before the same judge who had already refused a hearing about jury interference.

At the hearing the judge again ruled against us. He found that "rumors" were generated within the jury room, and did not originate outside. We appealed again. This time we lost. The appeals court usually gives great deference to the findings of trial judges who hear testimony, but in legal terms this decision was inexplicable and just plain wrong. Underlying it was the court's firm belief that the defendants were guilty. Requiring a new trial would have kept the case in the public eye and continued to harm business and tourism to St. Croix.

One of the defendants subsequently received a pardon. Three remain in prison, serving life terms. One, Ishmael LaBeet, was flown to the mainland to appear in federal court for a prior case he had pending. On his flight back to prison in St. Croix, he obtained a gun that had been left in the lavatory and hijacked the plane to Cuba. As far as I know, that is where he remains.

A few months after the conclusion of the St. Croix case, Margie moved to her own apartment in the West Village. Later she moved in with Bill. I moved in with Kris, though that relationship ended after a few months.

Today, more than four decades after our divorce, Margie and I remain the closest of friends. We live only blocks apart and share very similar politics, although she may be even more radical than I am. We still work on cases together and give each other unstinting support. Our respective families are one family. For many years after our separation, we shared our small cabin in upstate New York where her children with Bill—Sarah and Emily—spent part of the summer with my children. In the 1980s we all made a trip together to Cuba.

I also remained close with Bill, who continued to do work with the Center for Constitutional Rights for the rest of his life. I learned a lot from him. Even after major losses, Bill never got down or depressed. After all, he reasoned, it was the client's life, not his. His job was to keep fighting, which he did. Bill had a deep belief in juries—with juries he had at least a chance of convincing ordinary people of his client's defense. With cases argued solely before judges he had to appeal to the elite, who had less of a sense of justice. To his last breath Bill believed that racism was at the heart of our country's problems. His work reflected that. There was nobody like him—no one who could so dominate a courtroom, no one who cared so little about money, and no one who influenced so many others to become radical lawyers.

Three years passed before I made my second trip to Cuba. A lot had changed in the world. The movement was no longer about flower power, yippies, hippies, and ending the war. The Watergate scandal shook the country and forced President Richard Nixon to resign. The Paris Peace accords in 1973 mandated the withdrawal of U.S. troops, and in early 1975, with the fall of Saigon, the United States pulled out of Vietnam— although it left behind millions dead and a devastated country.

In the spring of 1976, my mother's cancer returned, and she was in and out of the hospital. I remember driving around the hospital block repeatedly, not wanting to go inside. It was just too painful. My entire family and my mother went to therapy together to try to deal with our emotions, but it was still awful.

I had already signed up to go to Cuba in April with the Venceremos Brigade—not as a lawyer, but as one of 300 brigadistas who had volunteered to do construction work for seven weeks. But given my mother's condition, leaving at all was a huge issue. Doctors assured me she was likely to live for several months. So I got permission from the organizers to go for three weeks. (I would make a different decision today.)

Arriving in Havana late at night, I went straight to the site where the brigade was working, an hour outside the city. The men's wooden dorm looked like a large summer camp cabin. Brigadistas were sleeping on triple metal-framed bunk beds with thin mattresses. Exhausted, I found an empty bunk and closed my eyes.

At 5:30 a.m., I was jolted awake by deafening, off-key singing blaring from speakers in the cabin. I have never forgotten the opening: *"Un hombre se levanta, temprano en la mañana, se pone la camisa."* ("A man gets up in the early morning and puts on his shirt.") The song may be beautiful when the famous Cuban troubadour Silvio Rodríguez sings it, but not when it's blasted from loudspeakers at 5:30 in the morning— every morning. It was so ear-splitting that no one could possibly stay in the dormitory.

Outside, it was still dark. Half-asleep, I ran out of the cabin dragging my clothes behind me. After breakfast, just as the sun was rising against a gorgeous, green Cuban landscape dotted with palm trees, the bus picked us up. We started early because later it got too hot to work. Our job was to help build concrete apartment houses. The most difficult job was digging four-foot foundation trenches in clay-like ground so that masons could cement the concrete blocks. None of us could dig for the entire day, so we took turns at different jobs.

One job I enjoyed was smoothing out concrete that had been freshly poured from a wheelbarrow into six-inch steel frames about the size of a door. I'd fill up the wheelbarrow with concrete from a hand mixer and pour it into a slab that would become a wall of the apartment. I then smoothed it with a wooden squeegee called a floater, a tool I'd used years before at my Dad's construction business.

It was hard physical labor. We took one 30-minute break called *merienda* (snack) when we ate wildly sweet pink yogurt. The work day ended by 1 p.m., when the bus carried us back to the camp for lunch.

In the afternoon we got some rest, but there were often also political education activities. Many brigadistas belonged to the U.S. Communist Party. However, the Cubans insisted that other progressives also join in the effort to build support for the revolution. These included members of Prairie Fire, whose politics were set forth in the book *Prairie Fire: The Politics of Revolutionary Anti-Imperialism*. Above a picture of Che, the book proclaimed in bold letters: "A SINGLE SPARK CAN START A PRAIRIE FIRE."

In our nightly discussions, factions within the brigade debated the relative merits of the accommodationist approach versus the "Che" approach. Che had employed the *foco* theory, which French radical writer Régis Debray described as a disciplined vanguard of guerrillas who would take armed actions to spark oppressed people to rise up. Although this approach had failed in Bolivia, it remained a driving ideology among leftists around the world. The *foco* theory could not have been farther from the politics of the U.S. Communist Party. My politics were then, and remain today, closer to those of Che.

IN THE CENTER OF THE SEVENTIES

We attended a series of talks on Chile and the 1973 coup. Members of the *Movimiento de Izquierda Revolucionaria (MIR)*, the Revolutionary Left Movement, dominated the dialogue. Some had been bodyguards for Salvador Allende, and they believed in arming the people. The debate among the brigadistas split, roughly, between members of the U.S. Communist Party and leftists who leaned toward the politics of Che, the Weathermen, and Prairie Fire.

The main question we discussed was: "Should Allende have heeded the MIR's warnings and armed the people against a possible coup?"

"That would have been foolhardy and impossible," the Communists argued. "It would have given the military and the United States an even better excuse to launch a coup."

The militant leftists replied: "Allende made a huge mistake. His unarmed supporters were like sitting ducks with no way to defend themselves. That is why thousands of them were killed and tortured."

Knowing what we know today about the military dictatorship that lasted almost a generation in Chile, I believe the MIR was probably right. Even back then, I think it was reasonable to believe that the United States would never allow an elected socialist like Allende to govern. After all, since 1959, a main Cold War goal of U.S. policy had been to overthrow the Cuban revolution and ensure that no other country would follow its lead. On the other hand, it's impossible to know how much blood would have been shed had Allende armed the people.

The Soviet Union, Cuba's main economic supporter, pushed a more gradual approach, not wanting to stir up trouble in the U.S's. backyard. The Soviets had pressured Cuba to end support for Che in Bolivia. Despite this, the Cubans supported, at least covertly, regional armed struggle. They trained, armed, and offered leadership advice to Central and Latin American revolutionaries in Cuba.

The brigadistas argued about these issues non-stop. The "Che" side believed in militancy and revolution. The U.S. Communists revered the Soviet Union and stuck with their gradualist approach. While the U.S.S.R. supported many Third World revolutions, I did not idealize the Soviet Union as the future. One time on our bus, to the tune of "We Shall Overcome," the Communists started singing "Brezhnev is our leader, we shall overcome." For me, a duller, more robotic, bureaucratic hero was hard to imagine.

After the brigade finished our work, the Cubans took us on a week-long trip around the country. One day we hiked 30 kilometers in the Sierra Maestra mountains, following Che's path as a guerrilla. We all lined up on a hot dusty road in the middle of a beautiful grassy land-scape. The Cubans provided doctors and ambulances for our group. Others carried water and split coconuts with machetes for us. But it was still a very hot, exhausting hike.

As we reached the top of a mountain, I could hear children singing in the distance. We got closer, and I saw 50 neatly uniformed children standing in front of a high school. Each was holding a handwritten plac-ard and singing the words: *"Seremos como el Che."* ("We will be like Che.") To be selfless, to make a family of one's comrades, to give up comfort and material gain for the revolution, to risk one's life to liberate humanity— that was the innocent, contagious idealism of youth, an idealism that in that moment I shared with all my heart.

Toward the end of our trip, the Venceremos brigadistas, dressed in our construction outfits with yellow hardhats and brigade scarves, joined the May Day parade in Havana. After marching for two hours, we joined hundreds of thousands of Cubans in Revolution Square, a large public space with a monument to the poet José Martí. The father of Cuban nationalism, Martí died in the struggle to free Cuba from Spain and wrote the lyrics of the famous Cuban song "Guantanamera." A steel sculpture of Che, perhaps 15 stories high, overlooked the square. Under it were the words *"Hasta La Victoria Siempre"* (Until Victory, Always).

IN THE CENTER OF THE SEVENTIES

I still recall a key part of Fidel's speech that afternoon. He explained why Cuban soldiers had been sent to support the leftist independence movement in Angola. "We are going there to fight against apartheid and South Africa," he said, "because in every Cuban's veins is the blood of Africa." It was remarkable for Fidel to speak this simple truth in a country which, until the revolution, had been deeply racist and denied its Black roots. On that beautiful day, I felt in complete solidarity with the people of Cuba.

In early May 1976, I flew back to New York and went straight to visit my mother. She lived in a spacious 17th-floor apartment on the Upper East Side. I rushed into her bedroom and there she was, under the covers, wan and much thinner. I lay on top of her and wept.

It was a difficult spring and summer. Though the cancer had spread throughout my mother's body, her mind was still sharp. One overcast day in May she revived enough to go with her children to visit our weekend homes in the Catskills. We stopped first at my brother's lovely old stone house. She had trouble walking, so we sat together on the wall of the front yard, under a leafy catalpa tree. A photograph shows me sporting a thick brown beard, sitting with my mother next to Kris's golden retriever. My mother's face looks puffy from chemotherapy, but she still seems beautiful to me. It is the last picture of us together.

She had never visited my upstate home. I helped her up the wooden steps to the small cabin, worrying that she expected me to have a fancier place. She sat on the deep blue couch, enveloped by its embroidered cushions, which she had given to Margie and me. I wanted her to see the cabin, and also to touch it physically. I wanted to have her presence there before she died.

For the next two months after her upstate trip, my mother was in and out of the hospital. We visited most days and sat with her for agonizing hours, even when she was unresponsive. Seeing my sister with her was most painful for me. Ellen was still in her twenties, and had gone through a tough time in the years since our father died, when she had been only ten. It all seemed too much to bear.

Near the end, my Uncle Max came from Cleveland. He had been very close to my father. However, like many of our relatives, he'd always looked down on my mother and resented her for moving away from Cleveland and remarrying. Max walked into the hospital room, sat down beside my mother, and told her she looked beautiful. She fixed him with a cold stare and replied, "It's taken you 25 years to tell me that."

On July 4, the 200th anniversary of the Declaration of Independence, tall ships, three- or four-masters, sailed into New York harbor. I sat with my mother as she slipped in and out of consciousness. That night, Kris and I rented a hotel room with a view of the fireworks show exploding over the Hudson River and I tried to forget what I was facing.

The next day, my mother slipped into a deep coma. I spent hours with her, sitting there as she labored to breathe. Nobody knew whether she had hours, days, or weeks left. Kris and I decided to take a short break at the New Jersey shore. Within a few hours of our arrival there, I got a call from the hospital. My mother had died.

Following her expressed wishes, we picked out a simple pine coffin. On Saturday night by the open coffin, we gathered and reminisced about her life. Our mother had experienced real poverty. We reflected on what such an intelligent woman might have done with her life if she'd had a full college education. Joking, I wondered if her early experience of hardship was connected to her abiding love of shopping. In a desperate attempt to cheer up a grim situation, I took one of her credit cards and placed it in the coffin beside her. "Never leave home without it," I intoned. We all laughed, but inside we were deep in mourning.

The following day we gathered in a Brooklyn cemetery at the family plot of my mother's surviving husband. As we lowered her casket into the earth, I leaned over and embraced it—and her—one last time.

IN THE CENTER OF THE SEVENTIES

Now there were just the three of us—Ellen, Bruce, and me—all orphaned relatively young. Still, we had each other, and the deaths of our parents brought us even closer together. From then on, we made sure that whatever our parents would have done for us, we would now do for each other.

I have kept some mementos from my mother. One that is especially important to me is a Japanese porcelain jar from the house we lived in until I was five. Another is the remnant of a white-and-purple cable-knit tennis sweater my mother gave me when I was 13. The garment remained intact until one day in the mid-'90s when I came home to find that my daughter Ana, unaware of its sentimental value, had cut it up to make clothes for her dolls. All that remained of the sweater was a four-inch square.

Today, it sits on my mantle, a last memory of my childhood.

Michael, one year old, Cleveland, Ohio.

Family photo 1955, Ann, Michael, Bruce and Harry.

Michael in Nicaragua, 1981.

Taking testimony from victims of Contra violence, Nicaragua, 1982.

Guild members (Michael top right) protest US funding of Contras against Nicaragua in front of the Federal Building, Manhattan, 1984.

Michael and Karen Ranucci's wedding invitation, 1987.

Karen Ranucci, Michael, Jake and Ana Ratner, at Jake's Bar Mitzvah, 2001.

Michael and Karen at Eres crossing to Gaza, which was being blocked by Israeli soldiers, June, 2009.

With Yoko Ono receiving the LennonOno Grant For Peace Award, Reykjavik, Iceland, 2006.

Michael, 2012.

With daughter Ana, daughter-in-law Elena Stein, and son Jake, 2013.

At a protest in New York City's Union Square, 2014.

6
THE REAGAN YEARS

Jimmy Carter was elected president in 1976. I liked him better than the presidents who came before or would come after. He did not start a major war, he did not intervene in some countries where revolutions succeeded, he briefly allowed travel to Cuba, and he at least talked about human rights.

For a short period after the U.S.'s defeat in Vietnam, the government was reluctant to begin another major foreign adventure. Congress passed the War Powers Resolution requiring congressional authorization or a declaration of war for the use of U.S. military force in a foreign country. And after President Nixon's abuse of power led to his resignation in 1974, Congress enacted laws intended to limit the powers of the CIA and the FBI, and curb warrantless wiretapping by national security agencies.

Abroad, particularly in Central America, revolution was in the air. Popular movements and armed revolutionaries confronted dictatorships and military regimes that had been propped up by the U.S. government. In 1979, revolutions in both Nicaragua and Grenada triumphed. Guerrillas in El Salvador were on the verge of toppling the right-wing dictator's government. And Guatemala looked as if it would be next.

But in 1980, the brief period of relatively liberal policies came to an end. The election of Ronald Reagan as president shocked me, everyone at CCR, and all of our friends. We had grown up under the Warren Supreme Court and spent our early years as lawyers working in the civil rights movement and actively opposing the Vietnam War. But now the "in-the-streets" Southern civil rights movement had waned. The anti-war movement had vanished. And the Black Panthers, Young Lords, and other militant groups had been virtually destroyed by the police, the FBI, and the CIA. The conservative backlash confirmed that the left counter-culture of the 1960s and 1970s was over.

From the beginning, Reagan's presidency plunged the country more deeply into militarism, nativism, and a cruel economic system that would mire huge swaths of the U.S. and world population in poverty.

During the '80s, I threw my heart and soul into resisting the Reagan agenda. I believed that legal work in the courts and political work outside the courts should go hand in hand. As legal director of CCR, as president of the National Lawyers Guild, and as a grassroots movement activist, I worked on many cases and campaigns to support budding revolutions in Central America and the Caribbean and to end U.S. intervention. I made more than 30 trips to Nicaragua, roughly the same number to Cuba, and quite a few to Grenada, El Salvador, Guatemala, Jamaica, and Costa Rica. I also spent a lot of time in Mexico, where I met with exiled revolutionaries.

In retrospect, though it was often not successful, I believe this work—always done in collaboration with other lawyers and activists—was the most important and fulfilling I have ever done.

CUBA

During this period, CCR and I worked closely with Cubans I'd known since the early '70s, who connected me with activists throughout the region and helped with issues directly involving Cuba. The U.S. embargo banned Americans from spending any money in Cuba or even traveling there. Many people—not just those from the Venceremos Brigades—broke the law by traveling to Cuba and were fined a thousand dollars or more. We decided to litigate every case we could. It proved a successful strategy. The government couldn't keep up with the time-consuming task of trying so many cases. Out of thousands of cases, only three or four went to trial and only a handful of people wound up having to pay a fine.

Early in the '80s, we brought litigation to challenge the ban on traveling to Cuba. Margie came up with a legal theory based on the Trading with the Enemy Act and the International Emergency Economic Powers Act, under which the regulations had been promulgated. The preeminent civil rights lawyer Leonard Boudin worked with my colleague Jules Lobel to develop the case. When it went all the way to the Supreme Court, Leonard argued it there.

Justice Anthony Kennedy, the swing vote, believed we were correct with respect to the law. But in conference, the other justices persuaded him that the court could not hand the president a loss on this issue. Kennedy switched his position, and, by a vote of 5-4, we lost our bid to legalize travel to Cuba. It was a disappointing defeat.

In *Nation v. Haig* we brought a more promising case involving Cuba. *The Nation* magazine was the lead plaintiff, and Secretary of State Alexander Haig was the defendant. The United States government had decided to ban distribution of the Cuban newspaper *Granma* in the United States. In a misguided attempt to publicize the ban, the government released a photo showing U.S. officials turning away a truck filled with thousands of copies of *Granma*. The photo provided all the evidence we needed. We knew we would win this one, and we did. The court held it was illegal to bar newspapers protected by the Constitution's First Amendment, even if they were coming from Cuba.

Through my work with Cuba, I met other activists supporting revolutions in Central America. Among them were Bill Schaap, Ellen Ray, Lou

Wolf, and ex-CIA officer Philip Agee, who together had co-founded a magazine called *CovertAction Information Bulletin*. I became the lawyer for *CovertAction* and its four editors. The magazine published articles about the CIA's efforts to overthrow governments and interfere with democracy around the world. In a column called "Naming Names," it printed the names of CIA officers and agents whose identities were supposed to be secret, thus making their covert work impossible.

The column was launched after Phil Agee published his book, *Inside the Company*. He described how CIA officials secretly used the cover of diplomatic posts in foreign countries to work with trade unions and other organizations to undermine local progressive movements. Phil's book named more than 200 people working for the CIA, which led to their expulsion from the countries they'd been working in.

Identifying CIA officials was not as difficult then as it later became. The Agency often recruited from particular universities—Notre Dame and Brown were two of the most prominent. The officers took diplomatic jobs in U.S. embassies abroad. Because the embassies published their biographies, we were able to track their careers. The "Naming Names" column caused untold trouble to the U.S. government and its security establishment. *CovertAction* became notorious, and the government labelled all four of its editors as public enemies and traitors. When the State Department later withdrew Phil's passport, he had to travel with papers from Germany, where he'd made his new home after being forced to leave the U.S.

In response to the "Naming Names" column, Congress passed the Agent Identities Protection Act of 1981, which made it illegal to name agents, except in the context of a news article. One remarkable aspect of the law was that it forbade the publication of information taken entirely from public sources—a direct attack on free speech. Along with many civil libertarians, we fought long and hard to strike this down, but we lost. My clients' column, which simply listed the names, could now land them in jail. As a result of the new law, *CovertAction* stopped publishing its "Naming Names" column.

Though it was still legal to publish an agent's name in the context of a news article, many journalists did not understand that or were too frightened to risk it. To this day, I still get calls from journalists who are concerned about naming an intelligence agent in an article. The lasting result of the law is a chilling effect on free speech.

In addition to our work on *CovertAction,* Bill, Ellen and I also started a publishing house, Deep Cover Publications, specializing in books about the CIA by former agents and other whistleblowers. Our first book was *White Paper, Whitewash.* The U.S. government had issued a "white paper" claiming to "document" shipments of arms from Cuba to El Salvador and asserting that Cuba was funding Salvadoran revolutionaries. A German writer, Warner Poelchau, analyzed the white paper and discovered many contradictions. He concluded that the documents it cited were falsified.

In his introduction to *White Paper, Whitewash*, Phil Agee pointed out that CIA operations typically use fabricated documents to implicate a country the U.S. government wants to harm or discredit. In this case, the CIA's goal was to undermine support the Salvadoran insurgents had built in the United States, particularly among Catholics and the human rights community. By publicizing Cuba's relationship to the rebels, it smeared the Salvadoran revolution with the communist label.

The documents cited in the white paper became a crucial factor in the ideological war between liberals, Catholics, and human rights people on the one hand and the Reagan administration on the other. Shortly after *White Paper, Whitewash* was published, an article appeared in the *Wall Street Journal* verifying our book's charge that the documents were fabricated. However, exposing the CIA's disinformation campaign was not enough to stop the U.S. government from continuing to arm the right-wing Salvadoran dictatorship.

A year later, we changed the name of the publishing house to Sheridan Square Press and released its first book, *Deadly Deceits: My 25 Years in the CIA* by Ralph McGehee, a former CIA case officer in Thailand, Vietnam, and Indonesia. I met him when he was in the process of risking his reputation, his pension, and possibly his family's safety by turning against the Agency. He was nervous, but proud that he'd broken with the CIA. He considered it the most important action of his life.

Sheridan Square went on to publish other books, including *Profits of War: Inside the Secret U.S.-Israeli Arms Network* by former Israeli spy Ari Ben-Menashe and the best-selling *On the Trail of the Assassins* by Jim Garrison, which became the basis of Oliver Stone's Oscar-winning film *JFK*.

The groundbreaking work of *CovertAction* and Sheridan Square helped bring to public attention for the first time the nefarious, illegal secret activities of the CIA.

EL SALVADOR

For me, law was becoming secondary to activism, politics, and winning revolutions. A lawsuit challenging intervention was nearly impossible to win and certainly was not going to stop imperialism. But it could still be a weapon in the larger struggle, a useful tool to expose and halt U.S. government intervention around the globe.

One of the most important cases CCR brought to try to stop U.S. intervention in Central America was *Crockett v. Reagan*. The plaintiff, Representative George Crockett Jr. from Detroit, was a member of the Black Congressional Caucus and the National Lawyers Guild. In the 1950s he had served six months in jail for contempt of court while defending those accused of being Communists under the Smith Act. He was the most radical member of Congress, and his Detroit constituency loved him.

Crockett v. Reagan questioned whether it was legal for U.S. military personnel to train El Salvador's armed forces to fight the Farabundo Martí National Liberation Front (FMLN), a coalition of five guerrilla groups working to overthrow the right-wing Salvadoran government.

Our first argument was based on the U.S. Constitution. Five hundred U.S. soldiers were "using force" in El Salvador, though Congress had not authorized the use of force as the Constitution requires. Our second argument was based on the 1973 War Powers Resolution, which says that no U.S. troops may be introduced into "hostilities" for more than 60 days without explicit congressional approval. If troops remain longer without approval, no vote is required to end the use of force. It ends automatically. On behalf of Crockett and 28 other members of Congress, we challenged the presidential use of force in El Salvador, which had been ordered without congressional approval.

We based our third claim on the Foreign Assistance Act to bring to light the terrible brutality of the government in El Salvador. The act prohibited U.S. aid to any country engaged in a consistent pattern of gross violations of internationally protected human rights: murder, torture, and disappearances. The appendix we attached with reports of human rights violations in El Salvador showed that right-wing death squads were routinely slaughtering and torturing people—everyone from politicians to priests. The most publicized example was Archbishop Óscar Romero, who had been assassinated in the chapel of a hospital while saying mass. He was one of thousands the military had murdered.

Brought in 1981, six years after the end of the Vietnam War, *Crockett v. Reagan* was the first case based on the War Powers Resolution. A mass movement in the U.S. had started mobilizing to oppose intervention in El Salvador. It included Catholic constituents based in Liberation Theology and others favoring democratic change in El Salvador, although not necessarily revolutionary change. We hoped our case would support and be part of that growing opposition movement.

MOVING THE BAR

I felt *Crockett v. Reagan* had a strong legal basis. The administration admitted that 500 U.S. troops had been sent to El Salvador as "trainers." But we had photographs of U.S. soldiers in the field with Salvadoran military personnel firing mortars against the FMLN.

After Vietnam, I thought the courts might be sympathetic to the argument that Congress had been denied its right to vote on whether to wage war. Of all the dozen cases we later litigated involving the wars in Central America, this was the one that I thought had the best chance of winning.

We argued the case in Washington D.C. federal district court before Judge Joyce Hens Green. She ruled that Crockett, as a member of Congress, had the right to litigate this issue. Judge Green also upheld the principle that under the War Powers Resolution a declaration of war or the use of force required congressional approval.

But ultimately the judge did not rule in our favor. She said it was not clear exactly where in El Salvador the 500 U.S. troops had been sent or whether their activities met the threshold for "hostilities." In addition, she dismissed our claim of gross human rights violations as unenforceable.

This was how judges often dismissed our cases—upholding our right to bring the case with their left hand but finding a way to rule against us with their right hand. We appealed, but lost. The outcome of *Crockett v. Reagan* was a blow, but it laid the foundation for future litigation challenging U.S. military intervention.

CIA-backed death squads in El Salvador continued to operate with impunity. Under pressure from human rights activists, Congress eventually passed legislation requiring certification that human rights in El Salvador were improving before any aid could be approved.

I was a lawyer for Barbara Mikulski (later a senator from Maryland), one of the Congress members who opposed aid to El Salvador. In 1983, President Reagan certified that human rights were improving in El Salvador and therefore it could continue receiving foreign assistance. Mikulski called me and asked, "Michael, can the president call a duck an eagle?" I replied, "Yes, because the law requires the president to certify that human rights are improving—but it doesn't require any proof."

In 1983, the House and Senate again passed legislation requiring certification and sent it to the president for signature. As simple as this may sound, it resulted in a very complicated case, *Barnes v. Carmen,* that I ended up filing on behalf of Congress.

Rather than accept or veto the bill, President Reagan did nothing, invoking a "pocket veto"—a rule that applies if Congress is adjourned and the president fails to return a bill within ten days. However, if Congress is in session, as we at CCR believed it was, the pocket veto rule does not apply. After the president failed to act on the certification bill within ten days, we believed it had become law, thus forcing another confrontation with Congress on human rights.

David Cole, a student of mine who later became national legal director of the ACLU, worked on the case with me. The law hinged on the definition of a congressional recess, which proved to be a complex question. We argued that because its committees continued to meet, Congress technically was still in session. Thus the president's pocket veto did not apply and the bill should become law.

Rounding up plaintiffs to litigate was challenging. Representative Michael Barnes of Maryland opposed aid to El Salvador and agreed to be the lead plaintiff. Ultimately Congress itself, both the Senate and the House, joined in the litigation because the president had ignored the legislation they passed, and they wanted a decision on their powers.

According to the law, the human rights certification for El Salvador was good for a year. If I could win the case within that year, new certification would be required for the following year's aid to be approved. Because the appalling human rights situation had deteriorated so much in El Salvador, it would be difficult for the president to justify renewed certification.

Though the Senate and the House had their own counsel, I argued the case on their behalf. It was ironic that I should be representing Congress. Unfortunately, we lost in the district court and in the court of appeals, and by that time the legislation had expired.

We asked the Supreme Court for discretionary review, arguing that this was an important issue because the impasse between White House and Congress could be repeated. The government countered that the legislation had been pocket-vetoed while Congress was in recess and the case was moot since the legislation had already expired.

Amazingly, the court took the case. But as I expected, the court ruled against us. U.S. aid to El Salvador's military government continued.

GOVERNMENT SURVEILLANCE

During the Reagan years, CCR, still a fairly small organization, geared up to oppose government surveillance of movement groups organizing for social change. Given the FBI's ignoble history during the civil rights movement and with COINTELPRO, we assumed the federal government was spying on civil rights activists and on solidarity groups opposed to U.S. intervention abroad.

To monitor the FBI's activities, we launched a project directed by Margie Ratner Kunstler and Ann Marie Buitrago, an expert on the FBI and Freedom of Information Act requests. We wanted to document the surveillance of activists, publish a list of FBI intrusions, file FOIA requests on behalf of movement organizations, and increase public awareness to start a pushback against FBI harassment. We encouraged movement organizations to call us about suspicious government activity.

Activists called in daily to report that their offices had been broken into, their houses burglarized, their computers hacked into or destroyed.

We began to publish a monthly newsletter, documenting every complaint we'd investigated.

We were surprised to discover that the key target of the Reagan administration's surveillance was the Central America solidarity movement in the United States—all the people and groups calling for an end to U.S. intervention. Most prominent among them were the Nicaragua Network, the Committee in Solidarity with the People of El Salvador (CISPES), the Network in Solidarity with the People of Guatemala, and Cuba solidarity groups.

The Reagan administration believed that solidarity groups supported communists, and therefore the government had a right to spy on them. Margie and I testified at a congressional hearing on this issue, arguing that anti-intervention solidarity groups were engaged in constitutionally protected dissent. But to no avail. At virtually every meeting or protest march I attended government agents were taking photographs and names. And many of us assumed our phones were tapped.

Ultimately, we made FOIA requests to 50 separate FBI field offices. Remarkably, we received tens of thousands of documents, including FBI files on union leaders, religious activists, and well-known figures like actress Susan Sarandon.

In one case, a young college graduate named Edward Haase returned to the U.S. from a fact-finding trip to Nicaragua. When he passed through U.S. Customs, officials confiscated his address book. We immediately went to court to retrieve it.

The government had to concede it had no evidence that Haase or anyone in his address book had done anything illegal. The judge issued an injunction requiring the FBI and Customs to return the address book to Haase.

We assumed that the government had already copied the address book and opened files on every single person in it. The incident became a scandal, and even the major newspapers printed the story with head-lines such as "A Wise Traveler Leaves His Address Book at Home."

GRENADA

In March 1980, I traveled to St. George's, the capital of the island nation of Grenada, to celebrate the success of the revolution there. It was a hot, sunny day, and approximately a thousand people—including Sandinista leader Daniel Ortega and Jamaica's leftist president Michael Manley—gathered in a soccer field with an old viewing stand at one end. Bill Schaap and I sat in the front near the Cuban delegation.

Flags flapped in the breeze, and the crowd chanted the slogan of the revolution—"Forward Ever, Backward Never." I listened as Maurice Bishop, the charismatic young leader of the Grenadian Revolution, spoke about democracy and elections. Real democracy, he said, meant partic-ipation in decision making, not simply pulling a lever in a voting booth every four years. He was also critical of European-style social democ-racy, calling it a half-way house between capitalism and socialism.

Sitting there, I was optimistic. Back in 1980, we all believed more and more revolutions would be victorious.

Two and a half years later, in August 1983, I returned to Grenada for a legal conference on U.S. imperialism. By then, Reagan had targeted Bishop's Socialist government for overthrow, charging that the island jeopardized U.S. shipping lanes, had relations with Cuba, and with Cuba's support was building an airport to accommodate fighter jets. The White House made the absurd claim that this tiny Caribbean island of 90,000 people posed a security threat to the U.S.

Grenada was gorgeous, ringed by beaches and rainforest, with a mountain in the center. It was part of the Spice Islands, and the aroma of nutmeg, its major export, floated everywhere. While it was true that the government was building a new airport, its goal was to promote tourism, not war. Until then, only small propeller planes could land in Grenada.

At the conference, I presented a paper about CCR's anti-war litigation. Prime Minister Bishop, a lawyer himself, told me he loved the work we were doing. But two months later, in October, a coup toppled the Bishop government. Maurice was imprisoned briefly, released, and then murdered. His body was never found.

It turned out the coup leaders had originally been Bishop's comrades. I had even held a reception for them at my house in New York. Bernard Coard, the deputy prime minister, had apparently led the coup. Coard was a dogmatic Marxist whose supporters had split with the less hard-line Bishop. Eventually, Coard and others were convicted of Bishop's murder and sentenced to death. On appeal, the death penalty was overturned. Coard served 23 years in prison and was released in 2009.

To this day, we do not know if the U.S. was involved in the coup. But it seized the opportunity to invade the island. On October 25, 1983, U.S. forces attacked Grenada, on the pretext that they were protecting hundreds of U.S. citizens attending a medical school on the island. But a survey revealed that more than 90 percent of the students said they did not want to be "saved." During the four-day war, U.S. forces bombed a mental hospital, killing 12 patients.

This invasion was the first direct encounter between Cuban and American troops. Cuban workers fought a losing pitched battle at Grenada's airport. But not all the Cubans were that brave. American troops invaded the Cuban embassy in St. George's, where an old acquaintance of mine was the ambassador. His American wife had been my client, and they had a young baby. Rather than defend the embassy, the ambassador surrendered, allowing U.S. soldiers to enter inviolable Cuban territory protected under international law.

When the ambassador returned to Cuba, angry Cubans threw shoes at him. My acquaintance lost his job and was assigned to do construction work. I often wonder what I would have done with a small baby and an invasion force landing in front of my house. Would I take the risk of having the baby harmed? The ambassador's duty was to defend the embassy, but how many of us would?

The invasion of Grenada clearly violated U.S. law. We at CCR tried to stop it. But by the time we filed our lawsuit arguing that Congress had not approved the war, it was over. We pressed on, but the court of appeals dismissed our case as moot.

Once again we had failed to win a case under the War Powers Resolution. Despite the requirements of the Constitution and legislation enacted by Congress, the courts believed it was not their role to restrict presidential power when it came to war or foreign affairs.

NICARAGUA

Nicaragua's revolution had toppled the former dictatorship of General Anastasio Somoza in 1979, but by the early 1980s the new Sandinista government was struggling. It was at war with Somoza's former soldiers, known as Contras (counter-revolutionaries), who were backed by the United States. CCR sent research teams to Nicaragua to develop legal challenges, document U.S. involvement in the training and funding of the Contras, and expose the Contras' widespread atrocities.

I made many trips to war-torn Nicaragua, and occasionally I found myself in dangerous situations. One morning in early 1984, I awoke in a hotel room in Managua and headed to the Nicaraguan Ministry of Foreign Affairs—a simple single-story building located in what then was considered the downtown area. The 1972 earthquake had left very little of the capital city standing.

I arrived before 7 a.m. My closest friend at the ministry was Martin Vega, a very bright young Nicaraguan revolutionary who had lived in the United States and spoke perfect English. At the meeting, we decided to interview survivors of a recent Contra attack in which six Nicaraguans, four of them children, had been killed. Civilian U.S. pilots had flown the helicopter used in the attack. It subsequently crashed, killing all aboard. A group called Civilian Military Assistance, which the CIA supported, was behind the attack. Because U.S. citizens had died, the incident received widespread press coverage—one of the few Contra attacks in which U.S. involvement was publicly exposed.

I suggested that CCR might be able to bring a lawsuit against those responsible for the killings—the pilots, Civilian Military Assistance, and even the U.S. government itself. I thought a lawsuit might help slow the U.S. government's secret training and support of the *contras* and discourage actions by mercenaries and private counter-revolutionary groups.

To make a case, we needed to interview the witnesses and the parents of the children who had been killed. Getting to them would not be easy. The attack had taken place in the far north of Nicaragua in a perilous area within the battle zone. To assure my safe passage, I would ride in a Jeep in between two other cars carrying armed Sandinista soldiers.

But no one warned me that the soldiers would hand me an AK-47. The only gun I had ever handled before was a light .22 caliber rifle for target practice at summer camp when I was a kid. The semi-automatic weapon the Sandinista soldiers shoved into my hands was big, heavy, and powerful. I felt totally unprepared.

I got into the back seat of the Jeep. Not knowing where else to put the AK-47, I stood it up at the side of my seat. Frankly, I was terrified. In retrospect, I don't understand why I ever took such a risk, but back then I never questioned it.

As we drove along the bumpy dirt roads, Martin spoke to me in English (my Spanish was terrible). He told me not to look directly in front, but rather to look out further to a middle distance where we might spot the *contras*.

The drive was harrowing. Eventually we made it to a tiny village where a seven-year-old girl had been killed. We were overcome with sadness when we met her parents. They told us their daughter had been playing outdoors when a helicopter swooped down on the village and fired indiscriminately. The parents showed us photos of their precious child, dressed in her best, lying on a stone. Flowers surrounded her lifeless body, not only for decoration, but because the odor of death would soon become unbearable in the humid Nicaraguan heat.

I wept for her young life and her parents' loss. It was not the only time I couldn't hold back tears during my work in Nicaragua. The young were very often the victims. They also suffered when their parents were wounded or killed. To this day, the haunting images of these children occasionally come back to me, and I weep yet again.

CCR did not end up filing this case, mainly because at the time we were already deeply involved in appealing a similar major case, *Sanchez-Espinoza v. Reagan.* We had filed it in late 1982 on behalf of three sets of plaintiffs: Nicaraguan civilians murdered or attacked by the *contras*; Congress members denied their right to vote on whether to go to war; and Florida citizens seeking to close secret *contra* training camps in the Everglades. The 64-page complaint included affidavits from the injured and raped and relatives of the Nicaraguans who'd been murdered. It contained a list of attacks on civilian facilities and medical personnel.

Other human rights groups had discouraged us from filing the case. They thought we would lose and create bad precedents for the future. But CCR and I believed that even if we lost, lawsuits like this were an important way of focusing attention on U.S. involvement in the U.S.-backed *contra* war. The killing was going on right now. Our clients were suffering right now.

A key paragraph of the lawsuit said that it was brought "on behalf of Nicaraguan citizens who have been murdered, tortured, mutilated, wounded, kidnapped and/or raped as a result of U.S.-sponsored paramilitary activities designed to ravage the civilian population of Nicaragua, destroy its economy, and overthrow its government."

The stories of the Nicaraguan plaintiffs, cited in our brief, are blood-curdling. For example:

"... plaintiff Maria Bustillo de Blandon, a resident of Nicaragua, saw her husband and five sons murdered and tortured by members of the Nicaraguan Democratic Front (FDN)—the main counterrevolutionary group funded by the federal defendants. On October 28, 1982, the *contras* entered her home, seized her husband, a lay pastor, and removed their five children from their beds. In front of the parents, the children were tied together, castrated, their ears cut off and their throats slit. The father was then killed.

"In July 1982, 130 *contras*, members of the FDN, attacked San Francisco de Guajinaqulapa, with rifles, mortars and machine guns, ransacking houses and over-running the town. After the attackers left, plaintiff Elia Maria Espinoza found her husband, his head smashed, and brains falling out. Seven other members of her family were previously found dead. Plaintiff Jose Santos-Barrera found his son lying face up, his chest bullet-ridden and his legs destroyed. Plaintiff Maria Espinal Mondragon found the body of her husband, with holes in his neck, stomach and right leg. His throat, as well as the throats of other victims lying near him, had been slit [...].

"Plaintiff Myrna Cunningham, a Nicaraguan doctor working in a hospital, was captured by *contras* who ransacked the hospital. She was threatened with death and raped 17 times. Thirteen other women from the town were also raped."[5]

In addition to the Nicaraguan plaintiffs' testimony, our legal filing contained precise details about the U.S. funding of the *contras*, the locations of their training camps in Honduras and Florida, as well as the source of the expended mortar shells we found, which were stamped "USA."

Among the defendants named in our lawsuit were President Reagan, John Negroponte, ambassador to Honduras and point person during the war, and Alpha 66, a Florida-based Cuban-American group that had been involved in the 1961 Bay of Pigs invasion of Cuba and was now running the *contra* training camps.

A unique aspect of *Sanchez-Espinoza v. Reagan* was that it relied partly on CCR's success in the 1980 case *Filártiga v. Peña-Irala*—perhaps the most important human rights case in U.S. history. In that earlier case, the family of Joelito Filártiga, a 17-year-old Paraguayan citizen who had been kidnapped and tortured to death by Paraguayan police, sued Américo Peña-Irala, the inspector general of police in Asunción at the time. In 1980 both parties were living in the United States, and CCR's Peter Weiss and Rhonda Copelon brought the case to a U.S. district court. They lost, but on appeal, the circuit court reversed the decision, awarding Filártiga $10 million in damages. More importantly, the ruling established that torturers and other foreign human rights violators who come to the United States can be sued in U.S. courts under the Alien Tort Statute, even if their criminal acts took place abroad. The opinion contained these ringing words: "The torturer is like a pirate of old, *hostis humani generis*, an enemy of all human kind."

---

5   A Miskito Indian from the English-speaking Atlantic coast of Nicaragua, Myrna was a courageous and eloquent voice in the fight against the *contras*—especially when they tried to claim the Miskitos should not be governed by the Spanish-speaking FSLN. She became a lifelong dear friend.

I was not directly involved in *Filártiga*, but I soon realized that it created an important precedent and opened the door for a ground-breaking period of litigation by CCR, including *Sanchez-Espinoza*.

The question of U.S. responsibility for violations of internationally recognized human rights lay at the heart of *Sanchez-Espinoza*. CCR argued that U.S. officials who directed and assisted the *contras* in injuring and killing Nicaraguans were as responsible as those who inflicted the injuries.

We launched a major campaign to publicize the case and highlight the ongoing atrocities of the war. We brought Nicaraguan plaintiffs to the United States to meet with journalists and members of Congress. Myrna Cunningham was an especially effective speaker in both English and Spanish. And my friend Sara Miles wrote a play based on our legal papers, *Talking Nicaragua*, which was performed in New York.

Ultimately we lost the litigation—on procedural issues, not on merit. Judge (later Supreme Court Justice) Antonin Scalia wrote the circuit court's precedent-defying opinion. The precedent set by *Filártiga* allowed a Paraguayan citizen to file a suit in a U.S. court that charged a Paraguayan police officer with human rights violations committed in Paraguay. By contrast, in *Sanchez-Espinoza* the circuit court barred a suit brought in a U.S. court by citizens of Nicaragua for harm caused by officials of the United States government itself. The inconsistency was obvious, but the court avoided ruling on U.S. foreign policy, even if that policy violated important norms of international human rights. As a result, non-citizens were denied the right to sue high U.S. government officials for damages under the Alien Tort Statute.

Sanchez-Espinoza was one of many cases the Center brought in the '80s knowing that we probably would not win. Though we lost almost all, we considered these cases to be an important part of a bigger movement to stop war and torture. Jules Lobel articulates our philosophy in his book *Success Without Victory*. He cites three historic examples of using the courts this way: 1. Elizabeth Cady Stanton brought hundreds of cases trying to establish women's right to vote; 2. New Orleans activists brought hundreds of cases challenging the legality of slavery before it was abolished; 3. The Center's 1980s cases attempted to stop intervention and torture in Central America. All three of these legal campaigns lost many times in court, yet ultimately prevailed in the court of public opinion—success without victory.

CCR, along with many other activists, continued to work hard to end the wars in Central America. I accompanied congressional delegations to Nicaragua and El Salvador so members could witness first-hand the effects of their votes, and we had some positive responses.

Greg Craig, Senator Ted Kennedy's national security adviser, asked me to work on the senator's planned hearing on *contra* atrocities against the Miskito Indians. When Greg traveled to Nicaragua, I helped him set up interviews with Myrna Cunningham and other witnesses. We brought several Miskito civilians who had been wounded by *contras* to testify in Washington, and the hearing got major coverage.

Later, the *New Republic* magazine published an article about my role in finding the witnesses. Called "Manipulating the Miskitos," it caused a flap. Greg Craig said he did not know I was president of the National Lawyers Guild, or that the NLG had been designated as a Communist front. He explained that he had turned to me because he did not want the Sandinistas to provide the witnesses. In the end, the facts won out—no matter that a Sandinista sympathizer had helped obtain them.

I also became an adviser to a number of groups focused on ending the wars. Activist friends Dale Wiehoff and Annie Hess had decided to organize international work brigades to help labor-depleted Nicaragua with its harvest. I arranged a meeting with Tomás Borge, one of the Sandinista commanders, and he approved the project. Over the next few years, hundreds of activists traveled to Nicaragua to pick coffee and cotton in support of the Sandinistas.

Another activist friend, Kathy Engel, started an organization called MADRE aimed at helping Nicaraguan women affected by the war. Originally MADRE was an acronym standing for "mothers against death and repression everywhere." We joked that next we'd set up PADRE (papas) and CADRE (children) against death and repression everywhere.

Another friend, Reed Brody, went to Nicaragua to investigate Contra atrocities. Fluent in Spanish, Reed was a lawyer about ten years younger than me. He had quit his job as a New York state assistant attorney general to go to Nicaragua, where he spent six months traveling from village to village, compiling first-hand accounts of atrocities. When his report, "*Contra* Terror in Nicaragua," made page one of *The New York Times*, President Reagan denounced it and labeled Reed as "one of the dictator Ortega's supporters, a sympathizer who has openly embraced Sandinismo."

Sara Miles and I prepped Reed for his media appearances, warning him that he would be attacked by contra supporters. But Reed's thorough research withstood scrutiny. The report devastated the *contras* and helped turn public opinion against Reagan's war.

In 1984, Nicaragua was scheduled to hold elections for its president and a new national assembly. I did not agree with this strategy. Few revolutionary governments hold elections before they are able to carry out their programs for reform. I also thought elections could split the Sandinistas. There were nine leaders of the Junta of National Reconstruction, representing various revolutionary political factions, yet only one president could be elected. In addition, the *contras* were still waging a war against the government. If Nicaraguans really wanted peace, they might well elect a government more friendly to the United States—and the Sandinista revolution would be over.

Nonetheless, Nicaragua held its election on a beautiful sunny day in November. I traveled there with a delegation of observers from the United States and Europe. At a number of polling places I saw long lines but nothing I would call fraudulent. The Sandinista candidate, Daniel Ortega, won the presidency with almost 67 percent of the vote.

Despite this electoral victory, the Reagan administration escalated its war and placed a commercial embargo on Nicaragua the next year. To its credit, Congress tried to stop aid to the *contras*. While President Reagan signed the legislation, he secretly proceeded to violate the ban in what became known as the Iran-Contra affair. The U.S. government began selling arms illegally to Iran and using the proceeds to fund the *contras*.

In Nicaragua, inflation skyrocketed, people got poorer and poorer, and the *contras* continued to terrorize the countryside. It was in this context that one morning in 1987 my legal assistant buzzed: "Someone named Ben Linder on the phone."

I picked up and heard a quiet, nervous voice. "Michael, this is Ben," he said. "Friends in Nicaragua told me to call. I just got back to Portland from Nicaragua, and I plan to go back. But I'm worried that my passport could be canceled."

A recent college graduate and an engineer, Ben explained that he had been working in northern Nicaragua on a small hydroelectric project to bring electricity to the village of El Cuá. I knew that, to date, no U.S. citizen's passport had been revoked for working in Nicaragua, and I assured him that cancellation was not likely.

"My father doesn't want me to go back," he said. "He's worried about me working in a war zone."

I thought, "Here's this young man worried about his passport, not about getting killed in a very dangerous area." Although he was not a soldier, I was well aware that the *contras* often directed their attacks at international aid workers.

I never forgot that conversation with Ben. The question for me remains, "Did I do anything to discourage him from returning?" Sadly, I think not.

A few days after we talked, Ben ignored his father's wishes and returned to El Cuá. On April 28, 1987, he and several Nicaraguan workers were building a small dam for the electric project when the *contras* attacked. Ben and two Nicaraguans were killed.

The attack made front-page news around the world, especially in the United States where it further inflamed sentiment against the war. We at CCR knew few facts about the attack, but we knew a bit about Ben's life in Nicaragua, his work, and the love people had for him. He was a slim, good-looking, lightly bearded young man with glasses. Trained as a clown, Ben would unicycle around the village juggling and encouraging kids to go for vaccinations.

The murder of civilian aid workers was a war crime, and I wanted CCR to sue the killers of this wonderful young man. The Linder family had consulted other lawyers, but no one had the stomach for such a challenging case—a killing in a foreign country, by foreigners, where witnesses lived in dangerous areas, the facts would be difficult to verify, and establishing jurisdiction in a U.S. court would be complicated.

Once the Linder family decided on CCR to represent them, Jules Lobel, a brilliant professor at the University of Pittsburgh, and I began the work on a civil suit. Later Beth Stephens, an excellent lawyer who had lived in Nicaragua, joined us.

Ben's entire family was anti-war. His father David was a doctor in his 60s, with a shock of gray hair. He, his wife Elisabeth, and Ben's brother and sister were utterly devastated, as was the extended family. They urgently wanted justice.

I have rarely seen someone whose face showed such intense pain as Ben's dad's. A photo of David at Ben's funeral in northern Nicaragua reveals his agony. In a tie and jacket, literally being held up by Elisabeth, he is walking behind Daniel Ortega. On Ben's gravestone there is an engraving of a unicycle. The inscription reads: "Benjamin Ernest Linder, Internationalista: the light he sparked will shine forever."

Within a few weeks of Ben's death, Congress member George Crockett held a hearing on the U.S. government's failure to protect Americans volunteering in Nicaragua. I heard both of Ben's parents testify.

Elisabeth Linder told the subcommittee: "My son was brutally murdered for bringing electricity to a few poor people in northern Nicaragua. He was murdered because he had a dream and because he had the courage to make that dream come true... Ben told me the first year that he was here, and this is a quote, 'It's a wonderful feeling to work in a country where the government's first concern is for its people, for all of its people.'"

I was stunned when a Republican representative on the subcommittee, Connie Mack from Florida, interrupted Elisabeth. "I just don't understand how you can use your grief to politicize this situation," he said. "I don't mean to be cruel, but I think by coming here today, you asked for it."

"Asked for it?" Elisabeth responded. "That is about the cruelest thing you could have said."

"You came here to blame this government," Mack charged.

"Yes," she replied.

"... to blame the president," Mack added.

"Yes," Ben Linder's mother said.

From the beginning, I had to warn the Linders that our chances of winning the lawsuit were slim. Unless we could show that some of the conduct—the decision to kill Ben or the formulation of a policy to execute volunteers—had occurred in the United States, no American court would hear the case.

I guessed that Ben's killing was pre-planned, and that the planning probably took place in Miami where the *contra* leadership was concentrated. Even if this particular attack had not been planned, I thought that the *contras'* ongoing policy of attacking and murdering aid workers had probably been formulated in Miami.

My guess proved correct. For the lawsuit, I interviewed a former *contra* leader who had no specific knowledge of this attack, but told me, "Ben would not have been randomly killed. It was our practice to frighten away supporters through such acts. That planning would have occurred in Miami. The *contras* would not kill an American citizen without high-level approval."

Now a reliable source had confirmed that planning of the murders of aid workers took place in the United States. That meant a U.S. court had jurisdiction and might hear such a case.

The next question I needed to answer was how Ben was killed. Was it in a firefight permitted by the laws of war? Was he carrying a gun, possibly making him a legitimate target? Even if he was not, Sandinistas with guns may have been guarding the project he was working on. If so, an attack might be considered legal. Beth Stephens and Jules Lobel spent a lot of time in Nicaragua interviewing witnesses. We could not say with certainty that no one had guns.

But we had more—photos of a deceased Ben and an autopsy report from Nicaragua. I took them to the respected New York City coroner, Dr. Michael Baden. At his small red-brick house on the Upper East Side, I explained the circumstances of Ben's death.

Dr. Baden looked at the photos. One showed a bullet hole in the skull surrounded by powder burns that create powder tattooing. As he explained, "The tattooing or powder burn will be smaller and denser, the closer the gun is to the wound. In this case the burn indicates that the gun was quite close to Ben's head, less than a foot away, and it appears that Ben was executed."

If Dr. Baden was right, our lawsuit had a chance. While a killing in a firefight might not violate the laws of war, an execution clearly did.

Dr. Baden also noticed a number of pin-prick injuries on Ben's forehead. The Nicaraguan autopsy said that Ben had been poked with a sharp instrument, likely while he was still alive. According to Dr. Baden, it appeared Ben was tortured before he was murdered.

I found this story unbearable and dreaded telling Ben's parents. But I had to, and I did. David refused to believe the torture story and did not want to talk about it. It was just too painful.

We brought the case in Miami, since that was where the key *contra* defendants lived. The night before I was to argue it in court, the Linder family arrived to witness the proceedings. I was always a bit nervous before arguments, but having Ben's family there made me all the more so. The opposing attorney was John Kirkpatrick, the son of Jeane Kirkpatrick, Reagan's ambassador to the United Nations. While Kirkpatrick didn't make a strong argument, his presence sent a clear message that President Reagan, or at least John's mother, was watching.

The district court dismissed the case before we got to trial. We appealed. I argued in a large, almost empty appeals courtroom in Miami. The court challenged our facts, but eventually had to agree that our allegation that the murder had been planned in the U.S. was sufficient to allow the case to go forward.

We now had the right to question the defendants before trial. Beth and Jules traveled to Nicaragua and looked for eyewitnesses but found none. We also requested documents from the *contra* leadership. They claimed they had none and knew nothing. I still believe that documents existed both before and after the killing. Even assuming the *contras* had nothing, the CIA, which was deeply involved in running the war, must have had some documentation of its efforts. But we never got it.

Ultimately, we had to tell the Linders we had not uncovered enough proof to be able to go to trial. David expressed dismay, and I felt awful—a very sad ending.

However, about seven years after Ben's death, his family raised money for his friends and other volunteers to complete the project Ben had been working on. In May 1994, in front of hundreds of people, the Benjamin Linder Hydroelectric Power Plant was inaugurated. It now serves all of the people in the Bocay area of northern Nicaragua.

As I did this solidarity work throughout the '80s, I often made mistakes that I now regret. My enthusiasm for revolutionary movements sometimes blinded me to policies that were simply wrong, and made me intolerant of dissenters within those movements.

One of my most glaring mistakes involved the indigenous people of Nicaragua. The U.S. government and the *contras* were arming the indigenous and Black, English-speaking population of the Atlantic Coast to encourage revolt against the revolutionary Sandinista government. Many Miskito and other indigenous tribes wanted to break away from the dominant central Spanish-speaking government and set up their own autonomous zones, if not a sovereign nation.

Some members of the American Indian Movement (AIM) in the U.S. were supporting the indigenous struggle in Nicaragua. I could not accept this. As president of the National Lawyers Guild, I issued a statement: the *contras* were using Nicaraguan indigenous groups and their U.S. lawyers to undermine the Sandinista revolution, and this was not the time to fight for indigenous autonomy.

An AIM lawyer, a former classmate of mine, called me. "Michael, you had no right to condemn the Indian struggle in the name of the Guild without any discussion," he said. "I want you to reopen the question."

But I didn't budge. "The actions of some people in AIM and on the Atlantic Coast are harming the revolution during a war," I said. Then I added, "You are an enemy of all humankind."

Intemperate and dogmatic, to say the least, perhaps even dead wrong, but that was how fervently I was wedded to my views back then.

Another difficult lesson I had to learn was that revolutionary movements can be full of intrigue and corruption. In 1983, the second in command of one of the Salvadoran FMLN's five factions, Mélida Anaya Montes, nom de guerre "Ana María," was killed with an ice pick in the house where she had been living in exile in Managua.

I happened to be at the U.S. embassy in Honduras with about 20 other activists when the murder occurred. "The United States is not responsible for the death of Ana María," a U.S. diplomat told us. "Her own fellow revolutionaries killed her."

I was enraged. Right-wing death squads backed by the U.S. government had murdered thousands of Salvadorans. The CIA was distributing a "how to" torture pamphlet and directing the Salvadoran army's murder and torture as well.

"I don't believe it," I told the diplomat. "The CIA killed her."

He shook his head. "We have confidential evidence. It was not us."

The diplomat was right. Eventually it was verified that FMLN hard-liners seeking to continue armed struggle against the military dictatorship had killed Ana María in a power struggle against moderates like her who favored peace negotiations. Cayetano Carpio, the head of the FMLN, was accused of organizing the murder. Soon after, he committed suicide.

The murders of Ana María and others, as well as the self-aggrandizement and opportunism of some leaders such as Nicaragua's President Daniel Ortega, made me realize that revolutionary leaders, too, could be corrupt and ruthless. The truth I finally understood was that broad social movements and grassroots groups make change, not charismatic heroes. It is a mistake to encourage cults of personality or to place too much power in the hands of any individual.

By 1990, as a presidential election loomed, most Nicaraguans were tired. They wanted the war to end and the economy to improve. President Daniel Ortega and his wife Rosario Murillo's personal extravagances hadn't helped the Sandinistas' cause. The opposition found the perfect candidate to run against Ortega. Violetta Chamorro was the widow of the courageous newspaper publisher Pedro Chamorro, who had been murdered by Somoza's thugs before the revolution. Viewed as both anti-Somoza and anti-Sandinista, Violetta Chamorro won the election and took office as the new president. The Sandinista revolution, barely a decade old, had lost power.

While depression would be too strong a word for what I was feeling, I did think that the work I had done in Central America and the Caribbean over the course of the previous decade had come to an end. The revolution in Grenada had been crushed, the FMLN was unlikely to overthrow the right-wing government in El Salvador, the Guatemalan military had killed hundreds of thousands, and the Sandinista revolution in Nicaragua had failed.

In the early '80s, my friend Dale Wiehoff used to say that the Central American revolutions presented a serious threat to the U.S.'s hold on the region. I agreed with him. But now, at the end of the decade, the power of the United States seemed more overwhelming than ever. "These revolutions may not have really dented U.S. hegemony," Dale told me. "Maybe they were just a blip on the screen."

Nearing the end of the '80s, like the Nicaraguans, I wanted to make major changes in my life. At the age of 44, I joined a therapy group.

"How do you see your life in ten years?" the therapist asked. "Are you still going to be serially dating, traveling abroad all the time, and living the way you are now?"

"No, I want to find a life partner and have children," I told her. I wasn't getting any younger, and didn't want my kids to go through the early loss of their father as I had.

MOVING THE BAR

"Michael, I want you to go out with at least six different people once or twice, and bring your experiences back to the group," she said. "You can hear their reaction and decide whether you're on the road to finding a suitable partner."

The first woman I described to the group was a Salvadoran guerrilla who belonged to the ERP (People's Revolutionary Army). Fifteen years my junior, she had lived in my house with a couple of other Salvadoran revolutionaries. The therapy group was not enthused. "Michael, she will not be a serious life partner," one person said. "Just move on." As it happened, the young revolutionary wasn't ready for the permanence I wanted, and her guerrilla group didn't approve of the relationship either.

After following the therapist's suggestions for a few months, I went out with a 32-year-old video journalist, Karen Ranucci. A mutual friend, Monica Melamid, had introduced us and warned Karen, "Michael will be a good date, but he won't get serious."

On our first date we went jogging. Karen was very pretty, small and thin, with olive skin and dark, curly hair. She worked at Downtown Community Television, a progressive independent outfit housed in an old firehouse below Canal Street. In the late '70s, when she was only 27, she had won an Emmy for reporting on a factory that was poisoning its workers.

We had a second date on a warm May evening, jogging at sunset, this time across the Brooklyn Bridge. Sharing a romantic drink under the bridge, Karen told me a bit about her background. "Both sides of my family were southern Italian," she said. "We lived in a middle-class section of Long Island, and I hung out with other Italians. A lot of them were into drugs. When my boyfriend died of an overdose, I went to the church service, and they gave me a little card with prayers to recite. Afterward, I spoke to the priest because I didn't understand what daily prayers I'd have to say to save him from purgatory or hell. The priest asked me: 'What were your boyfriend's sins?' I replied, 'Drugs and robbery.' The priest said, 'With those sins your friend can't get out of purgatory no matter how much you pray.' I was sixteen, and that was the last day of my being a Catholic."

Karen was the only one of five siblings to go to college. "My father discouraged me," she said, "but I told him I was going and would meet a nice Jewish boy."

That made me laugh. So did her story about taking the college boards. "I went into the testing room, never read the questions, and arbitrarily filled in the answers," she said. She ended up going to Old Westbury State College on Long Island. To pay for her education, she worked as a waitress and took out loans. Karen told me that college had changed her life and her politics.

My therapy group encouraged me to see her again, which I wanted to do in any case. On our next date we spent the night together in DCTV's firehouse, a Stanford White-designed landmark where Karen was living.

Karen had traveled all over the world. Along with DCTV's director Jon Alpert and his wife Keiko, she'd been to Salvadoran guerrilla camps and was one of the first American journalists in North Vietnam after the end of the war. She had covered Fidel Castro's visit to New York in 1979 and flown with him back to Cuba. On the plane she snapped a photo of Fidel holding up an "I Love NY" t-shirt—an image that was later made into a popular postcard. When we met, she was hawking the postcards to local tourist shops for five cents each.

But now she was ready to settle down.

After we'd been going out for about six months, we took a Christmas vacation to the idyllic Caribbean island of St. Martin with my brother Bruce and sister Ellen. On New Year's Eve, Karen said to me, "I need you to make a commitment. I'm getting older and I want to have kids. So if you aren't serious about me, I want to move on."

That kind of statement was typical of Karen. She could give an ultimatum fearlessly. Unlike me, she was not neurotic and had never been to a psychiatrist. I answered her then and there, and soon afterward, Karen moved into my apartment.

By the summer of 1987, Karen got pregnant. We were not then married, and this drove my sister Ellen crazy. A lesbian and an iconoclast in her own romantic life, Ellen was traditional in other respects.

I proposed, but Karen said, "I won't marry you unless you ask me in a romantic way."

I thought that was a bit silly, but the challenge sparked my imagination. I went to a Times Square tourist store and ordered this headline to be printed on a newspaper-size page: "Michael Asks Karen to Wed: Response Awaited." One morning I slipped the custom-printed page into the *New York Times*. We were upstate in my cozy cabin, sitting on the couch, drinking our coffee. It was fall, and Karen was getting bigger and bigger. Reading the *Times*, Karen turned a page and discovered my insert. Suddenly, she jumped up and hugged me, totally excited, and I knew her answer was yes.

Karen designed the wedding invitation—a photo of a very pregnant Karen pointing a wooden AK-47 at me with my hands held up. The caption, spelled out in individual block letters, read "Shotgun Wedding."

On January 31, 1988, 50 of our friends and immediate family attended our wedding. (We didn't invite the huge extended Ratner family—a decision I now regret.) Bruce performed the ceremony in the living room of his brownstone. A very big Karen looked stunning in a pink chiffon maternity dress, and I wore a tan suit and tie.

Considering our circumstances, Bruce did a remarkable job. He told a story written by the beloved Yiddish author Sholom Aleichem.

A man goes to the rabbi for advice.

Man: "Rabbi, I've been married for only three months, but my wife has just given birth. How can this be?"

Rabbi: "How long has she been married to you?"

Man: "Three months."

Rabbi: "How long have you been married to her?"

Man: "Three months."

Rabbi: "And how long have you been married to each other?"

Man: "Three months."

Rabbi: "Three plus three plus three—nine months. Everything is fine."

A little more than two months later, on April 5, 1988, our son Jake was born. We gave him the middle name Harry, in honor of my father.

I was a happy man.

7
THE END OF THE TWENTIETH CENTURY

Shortly after Jake's birth we took advantage of CCR's generous six-month paid parental leave policy. Karen, Jake, and I moved upstate to our small cabin. I went on long walks in the woods with Jake in a Snugli, while Karen rested after a wakeful night feeding him. To get the baby to fall asleep, we took long drives through the Catskills.

In early 1989, Karen received a grant to make a film about how Bolivians used popular video to further their work. Karen and I were excited, but nervous. It meant taking an eleven-month-old to a very poor country, where we'd live in La Paz, a city at an altitude of more than 12,000 feet, with almost no paved roads. What would we do if Jake became ill? There was no internet, no easy way to make phone calls, and we would be quite isolated. Bruce, Ellen, and Karen's parents all said we were crazy to go. We went anyway.

We arrived in Miami to discover that our flight to La Paz was cancelled because of a strike. We slept on the carpet near the gate until midnight, then took a ten-hour night flight on Lloyd Air Bolivia, an old colonial airline. We stopped in Caracas, Venezuela, then in Manaus, Brazil, a mining and timber town on the Amazon. With lightning flashing all around us, we waited on the ground for an hour and then took off into the worst storm I'd ever experienced, bouncing up and down like a ball in waves. We strapped Jake into two empty seats, and luckily he slept the entire flight.

MOVING THE BAR

We landed in El Alto, Bolivia, then the highest commercial airport in the world at 13,615 feet. Leaving the plane, I felt the ground shaking. "We're in an earthquake!" I said to Karen. It wasn't an earthquake, but the effect on our bodies of suddenly being thrust into extremely high altitude. Doctors in white coats stood at the gate, with oxygen masks for those who fainted or needed help.

While we waited for our taxi, we drank tea made from coca leaves. Popular (and legal) in Bolivia, the tea was supposed to help with altitude sickness. The taxi drove us through El Alto, the second largest city in Bolivia, where we saw small adobe houses clinging to the sides of the mountain, accessible only by very steep footpaths. We took the only road connecting the airport to La Paz. Block that road, and the capital is cut off from the rest of the country. In 1781, Túpac Katari led an indigenous uprising against Spanish rule and blocked this same road. In 2003, peasants and workers again blocked the road to La Paz, cutting off supplies of fuel and food. Their uprising led to the ouster of then-President Gonzalo Sánchez de Lozada and to the election of the nation's first indigenous president, Evo Morales.

When we reached La Paz, we saw many women dressed in traditional clothing: bowler hats, red- and orange-striped layers of skirts, and a baby in a carrying cloth. But other women were wearing shabby brown rags, begging on the streets, or selling the most meager fruit. Most were Aymara or Quechua Indians, many of whom spoke indigenous languages, not Spanish.

Our apartment, located in an upper-middle-class neighborhood, was on a high floor with views of the majestic snowcapped mountains that surround La Paz. The first week I suffered from *saroche*, altitude sickness. I drank coca tea and hardly got out of bed. Karen wasn't affected by the altitude and was able to work. Soon I felt better and began taking Spanish lessons. Jake, who learned his first words at ten months, already understood a lot of Spanish—the only language his babysitter in New York spoke.

Karen and I took wonderful walks in the neighborhood, often stopping for *saltenas*, a sweet spicy pastry filled with meat or seafood, peas, raisins, and olives. In the first week we came across a parade with many marching bands and thousands of soldiers dressed in uniforms from the late 1800s, each with a large pompom on his head. The president of Bolivia, wearing a pink sash and a uniform covered with medals, waved to schoolchildren lining the street. Four horses pulled a caisson with a small box on top. Behind the caisson a soldier was carrying a glass box. Karen asked a child what was going on.

"*Los restos de Abaroa,*" she replied—the mortal remains of Avaroa, a hero, posthumously recognized as a colonel, who had had been killed by Chilean soldiers in 1879 while defending Bolivia's only outlet to the sea.[6]

This annual parade celebrated him.

That same week we walked to the main street, La Prado. Normally traffic was bumper to bumper, but this day it was empty. Miners had come to town and were blocking the streets to protest against thousands of layoffs, severe cuts in pensions, and the recent privatization of the tin mines, which had been nationalized since the 1950s.

The most dramatic protest took place at the university, not far from our apartment. Twenty-five miners tied their hands and feet to poles and fences at the university entrance and on flagpoles atop the buildings, as if they were crucified. Despite freezing nights in March and April, the miners remained tied in their positions, wrapped up in blankets. A large group of miners and families protected them and brought them food. The papers featured bold front-page photos with headlines in capital letters: "¡CRUCIFICADOS!"

One night in late April, we were on the campus when government forces stormed in and cut the miners down before they died of exposure. We wept as Karen filmed it all. She later took the videos to

---

6 Bolivia is landlocked. Support for regaining a seaport was strong. On the back of every phone were the words, "Bolivia demands its right to access to the sea."

the Siglo XX tin mines and showed them to the families of the miners living there.

In the course of her work, Karen brought home many local videos, including *Camino de Las Almas* ("Path of Souls"), a documentary I found particularly intriguing. It had been produced to help the effort to recover textiles stolen from the village of Coroma. Hundreds of years old (some may have been pre-Colombian), the textiles were sacred to the people of Coroma, a remote Aymara village with no electricity or public transportation. It took a bus ride and then a two-hour walk with burros to get there. To the people of Coroma, the textiles, originally worn as clothing, embodied the souls of their ancestors. A living, breathing part of village life, the fabrics were kept in bundles, called *q'ipis*, that marked the geographical boundaries of the village. The Coromans consulted them on important issues such as marriage and planting times.

Once a year, the villagers removed the textiles from their bundles and wore them in a ceremony for All Saints' Day. A few tourists were permitted to witness the traditional ceremony. Unfortunately, in the 1970s, unscrupulous foreign dealers had hired Bolivian middlemen to bribe the keeper of the textiles, and 400 pieces had been stolen. According to the video, the villagers noticed that crop plantings soon started to fail. During a consultation with the *q'ipis*, villagers got a message that the textiles had been taken from Coroma and were lonely. The video ended with a villager riding his bike on the dirt path out of town, seeking help to recover the textiles.

The villager contacted a Bolivian sociologist, Cristina Bubba Zamora. She appealed to the United Nations, which passed a resolution prohibiting the textiles from being exported from Bolivia, traded, or sold. Not long afterward, the U.S. government imposed restrictions on the import of cultural artifacts from Bolivia. However, the new rules could not be applied retroactively to textiles already in the U.S.

THE END OF THE TWENTIETH CENTURY

Karen invited Cristina Zamora to our apartment in La Paz. Cristina explained that she and the Coromans had been creating an inventory of the remaining textiles and trying to publicize the losses. They had received a tip that a Coroman weaving was in an exhibition of Andean art in San Francisco. The Bolivian government informed U.S. Customs, which then seized 1,000 objects, including many Coroma textiles, from a San Francisco antiquities dealer named Steven Berger.

Cristina asked if CCR could help retrieve the weavings. I told her that recovering cultural patrimony was not my specialty of law, but I'd do what I could. Since this case didn't involve taking on the U.S. war machine, I knew a major law firm might work pro bono with CCR. I was able to recruit Bill Verick, a young lawyer from the respected San Francisco firm of Morrison and Foerster, and U.S. Customs provided us with a list of collectors who had bought the textiles from Berger—for as much as $25,000 each.

After threatening a lawsuit, we recovered some of the textiles from Berger. To track down others selling Bolivian textiles, I regularly checked "art for sale" ads. Responding to one ad, I called a wealthy man offering textiles. After he confirmed they were from Coroma, I told him about the U.N. ban and explained that they had likely been stolen. He asked if he could get a tax deduction by donating the textiles to a foundation that could then return them to Coroma. I gave him information on how to do it, but did not hear back. A few weeks later, a museum curator called me and said, "Someone came into the museum offering to donate textiles from Bolivia." It was the same collector. The museum refused the gift. The collector had to surrender them to me, and they were returned to Coroma.

U.S. Customs records also pointed us to an Episcopal priest in downtown New York who owned seven of the sacred Coroma textiles. I kept calling and writing him, but got no response. I appealed to the head of the Episcopal Church who just said the priest could be trusted. After a couple of months, I approached the director of the American Indian Community House, a non-profit organization serving the needs of Native Americans living in New York.

"What can we do about this Episcopal priest?" I asked. "For the Aymara people, the textiles are as sacred as pieces of the true cross would be to Christians."

"Why don't we organize a demonstration of indigenous people in front of the church and demand the textiles be returned?" she suggested.

I loved this idea. But before it ever happened, plans for the protest were leaked to the *Village Voice,* which printed an article about it. Within hours of publication, the priest called me and agreed to bring over the fabrics he had.

The textiles were strikingly beautiful, hand-woven with a few broad brown and reddish stripes, on naturally dyed fabrics. Considering their age, they were almost without a flaw.

"These aren't from Coroma," the priest said at first. "There are thousands of Bolivian textiles."

I showed him the bill of sale we'd obtained from Customs proving they were from Coroma.

The priest then argued, "The textiles would have been destroyed or damaged if left in Coroma." I call this the "Elgin Marbles defense," the excuse the British Museum uses to defend the friezes stolen from the Greek Parthenon.

"They were intact for hundreds of years when kept in Bolivia," I replied.

Finally the priest said, "I bought these, hoping they'd increase in value and help pay my children's college tuition."

That didn't merit a reply. "I'll keep them and send photos to the tribal elders and Cristina Bubba," I said. "They'll figure out what to do."

That night I stored the box under my bed. Even I, materialist that I am, felt there was something sacred about the textiles, that they were alive in a way.

The elders determined that the textiles did indeed come from Coroma. The case was important for Bolivia, for U.S. Customs, and for the Aymara people of Coroma. The Bolivian government planned a ceremony of return at their embassy in Washington. I took the train down, and the Bolivian ambassador and his wife met me. They were tall, thin, perfectly dressed, and of Spanish descent—not indigenous. Both had tiny gold coca leaves pinned to their lapels.

The embassy was spotless, painted white with intricate woodwork and 15-foot-high ceilings. The ambassador took me to a large closet and said, "Bolivia thanks you for this work. Forty of the textiles are in this closet, and I will have them brought out for you." Then an indigenous housekeeper came into the room, dressed in a black dress with a white apron. "I could not sleep last night," she told us. "The textiles were calling out to me that they wanted to be back with their ancestors."

The ceremony took place in a fancy ballroom with U.S. Customs officials, State Department representatives, Bolivian officials, our legal team, the press, and three Aymara villagers from Coroma dressed in colorful, woven ceremonial fabrics and headpieces. After the usual speeches, Customs returned the textiles and the Coromans played music on Andean panpipes. Bill Verick and I each received special thanks and a wooden scepter wrapped in tin and topped by a bird—an Aymara symbol of authority.

Then the ceremony was over, or so we thought. People left, but the Coroma villagers took Bill and me to a grassy courtyard behind the embassy. There, with a half a dozen of us watching, the Aymara began chanting. No one explained anything, but the Aymara dug a shallow hole in the lawn and brought out various powders, amulets, and talismans, including a llama fetus which they ritually burned. I stood next to the ambassador and his wife, who held a silver plate piled with coca leaves which she brought to each of us. In the middle of Washington, it all felt surreal.

I later learned that 30,000 Bolivians met the plane that finally returned the sacred textiles to their home.

After two months in Bolivia, we moved back to New York. I continued to work with CCR, but within a year, I stepped down from the job as legal director. On the evening of February 18, 1990, almost immediately after dinner at my brother's house, a very pregnant Karen went into labor. A few hours later, Jake's sister Ana, named for my mother and Karen's grandmother, was born. I witnessed the birth, and because it had gone so quickly I said, "That seemed easy." Karen looked ready to kill me.

Our daughter's birth gave me another six months' paid leave from CCR. We again took much of it upstate at our cabin in the Catskills, following the same baby routines with Ana that we'd enjoyed with Jake.

We wanted both kids to be bilingual, so we hired Yolanda Sanchez, who spoke only Spanish, to do childcare. Yolanda remained with us for the kids' early years. Today I am the only one of the four of us who is not fluent in Spanish.

Throughout the '90s, I taught human rights law at Yale and Columbia law schools. I often co-taught at Columbia with my friend Reed Brody, a Human Rights Watch lawyer I'd worked with in Nicaragua. Reed specialized in bringing human rights abusers to justice around the world—from Chile's former dictator Augusto Pinochet to the Chad dictator Hissène Habré.

My work at Yale began after a group of students asked if I'd co-teach a human rights litigation seminar one day a week with professor Harold Koh. The offer came at a perfect time. I wanted to step back a bit, not work abroad, and the idea of a brief commute to New Haven that allowed me to return home in time for dinner with my family appealed to me. I took the job, and for the next five years Harold and I jointly led a three-hour human rights clinic.

During this period, I also co-authored two books about international law, so other lawyers could draw on the work we'd done. The textbook I wrote with Beth Stephens was entitled *International Human Rights Litigation in U.S. Courts*. The other book, *The Pinochet Papers,* written with Reed Brody, compiled legal papers and precedent-setting decisions that led to the arrest in the United Kingdom of Augusto Pinochet.

While I concentrated on teaching and writing, I stayed involved in cases with CCR and the law school clinics. Most concerned international human rights issues, but I also took a few domestic cases. One day, the brilliant Native American activist Winona LaDuke called and asked for CCR's help to recover land stolen from her tribe—the White Earth Band of Chippewa (Ojibwe) Indians in Minnesota.

"Hundreds of Chippewas have filed claims," she explained. "But white landowners got a complex statute passed in Congress—the White Earth Reservation Land Settlement Act. It offers compensation to individuals who lost their land—if they drop their claim. But we don't want money. Native American culture depends on a land base. We want our land back."

Accompanied by one of CCR's law students, I hopped on a plane to White Earth Reservation, a few hours northwest of Minneapolis. Some members of the tribe picked us up at the airport in an old junker and drove us at 100 miles per hour on empty roads out to the reservation.

When originally created in 1867, the reservation spanned 830,000 acres. As a result of theft, it had shrunken to 100,000 acres, not all continuous. White-owned sportsmen's clubs, resorts, and businesses had been established on the stolen land. As we approached the reservation, the treeless landscape became bleaker and bleaker. We passed isolated trailers and run-down shacks with wrecked cars parked in front. Our driver explained that work on the reservation was hard to find and most people lived in utter poverty.

We met with some of the tribal leaders at a lodge. The men wore blue jeans and beads, with their hair pulled back in ponytails. It was a gray, gloomy day, and they invited us outdoors to smoke a peace pipe. We stood in a circle while the men chanted in Chippewa. That night we slept in a large tepee.

MOVING THE BAR

It took us a while to understand and challenge the White Earth Reservation Land Settlement Act of 1985. Each of the potential plaintiffs had land stolen in a different way in the early 20th century. As white settlers moved from the East, they wanted more land. They coveted the Native American reservations, which had been created by treaty with the U.S. government. Tribes owned the reservations communally, and it was impossible for anyone to acquire the land without the consent of both the tribes and the Bureau of Indian Affairs.

Beginning with the General Allotment Act of 1887, the Nelson Act of 1889 and subsequent legislation, white settlers convinced Congress to break the 1867 treaty the government had signed with the White Earth Band. The new laws divided the entire reservation into individual allotments of 80 to 160 acres for each member of the White Earth Band. The government insisted it was helping the Chippewa to "modernize" and learn to farm their own individual piece of land. But neither my clients nor I believed that for a second. After every Chippewa received an allotment, the communal reservation still occupied hundreds of thousands of acres. But the federal government gave or sold much of it to white settlers and held on to the remainder.

The allotment system destroyed the communal way of life. Now individuals, not the tribe, owned the land. Under the new laws, the Chippewas' individual allotments could not be sold for 25 years. The theory was that it would take that long for the "new owners" to learn farming and decide whether they wanted to stay on the land. After this 25-year period, the land could be sold, but not by full-blooded Chippewa. Only so-called "mixed bloods" could sell. I have no idea what the racist theory behind this rule might have been.

The whole system was absurd, but it got worse. Congress repealed a statute prohibiting taxation of Indian land. As a result, Indians lost more land for failure to pay taxes. After 25 years, unscrupulous white land traders swarmed the area. With outright lies, bribes, and liquor, they tricked the mixed-blood Chippewa landowners into signing over their deeds. Within a short while, that land, too, was lost.

But the land owned by full-blooded Indians could not be sold without the approval of the Bureau of Indian Affairs. With pseudo-scientific methods, speculators tried to prove that full-blooded Chippewa were actually mixed blood. We saw amazing pictures of white speculators taking head measurements with steel calipers to "prove" that Indians were "mixed blood" based on the shape of their heads. They also combed through a Chippewa's hair and mustache looking for "non-Indian hair." A single red hair in a mustache was enough for them to claim that a Chippewa had a non-Indian ancestor, was not full-blooded, and thus could legally sell his land.

CCR filed the White Earth Band's case against the federal government in Washington D.C. District Court. In *Littlewolf v. Lujan* (Manuel Lujan was Secretary of the Interior), we argued that the White Earth Reservation Land Act of 1985 failed to grant Chippewas a reasonable time to bring suits to recover their land and thus violated the Fifth Amendment's due process clause. Both the district and appeals courts ruled that the act's six-month statute of limitations was reasonable, and Congress had the right to appropriate Chippewa land under its power of eminent domain, as long as the Chippewas were paid for it. But the payment was a pittance—based on the land's value in the early 1900s, plus 5 percent interest, not compounded. The Indians were cheated again.

The loss set a bad precedent for other reservations where similar land grabs had occurred. "The federal court system basically slapped me and all the other Indian people in the face," said Winona LaDuke. "The court decision basically said your land was taken illegally, but the statute of limitations has expired so we cannot give you justice."

Stonewalled by the courts, LaDuke and the other White Earth Band leaders devised a new strategy. They created an organization,

Anishinabe Akeeng (Land of the People), to raise funds to buy back some of the stolen land. They have now recovered more than 1,200 acres.

Twenty years later, I visited the reservation with my son Jake. Anishinabe Akeeng had a beautiful office in a small building at the edge of the reservation, almost at the border with North Dakota. The Chippewa were continuing their work to regain the tribal land base and teaching Indian youth the Chippewa language and traditional skills.

In the 1990s and early 2000s, CCR brought civil lawsuits against several former dictators, torturers, and mass murderers who had set foot on U.S. soil. Once they'd entered the U.S., we could sue them in U.S. courts using the precedent established in Peter Weiss and Rhonda Copelon's land-mark case, *Filártiga v. Peña.*

I was particularly proud of our work in a case against Héctor Gramajo, a general and former defense minister of Guatemala. As a young man, Gramajo had attended the School of the Americas in Georgia, where the U.S. government trained thousands of Latin American soldiers in its brutal methods. Gramajo later played a prominent role in the massacre of more than 175,000 Mayans in the Guatemalan highlands.

U.S. foreign policy neo-conservatives had been grooming Gramajo to run for president of Guatemala. As part of that effort, he enrolled at Harvard's Kennedy School of Government, which advertises itself as "preparing leaders for democratic societies." However, the general could not control his predilection for mass murder. At the Kennedy School he wrote a paper bragging about his policy in Guatemala: "We have created a more humanitarian, less costly strategy, to be more compatible with the democratic system... which provides development for 70 percent of the population while we kill 30 percent. Before, the strategy was to kill 100 percent."

A journalist friend, Allan Nairn, told me that Gramajo was studying at Harvard and asked if we could sue him for his crimes. "I would love to," I replied, "but we need to find some of his surviving victims now living in the U.S. to be plaintiffs." We knew where Gramajo had worked in Guatemala and the name of the tribe, the Kanjobal, whose villages he'd decimated. Allan and CCR spent almost a year looking for survivors. But we were running out of time. In June 1991, Gramajo would be graduating from the Kennedy School and returning to Guatemala to run for president.

In late spring, we finally found a Kanjobal refugee community in Davis, California. I flew there, landing in a lush farming area of the Central Valley where the Guatemalan refugees picked vegetables for a living. With the help of the University of California at Davis's Law School Clinic, we arranged to interview some of these refugees seeking asylum in the U.S.

Their stories were hair-raising—particularly one told by a young man who had been nine years old in July 1982 when Gramajo's soldiers stormed into his village. The soldiers took all of the men out to be killed. They forced the boy to watch as they tied his father to a tree and cut off chunks of his chest while he was still alive, then doused him in gasoline and burned him to death. They then threw the boy's father and the other men into a hole filled with burning mattresses. The boy, called Juan Doe in the legal papers, ran home, found his house burned to the ground and his mother and siblings missing. He assumed they were all dead and fled to Mexico, where he worked in the fields. A true survivor, as a teenager, he made his way to Davis, California.

Just re-reading the affidavits gave me nightmares, but we'd found our plaintiffs for the suit against Gramajo. We had to act fast to prepare the papers and serve him with the legal complaint. We didn't know where he lived, but we were confident he would appear at his graduation.

My co-counsel Beth Stephens and I traveled to Cambridge with Allan Nairn, who had interviewed Gramajo in person and could identify him. We also arranged for a photographer and hired a process server to serve the papers. It was an overcast, warm morning. We waited in front of the school as the graduates, in robes and mortarboard hats, walked toward us from Harvard Yard to their ceremony.

"There he is," Allan said.

Gramajo, stocky and square-jawed, passed right in front of us. The process server handed him the papers and said, "You are served." At that moment the photographer snapped a picture of the former general receiving the legal papers, with Beth and me by his side. We sent out a press release, and the next morning the front page of the *Boston Globe* featured the photo.

We filed *Xuncax v. Gramajo* in the District Court of Massachusetts on behalf of eight plaintiffs, representing thousands of indigenous Guatemalans who had been murdered, tortured, and falsely imprisoned in what was known as "the Guatemala Solution." As the chief military commander of seven provinces, Gramajo had directed the operation. Because *Xuncax* was a civil case, Gramajo was allowed to return to Guatemala. He refused to cooperate with the court, so the judge found him in default, in effect acknowledging the veracity of our allegations. To publicize the judge's ruling, we bought full-page ads in Guatemalan newspapers, which had a major impact, ending Gramajo's bid for the presidency.

Later, the court issued a lengthy opinion stating that Gramajo "was aware of and supported widespread acts of brutality committed under his command resulting in thousands of civilian deaths." Furthermore, the court said, Gramajo "devised" and "directed" an "indiscriminate campaign of terror against civilians."

The judge ordered Gramajo to pay $47.5 million in damages to the plaintiffs. Although the damages were never paid, Gramajo's career was over. A few years later, he died of an allergic reaction to bee stings. As I write this, Guatemalan courts are putting some of the country's former killer generals on trial—even if only for corruption.

CCR also brought cases against Haitian, Argentinean, Israeli, Bosnian, Indonesian, and other human rights abusers whose home countries would not bring them to justice. We were akin to private attorneys general enforcing the law, even against officials of regimes the U.S. supported. For example, we won a judgment against former Haitian dictator Prosper Avril, who had tortured the mayor of Port-au-Prince and other Haitian political activists. The plaintiffs were awarded $41 million in damages. We brought another successful suit against Indonesian General Sintong Pandjaitan, who oversaw the 1991 massacre of 271 people at a memorial service in East Timor, which Indonesia had occupied. The mother of one of those executed was awarded $14 million in damages.

Although the courts often awarded us large judgments, the defendants fled the U.S. and the plaintiffs never recovered a penny. However, compensation wasn't my main goal. I wanted to focus public attention on the atrocities and stop the United States and the oppressive governments it backed from denying democratic rights, torturing, and killing people.

One case that caused an internal conflict at CCR involved the Bosnian Serb leader, Radovan Karadžić. I had little doubt he was guilty of war crimes, including mass rape, but I wasn't in favor of CCR bringing a case against him. I wanted to limit our work to cases that would strike a blow against the United States government's power and the repressive regimes it was supporting. Haiti fit my criteria, as did Guatemala. But by taking on the Karadžić case, we were siding with the U.S. government, which wanted to prosecute him as well.

Others at CCR disagreed. After hearing me out, one of my colleagues responded that there had to be accountability for mass killings and rape, and that this case would establish rape as a war crime. Ultimately, my colleague's view prevailed and CCR brought the case against Karadžić.

My friend Ramsey Clark, former attorney general of the United States and a member of CCR's advisory board, thought that none of our lawsuits against human rights violators should be brought in U.S. courts. Allowing a U.S. court to adjudicate human rights violations committed by other country's leaders, he argued, legitimizes the United States as a fair judge of the conduct of others. Ramsey felt that only a world court, where poorer countries participated, should try these cases. He believed this so strongly that he decided to represent Karadžić against CCR's lawsuit.

I will never forget the day when the tall, gangly Ramsey faced off against CCR's petite Beth Stephens, who was arguing one of her first cases in an appeals court. CCR won the Karadžić case, with a judgment of $4.5 billion. But again, the plaintiffs could not collect.

Ramsey's defense of Karadžić caused CCR to remove him from its advisory board. Despite this difference, Ramsey and I remained friends.

Year after year, the students in the Yale law clinic were brilliant and hard-working, and I loved teaching with Harold Koh. Nine years my junior, Harold was one of Yale's most beloved professors. His family was from South Korea, where his father was revered as one of the smartest men of his generation. "In the '50s, my father was Korea's U.N. ambassador when a military coup overthrew the Korean government," he told me. "To gain legitimacy, the coup's leaders asked him to return as prime minister. He refused and gave up his job."

Harold and I were both children of immigrants, which was to be a driving force in our work together. But we had our differences. One student of ours apparently thought of me as the "anti-Koh," and would later describe me as "bearded, bald, and fond of quoting Che Guevara." Harold mainly taught international business law at Yale. He knew little about human rights, and he had been a lawyer for the Reagan administration during the 1983 invasion of Grenada—the same invasion I'd gone to court to try to stop. Despite our different politics, we became great workmates and fast friends.

What made the Yale clinic truly special to me was our collective work representing Haitian refugees detained at the U.S. naval base at Guantánamo Bay, Cuba. At the time, I didn't really want to take on another major case involving U.S. foreign policy. For ten years I'd brought suits to stop the U.S. government's illegal interventions in Latin America. Although our cases had solid constitutional grounds, we'd lost every one. Tired and frustrated, I felt as if I'd been tilting at windmills.

But there was no way I could ignore the September 1991 military coup that overthrew the elected president of Haiti, the popular priest Jean-Bertrand Aristide. The coup unleashed a bloodbath. Within four days, the military murdered more than 2,000 Aristide supporters and tortured and jailed many more. Soldiers invaded the poorest neighborhoods, including Cité Soleil, where Aristide had his strongest base of support, and fired at will into people's homes. Fleeing the terror, thousands of refugees took to small boats that were barely seaworthy. Often more than 100 men, women, and children jammed into one 20-foot open rowboat with a jury-rigged sail. Without sufficient water or food, many died or suffered from sunstroke.

While some made it to neighboring countries, U.S. Coast Guard cutters patrolling the windward passage between Haiti and Cuba stopped the majority of the boats on the high seas. For a couple of weeks, the George Bush administration admitted these refugees to the United States. But soon the administration reversed its policy, claiming that many of those fleeing were economic, not political, refugees. U.S. border patrol agents began forcibly returning almost all the refugees to Haiti.

Refugees who come to the United States have the right to assert a claim for asylum if they face political persecution in their home country. A lawyer friend of mine from Miami, Ira Kurzban, had long worked on Haitian immigration issues. In the fall of 1991, Ira brought a class-action lawsuit, *Haitian Refugee Center v. James Baker (Secretary of State),* to stop the forcible return of the refugees to Haiti and assure that they received hearings on their asylum claims. A federal district court in Southern Florida issued several injunctions, halting forcible return. While it appealed, the administration ordered the Coast Guard to bring the refugees to the U.S. naval base at Guantánamo. At peak, nearly 15,000 Haitian refugees were held at the base.

In January 1992, the appeals court dismissed Ira's case, ruling that Haitians outside of the United States had no claims and the Constitution did not apply to them. It was a terrible defeat. Most of the Haitians were political refugees who had supported Aristide after the coup. Now, the U.S. Coast Guard could continue to stop them at sea and, with no legal due process, send them back to Haiti, where they likely faced prison or execution.

Ira called me to see if Harold or I had any ideas what to do next. Even though our chances were almost nil, a dozen of our Yale law clinic students wanted to try to litigate the issue again in a different federal court. Harold put them to work for two weeks, and they came up with a thin reed of a strategy that made us believe we might survive a government motion to dismiss: because the Supreme Court had not considered the issue, *res judicata*, which prohibited the same parties from re-litigating the same issue in another court, it would not apply.

I wanted our case to be filed in the U.S. District Court for the Eastern District of New York, where I felt the judges would be sympathetic. It was located in Brooklyn, a diverse community with a large immigrant population, including 100,000 Haitians. For the court to have jurisdiction, we needed a plaintiff with a Brooklyn connection. We found Haitian Centers Council, a Brooklyn-based group that wanted to travel to Guantánamo to counsel the Haitians held there. Right to counsel was a claim under the First Amendment, and we added it to our suit.

The night before we filed *Haitian Centers Council v. Gene McNary, Commissioner, Immigration and Naturalization Service*, Harold, the students, and I worked late at the office of a top New York law firm, Simpson Thacher & Bartlett, which had agreed to give us pro bono help. Joe

Tringali, a young litigation partner at Simpson, helped us finalize the papers. Harold and I were not trial lawyers. By contrast, Joe actually knew how to try a case.

Late that evening, Joe had a eureka moment. Buried deep in the government's papers, he noticed that a class of Haitian immigrants on Guantánamo were to be given a second hearing to determine if they qualified for entry into the United States. These immigrants had already been screened and found to have a "credible fear" of persecution if returned to Haiti. Normally, they would be admitted to the United States. For some reason we didn't understand, though, this group had to go through a second hearing and prove not only a "credible fear," but a "well-founded fear" of persecution, a more demanding standard. We were well aware how difficult it is for refugees to litigate that higher standard from inside the United States. But on board a ship, outside the country, or at a place like Guantánamo, it is far more difficult because the refugees are allowed no attorneys or appeal rights.

Our case was randomly assigned to Judge Sterling Johnson Jr., a Black federal judge and the former drug czar of New York. He had a reputation as a very tough guy—rumor had it that he kept a baseball bat under his bench. We immediately asked for a temporary injunction (restraining order) to halt the already "screened-in" refugees' return to Haiti until the case was resolved. The government responded aggressively, arguing that the issue had already been decided by another court and the case should be dismissed. But Judge Johnson granted us a temporary injunction and set a date for a more thorough hearing.

All of us worked intensely the next few days to prepare. Harold's work capacity was daunting. I sometimes stayed at Yale working into the early morning and then fell asleep in the faculty lounge, a comfortable room with oil paintings of deans and professors on the walls. Harold never stopped. He drank Diet Coke to keep himself awake, spending the entire night at the computer.

One early morning I was hidden on one of the sofas in the lounge and overheard a couple of faculty members talking.

"What do you think of Harold and the Haitian case?" one asked.

"He's too involved as an advocate," the other replied. "He has lost his objectivity."

I often think of that conversation and those ivory-tower law professors, who sit on the sidelines and don't get involved in working for social change. It's not what I ever wanted to be.

As part of the discovery process, Joe Tringali and I, along with a student, took depositions from numerous government witnesses while Harold and a group of other students prepared briefs. In their depositions, the government witnesses revealed a crucial fact: the 400 "screened-in" refugees inexplicably still on Guantánamo were HIV-positive, or were accompanied by a child or parent who was HIV-positive. Under U.S. law at the time, HIV-positive immigrants could not be admitted to the United States without the consent of the U.S. attorney general—and he would not consent unless each member of this group went through a second hearing.

At the time of Ira's litigation, neither the plaintiffs nor the public knew that "screened-in" HIV-positive refugees were required to have a second hearing. Our newfound awareness of this requirement meant that there was an important difference between the plaintiffs in our case and the plaintiffs in Ira's class action. Now we could insist that because the HIV-positive Haitian plaintiffs in our case had been "screened in," they had a clear right to consult attorneys, and to have counsel present at those second hearings.

I tried to recruit other human rights groups to join our lawsuit. The San Francisco Lawyers Committee for Urban Affairs signed on, but the ACLU was concerned about possible sanctions and fines for filing a frivolous lawsuit. We really wanted their support, so although CCR was a tiny organization compared to the ACLU, I promised CCR would pay any fines.

Predictably, the government briefs repeated their previous argument that the Constitution did not apply to aliens outside the United States. But they made another argument—that the case was frivolous. They asked for $50 million in sanctions against the lawyers and institutions that filed it, which included Yale and CCR. I'd often seen similar tactics from our opponents and believed sanctions would never be granted against human rights litigators seeking to protect refugees. But Harold and the dean of Yale's law school were extremely concerned, not just for their own personal liability but also for the future of the Yale law clinic.

A few days after the initial hearing, the second hearing took place. Judge Johnson ruled that the refugees could not be returned to Haiti until the case was resolved. He also decided that none of the refugees could be given a second hearing on Guantánamo until the issue of whether they had a right to an attorney had been resolved. And he rejected the government's demand that plaintiffs post a $10 million bond to cover the government's costs incurred because of the injunction.

I was elated. This was the first time CCR and I had ever won even a preliminary ruling in a major case challenging a U.S. foreign policy.

But the legal battle was far from over. One issue we had not litigated was the government's exclusion of HIV-positive immigrants from the United States. While an existing statute forbade entry to immigrants with communicable diseases, the issue was whether HIV fell into that category. After doing more research, I was surprised to discover the prevailing medical consensus: HIV was not communicable—that is, one could not become HIV-positive simply via physical proximity to an HIV-positive person.

Once I understood this, I wanted our lawsuit to challenge the exclusion of HIV-positive immigrants. I called the ACLU. "Michael, we have congressional legislation pending on this issue, and we have a good chance of winning," an ACLU lawyer told me. "If we add it to your lawsuit and lose, our congressional efforts will lose as well. So please leave it out."

Because the ACLU had taken the lead on this issue and was a counsel in our lawsuit, I reluctantly agreed to defer challenging the HIV exclusion. But Congress never passed the proposed legislation. It was not until many years later that the Obama administration eliminated the HIV exclusion from the regulations. The lesson for me—which I have learned again and again—was that Congress rarely has the courage to take on controversial issues. Sometimes it's better to raise these issues in the courts.

Early in the litigation process, Judge Johnson had to rule on whether we had the right to visit our clients at Guantánamo. By permitting Haitian priests, news reporters, and United Nations personnel to visit the refugees, the government had given us our strongest legal argument. If these others could visit, Judge Johnson ruled, then the government could not deny us our First Amendment right to visit and counsel our clients. A huge victory.

Traveling to Guantánamo, a secluded, 45-square-mile military base in southeastern Cuba under the exclusive jurisdiction of the United States, was difficult. No U.S. citizen could leave the U.S.-controlled base and go into other parts of Cuba, and only a few Cuban workers could come to work on the base. Harold and I flew with three others to Fort Lauderdale, where we boarded a single-engine propeller plane for a four-hour flight to the naval base.

U.S. military brass greeted us and took us to meet with our clients. The meeting was not in the refugee camp, which we were not allowed to visit, but it was on the military base. There wasn't much to see—just one-story cement-block buildings and Quonset huts on what looked like an old airfield. Still, I was excited to be there and looked forward to our work.

We met with five of our Haitian clients inside a large, empty hangar with offices on the periphery. Our team of five sat with them around a wooden table and began discussions with a translator.

"We are here to help you," we told them. "We are lawyers and students from Yale and will not charge a fee."

The meeting lasted a couple of hours. At one point one of the Haitians said, "We don't trust you to do a good job on our case. We have already been here a few months, and we have no results from you. We think you are not trying hard and it's because you are doing it for free. If we had lawyers that were paid, we would not be here."

This unexpected reaction upset us. We had worked literally night and day on this case, and our clients were angry at us.

The situation got quite tense. Luckily, Johnny McCalla, a Haitian-American activist who had accompanied us, intervened immediately. A member of the National Coalition of Haitian Refugees, Johnny spoke Creole, French, and English. "Be thankful these lawyers are here," Johnny told the Haitians. "They have worked hard and will not abandon you." Johnny saved the meeting and ultimately the case.

After he spoke up, we began to get along much better with our clients. I learned a lot from this incident. It showed how out of touch we were with people who had little reason to trust outsiders offering "help." Foolishly, I had expected gratitude.

The Haitians' plight was dire. They were detained here behind barbed wire, young children and adults crowded together into small concrete-block houses or tents. Bathroom facilities were often backed up and spewed nauseating odors. Banana rats ran freely through the camp. U.S. medical authorities had told the Haitians they were HIV-positive, which at that time meant certain death from AIDS. Most of the detainees refused to believe this diagnosis, claiming it was a U.S. conspiracy.

Over a few days, we talked at length with the detainees about their legal situation and living conditions. By the end of our trip, I felt a real affection had developed between us. We'd made real personal connections—and now our clients had become friends and comrades. At our last meeting, we sang beautiful songs together. As we left, I couldn't help but weep.

More than a year into the litigation, the Haitians demanded passage into the United States and began a hunger strike. A few of the law students opposed the strike because they thought it would embarrass our allies in the newly-elected Clinton administration and ruin our chances to negotiate an end to the detention.

One student expressed what many others were feeling: "The Haitians are very sick already. If they don't eat, they'll die. I can't stand watching them taking it out on themselves."

I had a different view of the hunger strike. Our clients felt desperate and hopeless, and the strike gave them a measure of control over their own lives. In the end, it didn't matter what any of us thought. The Haitians were going to make their own decisions.

When Harold and I met with Clinton's transition team in Washington, they were polite, but told us frankly, "People are terrified of AIDS. The chances of bringing an HIV-positive Haitian into the United States are zero." Harold and the Yale team continued with an "inside" strategy on the case, appealing to Harold's excellent contacts in the administration. But it was clear to me that we at CCR had to pursue an active "outside strategy" as well, and organize to free the Haitians.

As part of that effort, we invited the Black activist Jesse Jackson to visit Guantánamo during the hunger strike. Some of the students pleaded with him to urge the strikers to stop. Others, including me, wanted him to support and publicize the strike. We all hoped he would talk to President Clinton about ending the HIV detainment camp. Jackson, Harold, and I flew together from New York to Guantánamo on a private jet the administration had authorized.

This was our first trip since the strike had begun. As we arrived, we saw more than 100 strikers lying unmoving out on a field. I was horrified. Temperatures soared to 100 degrees. Some strikers had already been taken to the infirmary and force-fed. Jackson talked one-on-one to several people, and through a loudspeaker, he pleaded with the refugees not to risk their health and to end the strike. He also promised to talk to President Clinton about their situation, which boosted the strikers' morale and led to their eventual decision to end the strike.

One of my jobs was to handle communication with the assistant attorney general in charge of the case, Paul Cappuccio. Paul had clerked in the Supreme Court, was extremely bright, and very conservative. Most of the students could not stand him. Tough in court, he was the government lawyer who had pushed for the multi-million-dollar fine against us.

In court appearances, Paul argued the government's position that Guantánamo's medical facility was adequate for treating AIDS patients. We argued that once the T-cell count, a marker of AIDS, dropped below 200, the facilities there were insufficient. But as some of our clients—children and pregnant women—progressed from HIV to AIDS, Paul began to show a more humanitarian side. Despite the government's official position, Paul understood that many of the Haitians faced a life-or-death situation. I talked to him almost every day. Because he worked for the attorney general, he was able to get waivers of the HIV exclusion so that some of the very ill detainees and pregnant women could enter the United States. He also tried to make sure the pregnant women could give birth by Caesarian section, which reduced the risks of newborns contracting HIV.

In one instance, I asked Paul to arrange for a mother and baby with AIDS to go to a hospital near my house in Greenwich Village. Tubes poked out of the baby's tiny body. I stood helpless as this mother watched her baby die. The mother died shortly thereafter. Paul also arranged for a Haitian man with very advanced AIDS to come to Miami, where he died. People cried and screamed as they carried his coffin through the streets of Little Haiti.

Quite a few of our clients died at Guantánamo. Ironically, as the number of refugees in the camp dwindled, our chances of bringing all of the remaining detainees to the United States improved. But on this issue Clinton proved to be not any better than the first President Bush.

Once I even sat beside Clinton at a fundraising party and appealed directly to him. "There are about 300 Haitians living in unspeakable conditions at Guantánamo, and many are dying," I explained. "They're stuck because of the regulations on HIV. But you can grant waivers and get them into the U.S."

He dutifully took notes, nodded as if understanding, said he would talk to his people—and then did nothing.

Finally, we realized we could not depend on the politicians. The Yale students, particularly Michael Wishnie, began to organize constituencies of support to pressure the administration. He invited the gay activist group ACT-UP, which had a strong presence in New York, to be our advocates. After all, Guantánamo was the only detention camp for HIV/AIDS refugees in the world. ACT-UP trailed the president and his aides everywhere, demanding the closing of the camp. We also reached out to immigrant rights groups, Black groups, and Haitian-Americans. In addition, the students contacted activists across the country and began a rolling protest from college to college. They built cages on campuses and went on hunger strikes while sitting in the cages.

Ultimately, Clinton refused to close the camp, and in 1993 we had no choice but to go to trial with our case. The judge did not have the authority to force the government to allow the Haitians into the United States. Admission of "aliens" was at the president's discretion. So in his 53-page decision, Judge Johnson took another tack. He ordered the government to provide the Haitians with adequate medical care. And he ruled that Guantánamo's facilities were not equipped to treat detainees whose T-cells fell below 200. Judge Johnson wrote:

> Although the defendants [U.S. government agencies] refer to
> [the] Guantánamo operation as a *"humanitarian camp,"* the facts

disclose that it is nothing more than an HIV prison camp presenting potential public health risks to the Haitians held there [...] The detained Haitians are neither criminals nor national security risks. Some are pregnant mothers and others are children. Simply put, they are merely the unfortunate victims of a fatal disease... The Haitians' plight is a tragedy of immense proportion and their continued detainment is totally unacceptable to this Court.

Despite demands from 42 senators to appeal Johnson's ruling, the Clinton administration instead decided to release all of the remaining Guantánamo detainees and fly them to New York. We assembled an entire team of workers from human rights organizations, the Catholic church, and the government to help find care and housing for them.

I went to the airport with Harold, the other attorneys, and the students to meet the refugees. Out on the tarmac, we saw the plane land. Then our clients—women, men and children, who had spent almost two miserable years in detention at Guantánamo—slowly made their way down the ramp, one by one. When they saw us, they pumped their triumphant fists in the air, and I cried.

Together, we had won an impossible case. But tragically, many of the Haitian refugees were quite ill and would not survive long.

8
GUANTÁNAMO

September 11, 2001. A picture-postcard day. The air was still and dry as I took my morning run down the path that follows the West Side Highway to the southern tip of Manhattan. I glanced across the Hudson River to New Jersey, and suddenly, I heard an airplane fly low over my head, skimming down the Hudson. The jet engines roared. I looked up and watched in disbelief as the plane turned left and crashed into the North Tower of the World Trade Center. Was this really happening? A plume of black smoke confirmed that it was all too real. I thought it must be a freak accident and that emergency services would soon respond.

I looked at my watch: 8:46 a.m. I continued jogging, not far from the twin towers. Seventeen minutes later, a second plane came out of nowhere, flying low and loud. I saw it slam into the South Tower and explode, creating a fierce firestorm high up around the 70th floor. I knew then that this was no random accident. Something was terribly, terribly wrong.

I sprinted back to my home in the West Village. The house was empty, so I called to make sure my family was okay. Both kids were in school. Karen had just dropped off Jake, then 13, at Village Community School and was on her way home. Ana, 11, had gone with a friend to Little Red Schoolhouse. Everyone was safe.

But I knew that my brother Bruce and two of our cousins from Cleveland, Chuck and Jimmy, were scheduled to have a business meeting that morning somewhere downtown, and I couldn't get ahold of them. The TV news didn't have much information yet. Karen and I decided for the time being to leave the kids in school where they were well supervised. We went out into the street and walked over to Sheridan Square, where we had a perfect view of the towers straight down Seventh Avenue. Sirens screamed out as ambulances, fire trucks, and police cars raced toward what had already become an inferno.

I was worried about my brother and cousins, and I couldn't do a thing to help them. Hundreds of people from the neighborhood milled around on the street, some dazed, some crying, some hysterical. Nobody knew what was going on. We were all terrified and in shock. Strangers were hugging each other, just clinging to another human body to try to calm their fears.

We could see flames leaping out of the towers and dark smoke billowing up into the sky, blowing toward Brooklyn. Then, like an enormous tinker toy, the South Tower collapsed, from the top down, upper floors first, lower floors following quickly. Within ten seconds, the entire building was reduced to a heap of rubble.

Before I could process this nightmarish vision, I spotted Bruce and my two cousins in their business suits and ties running at full speed up Seventh Avenue toward me. We took them back to the house and as they caught their breath and cleaned up, they explained that their meeting had been on the top floor of World Trade Center 7. That building had not been hit and was still intact. When the planes struck the twin towers, the authorities told everyone inside Building 7 to stay put. But Bruce decided to ignore the warning, and he and the cousins ran down 40 flights of stairs. They barely escaped before the South Tower collapsed, casting a pall of dust everywhere.

While Bruce and I tried to figure out how to get our cousins back to Cleveland, Karen went to pick up Jake. A neighbor brought Ana home. How do you explain this to a 13-year-old and an 11-year-old? At that point we didn't know much more than they did. Karen and the kids busied themselves making dozens of peanut butter and jelly sandwiches, thinking that the survivors would need to be fed. They took the sandwiches over to nearby St. Vincent's Hospital. But the place was eerily quiet and empty. There were no survivors.

That night we didn't want to be alone in the house. All of us, including the kids, walked over to Union Square where hundreds of people had gathered for a candlelight vigil. It was silent and mournful, like a funeral, and everybody was scared. People just needed to be together.

The next day our friends Michael and Debby Smith, who lived within a few blocks of the towers, had to evacuate their apartment. They walked uptown, carrying their African gray parrot Charlie in a cage. "It's okay, it's okay," Charlie said to every passerby on the street. They arrived at our house and stayed with us for the next week or two. Mike had narrowly escaped disaster. He'd scheduled a business breakfast at 9 a.m. at Windows on the World atop the North Tower, but at the last minute it had been canceled.

In the next few days the details of a well-coordinated terrorist attack began to emerge—the hijacking of the planes by Saudi members of al-Qaeda, the nearly simultaneous hijacking of two other planes, one that slammed into the Pentagon and the other that crashed in a field in Pennsylvania after a struggle between passengers and hijackers. But more questions emerged than answers.

Many Americans, from the White House and the media to ordinary people on the street, immediately called for retaliation. Against whom or how or to what end was not clear, but there was a definite feeling in the air of "Let's just bomb the hell out of them." After witnessing this tragedy with my own eyes, I was skeptical of that kneejerk response and very concerned about the direction these events might lead us.

On September 13, two days after the attacks, I watched President George W. Bush's televised speech in my living room with friends, horrified by what I was hearing. Presenting a scary, black-and-white view of the world, he was ready to go to war and kill thousands with no understanding of who committed these acts or why. Referring to those responsible for the attack, Bush said, "They want to destroy our way of life." He went on to call the U.S. response a "crusade" and sent a message to the attackers: "We will hunt you down."

I did not accept Bush's idea that this was an attack on "our way of life." His speech did not show even the slightest understanding that terrorist acts at home might be connected to our government's policies abroad—such as the possibility that the U.S. role in the Israel-Palestine conflict or the U.S. military presence in Saudi Arabia could have motivated the attackers.

I always felt that it was just a matter of time before the U.S. government's interventionist policies would come back to haunt us. In those days, few non-Muslims here knew much about Islam. I had heard of Osama bin Laden, but I certainly couldn't tell you anything about Wahhabism. So there was a lot of learning to do very quickly about what jihad was and what extremist Muslims really wanted.

The day after Bush's speech, Congress passed the Authorization for Use of Military Force, and on September 18, Bush signed it into law. Only one member of the entire Congress—Representative Barbara Lee from California—voted against the bill.

The AUMF gave the president such unprecedented, disturbing, and broad power that I was not just concerned, but truly stunned. It essentially said the president can use military force to attack any country, organization, or person who aided, assisted, or harbored persons in the September 11th attacks. And that he could also use that military force to prevent any future attacks. He could start wars against all 37 countries where the U.S. government claims the al-Qaeda network is present, or against anyone else he suspects of involvement in the attacks of September 11 or any future attacks. The president could do all this without getting any further approval from Congress, even if he leads us into World War III.

So legally and politically, with the AUMF, Congress gave up its authority over war and handed it to one individual in the White House. There was no time limit. They even gave the president a fat $20 billion check to help him along in this endless war. This is not what the framers of our Constitution imagined. On the contrary, the Constitution was drafted to keep presidential wars in check. As I read the details of the AUMF, I could just see the excesses coming—illegal surveillance, indefinite detentions, torture, all in the name of national security.

As early as September 23, Jules Lobel and I wrote an article for *The Jurist* outlining why Bush's plan to launch a unilateral war against Afghanistan would violate international law.

"The United Nations Charter (Article 2(4) and Article 51) prohibits the use of force except in matters of self-defense," we pointed out. "A country is not permitted to use military force for purposes of retaliation, vengeance, and punishment. In other words, unless a future attack on the United States is imminent, it cannot use military force. This means that even if the United States furnishes evidence as to the authors of the September 11 attack, it cannot use military force against them."

Instead of an illegal war, I proposed an alternative approach in a speech I made at the NYC chapter of the National Lawyers Guild on October 3: "The attack on September 11 should not have been called and treated as acts of war by the government. The attack was a criminal act, a crime against humanity under international law—the mass killing of a civilian population. It doesn't lessen its seriousness. Crimes against humanity are what we tried the Nazis for at Nuremberg. It is a very serious crime, but it is not an act of war. Treat it as a criminal act, go to the United Nations and request the Security Council to establish an international court to try the perpetrators of September 11. That court should have the power to investigate, extradite, and issue warrants of arrests." The Security Council could also apply sanctions against non-cooperating countries or sever diplomatic and economic relations with them.

But there was no stopping the administration in its rush to war. On October 7 the bombing of Afghanistan began. The idea that the U.S. was going to bring devastation to another country was antithetical to me, particularly one of the poorest countries in the world—and particularly since not one of the 9/11 hijackers was Afghani. But people were so scared that they were willing to do anything. Even my friend Richard Falk wrote a piece in *The Nation* saying this might be a just war. Jules Lobel and I responded with a letter to the magazine. Then I debated Richard *on Democracy Now!*, but by then Richard said that the way the U.S. military planned to fight this war was so brutal that he could no longer accept that it was the right thing to do. You cannot drop cluster bombs from 30,000 feet and expect it won't be very gruesome and kill many innocent people.

I didn't have any idea how CCR or I would be drawn into all this. But within a week after the 9/11 attacks occurred, CCR started getting the first calls from the Muslim community. We had an Israeli Arabic speaker on staff who handled them. Hundreds of non-citizen Muslim men were being arrested for no reason other than that they were Muslims. Often their families didn't even know where they were.

We at CCR went to the prisons to help families locate their loved ones, and we too had trouble finding the missing people. By some estimates, nearly 3,000 people had been detained, 60 percent of them in the New York area. Instead of being deported, these immigrants—some documented, some not—were being held without bail or representation while the FBI investigated whether they had any connection to terrorism. Most stayed in prison for months before the FBI cleared them. Many were held at a prison in Passaic, New Jersey, and many were also held in solitary confinement at a specially-created Administrative Maximum Special Housing Unit at Metropolitan Detention Center in Manhattan. The conditions were horrifying. The young men were beaten, deprived of sleep, and verbally abused. They would come out shackled, under video cameras and lights.

CCR decided to launch a major civil rights case challenging the government's policy of imprisoning non-U.S. citizens until they got FBI clearances, even though there was no proof that they had ever done anything unlawful. *Turkmen v. Ashcroft*, filed on April 17, 2002, charged that the Justice Department and the Metropolitan Detention Center violated the First, Fourth, and Fifth Amendment rights of Muslim aliens by detaining them under brutal conditions for an unreasonable length of time, without access to lawyers, friends, or family. In November 2009, six of the plaintiffs who had been held at Metropolitan Detention Center settled their claims for $1.26 million. The others persisted. A depressing example of how slowly the wheels of justice grind, the case, later renamed *Ziglar v. Abbasi*, was still in the courts 14 years later.

The shameful persecution of Muslims in the days after September 11 revealed just how much fear, panic, and racism had been unleashed in the U.S. Then, in the six-week period beginning September 18, heightened emotions escalated into hysteria when the press reported that an unknown bioterrorist was using the U.S. Postal Service to deliver deadly anthrax spores. The first set of five letters containing the coarse brown grainy material were mailed anonymously from Trenton, New Jersey, to the New York offices of ABC, CBS, and NBC News, the *New York Post*, and the *National Enquirer* in Boca Raton, Florida. A journalist at the *Sun* tabloid, which shared the *Enquirer's* offices, was the first victim to die.

Three weeks after the first toxic mailing, two more letters containing an even more potent dry powder consisting of anthrax spores were sent from Trenton, addressed to two prominent members of Congress—Senator Majority Leader Tom Daschle and Senate Judiciary Committee Chair Patrick Leahy. Neither reached its intended target, but 34 members of Daschle's staff tested positive for anthrax, and many postal workers and others were exposed. By the end of November, 22 people had developed anthrax infections, and five died from inhaling anthrax.

You couldn't even open a letter without worrying. Once again, by chance, my brother Bruce found himself caught up in the mess. On October 17, when the second set of letters arrived, he had visited New York Governor George Pataki's city offices. That same day, traces of anthrax had been discovered in the governor's offices on the 39th floor. My brother had visited the floor below.

To be safe, I took Bruce to New York University hospital to be checked out. It was like a war room. Hundreds of people milled about. The doctors gave those at risk a test to see if they had been exposed to the spores. It turned out that Bruce had not been exposed, but his business partner sent gas masks over to our house as a precaution.

In this atmosphere of heightened fear and hysteria, Congress passed one of the most repressive pieces of legislation in its history. The USA Patriot Act was a hodgepodge of new laws that right-wing lobbyists and prominent members of the administration had failed to get Congress to enact for at least a decade. But now, on October 26, President Bush signed the Patriot Act into law. It gave law enforcement the authority to break into private homes to carry out so-called "sneak-and-peek" searches without the occupant's knowledge or consent. It opened the door for the federal government to carry out mass surveillance on citizens without a court order, including expanded tapping of telephones and e-mail and even monitoring of business and library records. It made it a crime to give material support to "terrorists"—which meant, for example, that if this law had been in effect during apartheid in South Africa, anyone who had donated to the African National Congress, then labeled a "terrorist" organization by the U.S. government, would have been subject to arrest. And now it meant that someone who gave a donation to a Muslim charity organization could face criminal charges.

And it authorized the indefinite detention of immigrants—providing a veil of legality to an indefensible practice that was already being carried out at the Metropolitan Detention Center and elsewhere. "If you overstay your visa even by one day, we will arrest you," Attorney General John Ashcroft told a conference of mayors. Criminal suspects who commit even minor infractions, he said, will be "put in jail and kept in custody as long as possible."

More than 300 pages long, the newly revised Patriot Act had been thrown together in little more than a month. And its sponsors presented it to Congress in the middle of an anthrax panic shortly after Senator Daschle's staff was infected. It's safe to say that most of the members of Congress had not even read the bill before they cast their votes and dashed out of Washington to avoid anthrax exposure. Despite opposition from both civil liberties groups and such prominent right-wing critics as the Eagle Forum and Phyllis Schlafly—who believed it allowed too much government intrusion into citizens' lives—the bill passed the House overwhelmingly with almost no debate. In the Senate, only one member voted no—Senator Russ Feingold of Wisconsin.

It all happened very fast because the right-wing proponents were ready. I'm generally skeptical of conspiracy theories, but something the neo-conservative think-tank Project for the New American Century had said in a report back in 1997 stuck in my mind. After outlining its program—U.S. military domination of the world, a reversal of the loser mentality of the Vietnam War by eliminating all challengers, regime change in countries that were not going along with U.S. policies, and a reshuffling of the entire Middle East power structure to assure Israel's security—the report said it would take a long time to implement "absent some catastrophic catalyzing event—like a new Pearl Harbor."

MOVING THE BAR

In 1997, when William Kristol and Robert Kagan founded The Project for the New American Century in Washington, 25 people signed its statement of principles. Ten of them went on to serve in the George W. Bush administration, including Vice-President Dick Cheney, Defense Secretary Donald Rumsfeld, and Deputy Defense Secretary Paul Wolfowitz. This group of seven or eight guys in the Pentagon shared their dreams, which included toppling Iraqi President Saddam Hussein who, to their chagrin, had managed to survive the 1991 Gulf War.

The Cheney-Rumsfeld faction had been waiting for years for some way to create a surveillance/national security state which could impose regime change in countries like Afghanistan and Iraq. The attacks on 9/11 finally provided the catalyzing event—"a new Pearl Harbor"—to turn their fantasies into law in the form of the Patriot Act.

CCR opposed the Patriot Act, but since many other groups had mobilized against it, we decided to focus on the increasing attacks on Muslim refugees and the frightening implications of a new military order that Bush had issued.

The Military Order on the Detention, Treatment, and Trial of Certain Non-Citizens in the War Against Terrorism took effect on November 13, 2001. The next morning, while eating my breakfast, I first read about it in an article in the *New York Times*. A few things about the Order immediately struck me. First, it went way beyond just arresting members of al-Qaeda. Second, it authorized detaining people anywhere in the world. Third, secret military commissions with hand-appointed judges could try detainees on charges that carried the death penalty. These commissions would allow evidence obtained from torture. No appeals to any court of law would be allowed. And the final appeal would be to the president alone. Fourth, the government could hold detainees indefinitely without any trial. And fifth, the Order abolished habeas corpus. One of the cornerstones of criminal law, a writ of habeas corpus is a court order to a prison authority to bring a prisoner before a judge to determine if the detention is lawful.

GUANTÁNAMO

I was stunned at how far this Order went. Now when you look it up it is called the Presidential Order. But it was originally called Military Order No. 1, implying that there would be others and implying, if not stating explicitly, that the military had taken over the country. I considered it then and I consider it today to be a coup d'etat.

After reading the details, I gulped down my breakfast and headed over to the Center. I sat down with Bill Goodman, our legal director, and said, "We have to do something about this."

Bill and I agreed that when the first people were arrested under this Order, we would be willing to take their cases and represent them. We called a reporter at the *New York Times*, and on November 30, 2001, the paper published an article headlined "Center Girds for Long Legal Fight on New Bush Anti-Terror Policies." It carried a photo of Bill and me with a caption saying that we were getting ready to challenge the Order. "My job is to defend the Constitution from its enemies," Bill said in the article. "Its main enemies right now are the Justice Department and the White House."

After the article came out and in the following months, we got plenty of hate mail—hundreds of e-mails and phone messages, some carrying implicit threats and others denying that those at Guantánamo should have any rights. A sampling:

"Well Mr. Ratner, you certainly are a piece of work. Is there any piece of worthless subhuman brute you won't stick up for? ...You have a vile hatred for this country, the only country in the world where it is safe for a coward like yourself to spit on the land that you live in."

"I guess the part you have not figured out yet is that Muslims hate us and will kill any Christian."

"You are a bald fat fuck. Go over to Iraq and let them cut your big ass head off, you idiot scum-sucking lawyer."

"You should be charged with treason against this country and thrown in jail for the rest of your life."

When we initially presented our plan to the rest of CCR, some of the lawyers thought we shouldn't get involved. Nancy Chang, who'd written CCR's pamphlet about the Patriot Act, argued, "Look, Rumsfeld and others are saying there are sleeper cells of terrorists. We could end up representing some of the people who actually planned to fly planes into the World Trade Center. Do we really want to do that?"

She is now pleased that we went ahead and represented the Guantánamo prisoners. But at the time, Nancy's point could not be dismissed. To myself, I thought, "I'll defend the people on habeas, because that is crucial, but I do not necessarily want to represent them at the criminal trials." I made that distinction in my mind—but not publicly and, in the end, I did not act on it. I would later come to realize that most of those the Bush administration claimed were terrorists were not, that trials would be a complete sham, and that it was important to challenge every denial of rights the Bush administration attempted, on every front.

Others at CCR pointed out that this was not the kind of case the Center traditionally got involved in. In the past, the Center represented the civil rights movement, anti-war demonstrators, prisoners, all kinds of movements for social change. The case we were proposing was actually closer to ACLU-type cases, which generally defend the principles of the Bill of Rights. The idea of defending the fundamental democratic rights of groups or individuals we strongly disagreed with, as opposed to social movements we clearly supported, was a major departure for some of us at CCR.

In addition, when I met with the fundraisers at CCR, they expressed their concern.

"We're going to be defending terrorists?" they said. "This is six weeks after 9/11."

"We're going to be defending detainees," I replied. "We don't know if they're terrorists."

"Whatever you call them, we are not going to be able to raise any money," they said. "People are going to stop giving. We are going to be hated."

Because of the dissent, Bill Goodman scheduled a meeting at CCR to decide whether or not to take on these cases. Before the meeting, I copied two pages from Bill Kunstler's autobiography, *My Life as a Radical Lawyer,* and passed them around. I was not at CCR in 1990 when Bill represented Yusef Salaam in the Central Park jogger case. Salaam, a Black 15-year-old, had been taken into detention along with four other teenagers and coercively interrogated by prosecutor Linda Fairstein. Even though Salaam's parents and older brother, an attorney, were outside, she would not let them be present at the interrogation. Eventually, Salaam and the other four teenagers confessed to attempted rape of the "Central Park jogger," 28-year-old Trisha Meili. And at that point the media were screaming for blood. Donald Trump took out a full-page ad in all four of the city's major newspapers calling for the five teenagers to be executed.

After the trial ended in conviction of the Central Park Five based on their coerced confessions, Salaam's family asked Bill Kunstler to represent Salaam for his appeal. Bill came to the Center and said, "I want you to be co-counsel with me on Yusef Salaam's appeal." The Center's lawyers, of course, were well aware of the long history of Black men being falsely accused of raping white women in the South. But still, they turned down Kunstler's request. Maybe it was because the Center did not really do criminal cases back then. Maybe they thought Salaam was guilty. Or maybe it was because of pressure from the feminist movement at the time. Whatever the reasons, it was not easy for the Center to refuse Bill, one of its founders.

Bill represented Salaam by himself on the appeal. He asked the judge to grant Salaam bail so the teenager could participate in the appeal process. The judge refused, and Bill called him a racist. The judge held Bill in contempt of court, which certainly didn't help Salaam. He got a 15-year prison term.

For his contempt case, Bill asked the Center to represent him. Once again, the Center turned him down. Morty Stavis, also a CCR co-founder, represented Bill on his own and eventually got most of the contempt charges dropped. Rather than being disbarred, Bill got a slap on the wrist.

Before he died in 1995, Bill wrote about this case in his autobiography. A few years later, not long after the events of 9/11, a convicted rapist named Matias Reyes confessed to the rape of the Central Park jogger and said he had acted alone. DNA evidence and other details confirmed his account. After spending many years in prison, Yusef Salaam and the other four were totally exonerated. (In 2014, New York City agreed to a settlement awarding the five a total of $41 million—one million for each year they spent in prison.)

I copied those two pages from Bill's autobiography and attached a cover note. "We are not making this mistake again," I wrote. "We just have to show courage right now. This is not a time to worry about funding, not a time to worry about hate. They are taking away the writ of habeas corpus, a key democratic right. The only difference between a police state and a non-police state is habeas corpus. In the police state, there is no limit to the executive's power to jail anyone he wants without court review. That's the definition of a police state."

I wasn't there for the actual debate at CCR. But the result was that the Center would take the first case under the Military Order that we could find. Already the government was "scooping up," as Defense Secretary Rumsfeld put it, thousands of men from Afghanistan, Pakistan, and other countries, imprisoning and torturing them. These were not necessarily men found on the battlefield. Many of them wore civilian clothes. Many were taken in midnight raids that did not involve the Taliban or al-Qaeda. And most of them were detained not by U.S. forces but by the Northern

Alliance, a loose coalition in a small corner of Afghanistan whom the Taliban had been fighting to oust.

The Northern Alliance, in conjunction with a bunch of warlords, eventually imprisoned as many as 35,000 or 40,000 people. The U.S. dropped leaflets all over the country offering rewards of anywhere from $50 to $5,000 to anyone who turned over members of Al-Qaeda or high-level Taliban officials. In Afghanistan, these were huge sums of money. Villagers and warlords started turning over their enemies or anyone they didn't like, or, finally, anyone they could pick up. Among those eventually released were taxi drivers and even a shepherd in his nineties.

Initially, the U.S. military sent many of these people to detention facilities in Bagram and Kandahar, Afghanistan, where the first interrogations and torture took place. In a process called rendition, U.S. authorities sent some detainees to third countries where local security services would use torture to obtain information or forced confessions.

But the U.S. government operated in secrecy, and we had no way of knowing any of this at the time.

From the moment I read about the Military Order, I had a strong feeling that those detained under it would end up, like the Haitians a decade before, at Guantánamo. On January 11, 2002, the government sent a plane with the first detainees from Bagram Prison in Afghanistan to Guantánamo Bay Naval Station in Cuba. Rumsfeld called them "the worst of the worst." General Richard B. Myers, chair of the Joint Chiefs of Staff, wrote that the detainees were "the kinds of people who would gnaw through hydraulic lines in the back of a C-17 to bring it down."

Many of them would eventually become our clients, but at the time we still didn't have the name of even a single prisoner. The government refused to allow us access to Guantánamo or to any further information.

We started by putting together a legal team and preparing for the first client. The original team included Hofstra law professor Eric Friedman, Jules Lobel who was living in Pittsburgh, David Cole, the Legal

Defense Fund, Ted Shaw, and Steven Watt. Prominent anti-death penalty lawyers Joe Margulies and Sandra Babcock from Minneapolis contacted me and arranged a conference call with several other lawyers, including the British lawyer Clive Stafford Smith, who ran the anti-death penalty group Reprieve in New Orleans. Margulies and Stafford Smith committed themselves and really began to work hard with us.

After doing initial research, Cole and others thought there was no chance for us to win. The legal precedents were simply against us. I couldn't disagree. "It may be completely hopeless," I told Cole, "but that never stopped us before. Sometimes you just have to fight for the principle."

We tried to reach out to other organizations, particularly the American Civil Liberties Union, but they refused to join us until a year later. They were afraid the cases would lose and create bad precedent. And they were also afraid there was too much anger in the country at the time and they would lose support. A representative of the ACLU offered these explanations at a panel at Columbia Law School that I was on. An Arab woman in the audience stood up and said, "Thank god for the Center. Because when we were being put into offshore prisons, the ACLU was saying they were afraid of setting bad precedents."

"The Center is an institution that doesn't worry too much about precedents," I said. "We see the law as a malleable instrument that has some flexibility. We believe it can effect social change, even with losses."

A week after the detainees arrived at Guantánamo, the name and a photo of the man who would become our first client appeared in the press. David Hicks, an Australian citizen who had converted to Islam and traveled to Afghanistan, had been captured unarmed in the back of a truck by a Northern Alliance warlord and sold for $5,000 to U.S. Special Forces. He had received paramilitary training in Afghanistan, but the menacing photo of him with a rocket-launcher on his shoulder was actually taken when he was fighting with U.S. forces in Kosovo.

GUANTÁNAMO

The first prisoners at Guantánamo had been allowed to send a single-page letter to their families via the International Red Cross. Hicks had written to his father, Terry, in Australia who contacted a lawyer in Adelaide named Stephen Kenny to represent him.

Kenny's name appeared in the press, and I called him. Kenny told me that on January 18, the American government had officially notified the Australian embassy that the U.S. military had taken Hicks to Guantánamo under the President's Military Order Number 1. Kenny had asked to visit his client David Hicks, but the Australian Embassy told him that was up to the Americans.

After talking further with Joe Margulies, Steve Kenny asked CCR to represent David Hicks in the federal habeas corpus suit we were preparing. Technically, Kenny was representing Hicks's father Terry because the Americans would not allow Kenny to see David himself. There is a provision of American law called "next friend," which is normally used in mental incapacitation cases, when a person is rendered incapable of choosing a lawyer. The next friend is someone who represents the best interests of the person. We decided CCR would represent Terry Hicks, the father, as the "next friend" on behalf of his son, David. It was an unusual arrangement, and we didn't know if the court would allow it.

Within a week, we got our next two clients. Following the same diplomatic procedure as it had with Hicks, the U.S. government had notified the British embassy that it was holding two British citizens at Guantánamo—Shafiq Rasul and Asif Iqbal, both from Tipton, England. The families of the two young men contacted the remarkable British lawyers Gareth Peirce and Clive Stafford Smith to represent them in England. An expert on torture, Peirce was the original lawyer for Bobby Sands and the imprisoned Irish Republican hunger strikers back in 1981. Stafford Smith was born in England but had gone to Columbia Law School and devoted his legal career to defending death penalty cases in Louisiana.

MOVING THE BAR

On January 21, we were still figuring out our Hicks strategy when I got a call from Stafford Smith. Speaking in his cultivated British accent, he said, "Michael, we have two clients from Guantánamo and they want to work with you."

Soon after that, CCR lawyer Steven Watt found the name of another Australian detainee, Mahmoud Habib, who'd been identified in the press. Habib's family received the same kind of official notification that the Hicks, Rasul, and Iqbal families had received. We wound up representing all these families in the U.S. as next friends.

We had long discussions about the best legal strategy to pursue. I saw what we were doing as essentially a petition seeking a writ of habeas corpus for the detainees. The right to habeas corpus is in the U.S. Constitution, but it has also been a hallmark of Anglo-American law dating back to the Magna Carta in 1215. It was re-enforced and officially passed into British law in 1679, when some British officials were sending prisoners to remote islands and military bases to prevent any judicial inquiry into their imprisonment. Parliament passed the Habeas Corpus Act to prohibit this practice of offshore penal colonies beyond the reach of the law—precisely the practice the Bush administration had revived.

The administration had labeled the detainees with the newly invented term "enemy combatants," not the more traditional "prisoners of war." The entire world is a battlefield, the administration argued, and all people detained in that battlefield are "enemy combatants" because they are fighting against the United States. According to the administration, they were foreigners being held on land that technically belonged to Cuba. Therefore, they had no rights to a hearing or judicial review or representation. Furthermore, they could be held beyond the end of the war in Afghanistan, beyond the end of the war in Iraq, until the end of the war on terrorism—which could go on forever.

In my view, this was nothing short of an outrageous assault on the Magna Carta and the most fundamental rights guaranteed by our justice system. For legal precedents, the administration relied on two primary cases. The first, a famous World War II case called *Ex Parte Quirin*, involved German saboteurs who had sneaked into the United States supposedly to commit acts of sabotage. A military tribunal tried and convicted them, and some were immediately executed. Others were released at the end of the war. The U.S. Supreme Court upheld the military tribunals and executions and said the German prisoners had no rights to further judicial review in U.S. courts.

But we felt the *Quirin* case shouldn't apply to the Guantánamo prisoners. In that case, two nation-states were in a declared war, and the defendants were spies or saboteurs working directly for the German enemy. And even they got a trial—not one acceptable today, but at least a trial. They were not simply detained forever without any hearing. If any of the Guantánamo detainees proved to be from the Taliban army, we believed they should be treated as POWs, not as enemy combatants (a legally meaningless term), and the Geneva Conventions should apply to them.

The second precedent the government relied on was *Johnson v. Eisentrager.* This was a 1950 Supreme Court case involving 27 Germans who had been tried by a U.S. military commission for war crimes in China after Germany had surrendered at the end of World War II. Twenty-one of them were convicted and imprisoned in Germany. One of them filed a writ of habeas corpus. The U.S. Supreme Court rejected the petition, ruling that no enemy prisoner of war has a right to a writ of habeas corpus in an American court if he is outside the United States. In our case, the government was arguing that since Guantánamo was outside the country, U.S. courts had no jurisdiction.

We didn't actually think we would win, but there were differences between the *Eisentrager* prisoners and the detainees at Guantánamo. First, in *Eisentrager*, there was a military trial and the writ of habeas was requested in the context of hostilities. Second, in *Eisentrager*, the aliens convicted of war crimes were from an enemy nation in a formally declared war. Our clients were citizens of friendly nations and hadn't been charged with or convicted of anything.

Still, we knew *Eisentrager* was a formidable obstacle, and we wanted to find another way to deal with it. So we based part of our strategy on the Alien Tort Statute, which permitted suits by aliens for violations of fundamental rights protected by international law. The statute gave us a separate jurisdictional basis that did not depend on habeas. My view was that under international law the Guantánamo prisoners were being held by arbitrary detention—detention without any legal process, charges, or trial. We believed that even if the Constitution might not apply at Guantánamo, customary international law protected the detainees.

The Geneva Conventions of 1949 required prisoner of war hearings under the Third Convention. I thought the detainees should be treated as POWs under Article IV. In addition, both the International Covenant on Civil and Political Rights and customary international law barred arbitrary detention. We decided to file three counts of our complaint under the Alien Tort Statute, the Geneva Conventions, and ICCPR. Then we decided to make a number of claims under the due process clause.

On February 7, 2002, the president issued a new executive order saying the Geneva Conventions do not apply to al-Qaeda. According to the Order, they did apply to the Taliban—except if there was a military necessity, in which case they would not.

I was appalled. Bush was saying, "We're going to treat prisoners humanely, except when military necessity requires otherwise." No matter how Bush's lawyers twisted the law to his liking in their memos, the fact remains that the Geneva Conventions do not permit torture. There are no exceptions—even for so-called "military necessity."

The Order struck me as the equivalent of a war crime, and I spoke out about it. To his credit, Secretary of State Colin Powell dissented from the president on this issue. But he was fighting a losing battle—and so was I. Even friends doubted my position. One called and said, "Michael, are you out of your mind? How can Geneva apply to people who aren't wearing uniforms?"

"Well, maybe they're not POWs," I said. "But they need to have a hearing to determine that. And if they are found not to be POWs, then they are protected under the Fourth Convention. And if not, they are protected under Common Article 3, a bill of rights which applies to everyone."

My argument was that every human being must have a status under law. Someone who has no legal status or no rights is not a human being. That person is, in effect, nothing—and can be treated that way.

Not long before we were ready to file our suit, Tom Wilner from the Washington office of the prestigious Wall Street law firm of Shearman & Sterling called me and asked to meet. The wealthy families of 12 Kuwaiti young men being held at Guantánamo had hired Wilner to represent them. Several of the families had assembled files proving that their sons had long histories of doing charitable work in Muslim countries. One of them was a 40-year-old vice-president of Kuwait Airlines. While they were doing their humanitarian aid work, someone from Pakistan had turned them over to U.S. forces for a bounty.

Wilner had gone to Kuwait and during his research he found out we at CCR were working on our case. Now back in Washington, he wanted to talk strategy. So Clive, Joe, and I traveled to the nation's capital. Eric Freedman, who knows habeas law cold, joined us.

Walking into Shearman & Sterling's fancy building, we all felt scruffy. It's one of the biggest international law firms, based in New York and Washington, with more than 200 lawyers handling primarily financial and banking issues. The place reeked of money—huge, tastefully decorated offices, marble everywhere, views down Pennsylvania Avenue to the White House.

Everyone wore elegant, conspicuously expensive, hand-tailored suits.

MOVING THE BAR

We didn't know what to expect. Tom, a onetime high school wrestling champion now in his 50s, greeted us. He was bald with a big prominent forehead and dark bushy eyebrows. A quintessential insider who grew up in Washington, Tom knew everybody in the power circles down there. He'd graduated from St. Albans, the same school where Al Gore had gone. Among his classmates were Don Graham, publisher of the *Washington Post*, and several U.S. senators' sons. David Brinkley, Brit Hume, and many other big-name journalists in the capital were his personal friends.

Tom and his colleagues treated us graciously. Though they were clearly very smart, they'd never filed a habeas case and knew very little about the Alien Tort Statute. We had a lot of experience with both, so they wanted to hear how we were approaching our case. They particularly wanted to know what Harold Koh at Yale thought, and we called Koh right there from the room.

Then we talked about *Eisentrager*. "We are not going to make this a habeas case," Tom said. "We're just going to call it a civil action lawsuit. We are not going to ask for the release of our clients. We're going to ask to get them lawyers and get them into a court."

"Tom, it's not going to work," I said. "The court will consider it a habeas action no matter what you label it."

But he was stubborn about this. His entire petition, ultimately filed in May 2002 as *Al Odah v. United States,* ended up saying nothing about habeas. This strategy wasn't necessarily wrong, and we were going to have habeas in our petition, so it didn't make much difference. But by the end of that first meeting we decided to file our suits separately and consolidate them later.

Before we filed, we made one other strategic decision. Though David Hicks was our first client, we chose not to lead with his name. The photo in the newspaper that showed Hicks with a missile launcher on his shoulders sent the wrong message. Instead, we called the case *Rasul v. Bush.*

We were licensed to practice in New York, so we needed a local D.C. lawyer to file the case for us. The atmosphere was so poisoned with anxiety and fear that at first we couldn't find a single lawyer willing to do it. Eventually, Barry Boss, a very fine criminal attorney, agreed to work with us.

On February 19, 2002, Boss filed the papers. Joe Margulies and I were listed as the lawyers for Hicks, with Clive Stafford Smith and Gareth Peirce representing Rasul and Iqbal. By June 26, when the case was argued before District Court Judge Colleen Kollar-Kotelly, *Rasul* had been consolidated with Tom Wilner's case, *Al Odah v. United States,* and a third case, *Habib v. Bush,* in which Joe Margulies and CCR represented the Australian, Mahmoud Habib, who had been sent to Egypt and tortured before ending up in Guantánamo.

Our lead counsel Joe Margulies and Tom Wilner shared the oral argument before Judge Kollar-Kotelly in a nearly empty courtroom. Tom cited *Ralpho v. Bell,* a very good precedent from the D.C. Circuit Court about Micronesia in the Mariana Islands, which was a trust territory of the U.S. The circuit court's unanimous decision 20 years before affirmed that the residents of Micronesia had rights under the U.S. Constitution, even though Micronesia was not a U.S. territory and the U.S. did not have sovereignty.

But it was like talking to a wall. We were arguing for the rights of "terrorists" who supposedly attacked the U.S. on 9/11 and asking a district court judge to go against *Eisentrager.* In a different time there might have been a shot at that. But not in the current environment of fear and hysteria.

Judge Kollar-Kotelly ruled against us on every important point. She saw the word "sovereignty" in *Eisentrager* and said, "Well, the U.S. government is not sovereign over Guantánamo, so the prisoners have no right to habeas." She did not agree with our arguments based on the Alien Tort Statute or the Geneva Conventions either. And she didn't buy

Tom's Micronesia precedent or his claim that all his clients were asking for was a lawyer.

The judge's opinion was totally predictable. We would have been shocked to win at this level. We knew we had to get to the Supreme Court eventually, so we wanted to proceed as rapidly as we could. We immediately started working on our briefs for the District of Columbia Circuit Court of Appeals.

Our briefs tried to undercut the thinking of Judge Kollar-Kotelly. We argued that there are more than two ways to read *Eisentrager*. The question was whether habeas applied only in sovereign territory of the United States, or if it applied in any place where the United States exercised real control. We argued that "sovereignty" was simply an imprecise term. In *Eisentrager,* sometimes the word "sovereignty" is used, and sometimes "territory" is used. Our position was that *Eisentrager* was not just talking about technical sovereignty, but about real control. Control was the sine qua non and the equivalent of U.S. territory.

The D.C. Circuit Court consisted of three judges—A. Raymond Randolph, Merrick Garland, and Stephen Williams. Tom Wilner knew two of them very well. He'd been good friends with Randolph at University of Pennsylvania Law School. Tom described him as "brilliant, a right-wing conservative, and a hard-ass guy." And Garland had worked as a lawyer under Tom's supervision at the prestigious Washington law firm of Arnold & Porter. (In 2016 President Barack Obama nominated Garland to the U.S. Supreme Court, but the Republican Senate refused to give him a hearing and the nomination died.)

On December 2, 2002, Joe and Tom presented our oral arguments to the D.C. Circuit Court. It went terribly. Each of them had five minutes, not nearly enough for such complicated cases. I watched helplessly from the courtroom as Randolph peppered Joe and Tom with questions about the Alien Tort Statute and two D.C. circuit cases for which Randolph himself had written the court's opinions, relying on *Eisentrager*.

"How can aliens sue for something like arbitrary detention when American citizens cannot?" Randolph kept asking. Joe and Tom did their best, but not having argued any cases before under the Alien Tort Statute, they didn't have an answer. There is an answer, which is that there is a separate statute now that allows U.S. citizens to do what the Alien Tort Statute does. I was aware of this, but I was stuck in the audience and couldn't say anything.

The oral argument was an exercise in futility. This hostile court was not going to side with us. And it didn't. In March 2003 the circuit court's decision affirmed the district court's ruling and basically rejected all our arguments.

There was never any question that we would appeal to the Supreme Court, though I must admit I was pessimistic about our chances. In the context of *Eisentrager* and the so-called "war on terror," we figured we had about a 10 percent shot at winning. But we weren't going to avoid the Supreme Court for fear of creating bad precedent.

Joe, Tom, and I consulted with three law professors—Tony Amsterdam, Doug Cassel, and Eric Freedman—to come up with a strategy to get the Supreme Court to grant *certiorari* and accept our case for review. We decided the key was going to be the swing voters, Justices Sandra Day O'Connor and Anthony Kennedy. Based on research of their previous decisions, we thought the issue that would appeal to them was basic separation of powers. In our brief we emphasized that if the government's position was accepted, the court would be handing over to the executive the unilateral power to manipulate when the judiciary can and cannot review a case. That would strip the court of both its power and its responsibility and violate the basic separation of powers established by the Constitution.

Wilner came up with another novel argument after a producer from CBS's *60 Minutes* told him that iguanas were protected on the base under the Endangered Species Act. It was true. Anyone who harms an iguana at Guantánamo can be prosecuted. So iguanas are safe at Guantánamo, but if they wander off the base anywhere else in Cuba, they get eaten. "It struck me," said Tom. "Here the government was arguing that the detainees down there were not protected by U.S. law, but the iguanas were." He noted this in his brief for *certiorari*. It had an impact because later, at the Supreme Court oral argument, Justice David Souter mentioned it in one of his questions from the bench.

The other issue that came up when we wrote our briefs was whether to assert a claim for jurisdiction not just under the habeas statute, but under the Alien Tort Statute. Harold Koh reviewed our brief and urged us not to raise the issue. He thought it would be a bad test of the Alien Tort Statute and could jeopardize future claims under it. Normally, I would have included it. But because Harold and I were so close and we didn't want to cause a split in our legal team, we decided not to include the claim. Tom Wilner, however, insisted on putting it in his brief.

The second part of our strategy for getting *certiorari* involved gathering *amicus curiae* briefs from key supporters. Doug Cassel headed the effort and got eight *amicus* briefs from former federal judges, U.S. diplomats (including former Secretary of State William Rogers), top U.S. military officers, American prisoners of war and, perhaps most important, from Fred Korematsu who, in a landmark lawsuit, had challenged the U.S. government's internment during World War II of Japanese-Americans and anyone of Japanese descent. Korematsu lost his case in 1944 when the Supreme Court sided with the government.

However, as Martin Luther King, Jr. once said, "The arc of the moral universe is long, but it bends toward justice." And so, over the years, the prevailing view of Americans toward Japanese internment changed and bent toward justice. In 1983, a U.S. district court overturned Korematsu's conviction for evading internment when he proved that the government had suppressed a report of the Office of Naval Intelligence indicating that no evidence existed that Japanese Americans were acting as spies.

GUANTÁNAMO

Korematsu's 28-page brief, written with law professor Geoffrey Stone in support of our case, showed a pattern of unnecessary executive branch curtailment of civil liberties during wartime and pointed out the parallels between Japanese internment during World War II and the plight of Guantánamo prisoners after 9/11. Korematsu's moral authority proved to be very powerful. In his book *Engines of Liberty*, David Cole makes the case that this *amicus* brief was the key piece of our strategy to win *certiorari*. Without a doubt it was very important.

Meanwhile, in the summer of 2003, the military commissions created under the Presidential Military Order of November 13, 2001 were finally starting. CCR still had only five clients—Hicks and Habib from Australia and Rasul, Iqbal, and Ahmed from England. And Tom Wilner had the 12 Kuwaitis. By this time, they and the other detainees had been at Guantánamo for a year and a half.

David Hicks was one of the first to be charged before a military commission. A small group of military lawyers—Charlie Swift, Michael Mori, Mark Bridges, Sharon Shaffer, and Philip Sunde—had been appointed to represent Hicks and our other clients. Clive Stafford Smith, who had tried approximately 200 death penalty cases in the South, took the lead and started working on a strategic handbook about how to deal with military commissions. He urged us at CCR to meet with the military commission lawyers appointed to defend our clients and to explain that these were not just typical trials. It was critical that we get civilian counsel involved and use every tool at our disposal, including publicity.

Clive, Joe, Tom, and I met for several hours with the five military lawyers at the Pentagon in Washington. I was nervous. Meeting with the military is not what I normally do, and I was particularly distrustful because these were not reserves. They were career military lawyers.

But to my surprise, they turned out to be excellent, courageous lawyers. They brought us into a room and whispered to us because they didn't want their boss, a political appointee who reported directly to Donald Rumsfeld, to hear what we were saying. They knew that the military commissions were being controlled by the politicians in Washington. A couple of them said that from the very beginning they were appalled by the inherent unfairness of the commissions.

At that first meeting we discussed Hicks. The government chose Hicks to go first because he was Australian and they could talk to him in English. They hadn't charged him yet, but supposedly they had a confession from him and wanted him to accept a plea bargain of 20 years. The military defense lawyers thought this was crazy. We decided we needed to get an outside civilian criminal lawyer involved. Josh Dratel, a trial lawyer who handled many of the big terrorist cases in New York City, took the case on, along with us.

The government didn't charge Hicks until nine months later. He refused the plea bargain. Ultimately the military commission sentenced him to time served and nine months for "providing material support to terrorism." He ended up serving six of those months in an Australian prison and then was released. Eight years later, in 2015, a U.S. Military Review Board overturned the conviction against David Hicks.

While we waited to hear whether the Supreme Court would accept *Rasul* for review, we launched a solidarity campaign led in large part by Clive Stafford Smith. Having lots of experience with his death-penalty work, Clive understood the importance of publicity in any trial. Over the next two years, I spent much of my time speaking at forums around the country organized by the Guantánamo Testimonials Project and doing media interviews about the plight of Guantánamo's prisoners.

In late summer of 2003, after hearing several of these interviews on the radio, my good friend Ellen Ray, co-editor of *CovertAction Quarterly*, and Margo Baldwin, publisher of Chelsea Green Publishing, asked me to participate in another project to get the facts about Guantánamo out to the public.

GUANTÁNAMO

Ellen read and analyzed my files and then forced me to sit down for an extensive interview. After transcribing the tapes, Ellen, her husband Bill Schaap, and I edited them down into a simple, accessible question-and-answer format. We covered the history of Guantánamo, the Bush administration's invention of the term "enemy combatant," the Geneva Conventions against torture, the administration's use of rendition, the unreliability of false confessions obtained under torture, and much more. Then we added an appendix of key documents, including the Military Order of November 13, 2001, Article V of the Geneva Convention, and a letter from released British detainees Shafiq Rasul and Asif Iqbal to the Senate Armed Services Committee. The result was the short book *Guantánamo: What the World Should Know*, by Ellen Ray and me, published by Chelsea Green.

Another creative effort to inform the public was CCR and Culture Project's production of *Guantánamo: Honor Bound to Defend Freedom*, a deeply moving documentary play about the experiences of four detainees. Originally staged in London and then moved to New York and San Francisco, it was written by British journalists Victoria Brittain and Gillian Slovo, based on actual testimony and interviews with the detainees and their families, lawyers, and politicians. Every night lawyers from CCR, including myself, stayed at the Bleecker Theater after the play to lead a discussion and answer questions from the audience. And on some evenings well-known guests like the South African Nobel Peace Prize winner Bishop Desmond Tutu and actors Tim Robbins and Danny Glover would join the cast.

I'll never forget one night when the father of Moazzam Begg, one of the detainees featured in the play, appeared in the audience. A British Pakistani, the younger Begg had been arrested at his home in Pakistan and held first at Bagram in Afghanistan and then at Guantánamo for three years. As a father of two children, I couldn't imagine the pain that Moazzam's father was feeling as he watched the real-life testimony about his son's cruel and humiliating torture.

As part of its solidarity effort, CCR also sponsored a rally at Cooper Union featuring the renowned British actors Vanessa and Corin Redgrave. They had started a campaign to close Guantánamo and had brought attention to the plight of British citizens imprisoned there. British public opinion turned against the detainments when the Bush administration announced that two British citizens, Feroz Abbasi and Moazzam Begg, were going to be tried by U.S. military commissions. It enraged the British public that their citizens could be tried at Guantánamo by a secret military tribunal and could even face the death penalty. Lord Steyn, a respected retired British Law Lord, called Guantánamo "a monstrous failure of justice" and "a hellhole of utter lawlessness."

The public pressure had an effect. Bush met with British Prime Minister Tony Blair and agreed to suspend the proceedings against Begg and Abbasi. They, along with two other British citizens, were finally released more than a year later. This confirmed my view that grassroots organizing and solidarity campaigns always play a crucial role in any legal case.

On November 10, 2003, the Supreme Court announced that it would grant *certiorari* and hear the three cases (*Rasul v. Bush, Al Odah v. U.S,.* and *Habib v. Bush*) now combined and known as *Rasul v. Bush*. When I look in retrospect at why the justices took the case, I believe they viewed it as an executive-detention case, not as a prisoner-of-war case. What concerned them most, I suspect, was precisely what had bothered us from the beginning: this was not a conventional war. People were being rounded up and imprisoned indefinitely in a "war" that had no ending. When you have detainees who might be held forever, you simply have to give them some kind of due process.

CCR lawyer Barbara Olshansky did the bulk of the writing of our brief for *Rasul*, though Joe Margulies and I are also listed as co-authors. Tom Wilner wrote a separate brief for *Al Odah*. More than a dozen *amicus* briefs came from many of the same groups who had supported us in our appeal for *certiorari*. But one new *amicus* brief was historic: in January 2004, 175 members of the United Kingdom's Parliament filed a brief in support of the British citizen Shafiq Rasul. Never before had members of Parliament filed a brief in the U.S. Supreme Court.

With international pressure mounting, President Bush decided in March 2004 to transfer five of the British detainees, including our Tipton Three clients—Rasul, Iqbal, and Ahmed—to the United Kingdom before the U.S. Supreme Court heard the case. Within 24 hours, British authorities cleared them of all charges and released them.

That same month, I went to a three-day conference at Oxford, England featuring a series of lectures on the challenges of legal representation of Muslim clients. Clive Stafford Smith had organized it, and about 20 lawyers attended, including the military lawyers from Guantánamo. We learned a lot about Wahhabism and what we could expect when representing Muslims who'd been confined, but we also spent time drinking, chatting, and building the relationship between military and civilian lawyers.

While at the Oxford conference, I met our clients, the Tipton Three, for the first time. Clive and Gareth Peirce, their British lawyers, introduced us, and I was floored. Contradicting all media stereotypes, there before me were three personable, respectful young men. One of them was a bit shy and withdrawn. Raised in a Muslim community in Britain, they all had long beards. They seemed quite British, laughing and joking even though they had just endured an unspeakable two and a half years of imprisonment. They reminded me of my own kids—young, innocent, earnest.

We spent two or three hours together—our first personal contact with Guantánamo detainees. They sat and told us their story. The three had gone to the same school and were friends in Tipton. In October 2001, when they traveled together to Pakistan, Rasul was 24 years old. Iqbal and Ahmed were both 20. Rasul said he went to Pakistan to visit relatives, explore his culture, and pursue his computer studies. Iqbal had gone to Pakistan, intending to marry a woman from his father's village. And Ahmed said he went to attend his friend Iqbal's wedding.

Not long before the wedding was to take place, the three left the village on a short trip to Northern Afghanistan and on November 28, fighters loyal to a local war lord, General Rashid Dostum, took them prisoner. Dostum and other war lords routinely picked up foreigners to sell to American forces. Dostum held them and approximately 200 others in shipping containers. When they complained that they were suffocating, Dostum's soldiers fired shots randomly into the containers, killing several people and wounding Iqbal in the arm. Dostum sent the prisoners to Sheberghan Prison in Northern Afghanistan, where U.S. soldiers questioned them as they kneeled with guns held to their heads.

Of the 200 prisoners, nearly 180 died from heat, starvation and the gunshots, but the three young men from Tipton somehow survived. For nearly a month, they endured torture and horrifying conditions at Sheberghan. In December 2001, Dostum sold them to the American forces, who flew them to Kandahar, where they slept in tents on the freezing ground, were fed only two biscuits a day, and underwent interrogations at gunpoint.

In a letter to the Senate Armed Services Committee, Rasul and Iqbal reported what happened next:

"We were kicked and beaten. They kept us in 'three-piece suits' made up of a body belt with a chain down to leg irons and hand shackles attached. Before we boarded the plane to Guantánamo, they dressed us in hoods, earmuffs, painted-out goggles, and surgical masks so we were completely disoriented. On the plane, they chained us to the floor without access to a toilet for the 22-hour flight."

After landing at Guantánamo in January 2002, the young men were kept in cages six feet by six feet, with a hole-in-the ground toilet, a sink with running water, and a bunk with a mattress. They stayed in their cages 24 hours per day, except for two minutes a week to take a shower. Guards paced outside constantly, and the powerful floodlights surrounding the camp never dimmed. In the first few weeks they could not exercise at all. "During the day we were forced to sit in the cell in total silence," said Iqbal. "We couldn't lie down. We couldn't lean on the wire fence or stand up and walk around the cage."

Iqbal explained that the guards "were told that we would kill them with our toothbrushes at the first opportunity, that we were all members of al-Qaeda, and that we had killed women and children indiscriminately." As a result, the guards treated the inmates brutally, verbally and physically abusing them, and showed disrespect for Islam, often kicking the Koran or throwing it into the toilet.

When taken to interrogation rooms, the inmates wore shackles. "Our interrogations in Guantánamo," Rasul and Iqbal said, "were conducted with us chained to the floor for hours on end in circumstances so prolonged that it was practice to have plastic chairs for the interrogators that could be easily hosed off because prisoners would be forced to urinate during the course of them and were not allowed to go to the toilet."

During interrogations, guards "short shackled" them—forcing them to squat without a chair with their hands chained between their legs and to the floor. "If we fell over," they said, "the chains would cut into our hands. We would be left in this position for hours before an interrogation, during the interrogations (which could last as long as 12 hours), and sometimes for hours while the interrogators left the room. The air conditioning was turned up so high that within minutes we would be freezing. There was strobe lighting and loud music played that was itself a form of torture. Sometimes dogs were brought in to frighten us. We were not fed all the time that we were there, and when we were returned to our cells, we would not be fed that day."

MOVING THE BAR

The interrogators showed Rasul a grainy video from August 2000 in which Osama bin Laden gave a talk to about 40 men in an open field in Afghanistan. Mohamed Atta, later one of the 9/11 plane hijackers, was supposedly identifiable in the video. Insisting that the young men from Tipton were in the video and had prior knowledge of the 9/11 attacks, the interrogators pointed at figures in still photos that didn't remotely resemble the young men.

"That's you in the picture," one adamant interrogator kept saying. "I've put detainees here in isolation for 12 months and eventually they've broken. You might as well admit it now so that you don't have to stay in isolation."

"No, no, we were in England at that time," the young detainees answered repeatedly. Rasul told the interrogators that they could check the records of the university where he was enrolled then, and also of Curry's electronics store where he worked at the time. Iqbal told them that "during the relevant period, I had been in trouble with the police in England. I said I could get ten policemen who could be witnesses, if necessary. I told him that I had court records."

But the interrogations continued unabated. Ahmed said that each of the three was interrogated at least 100 times. "After three months in solitary confinement under harsh conditions and repeated interrogations, we finally agreed to confess," they said.

"The reason I did this," explained Rasul, the only one who was actually shown the video, "was because of the previous five or six weeks of being held in isolation and being taken to interrogation for hours on end, short shackled, and being treated that way. I was going out of my mind and didn't know what was going on. I was desperate for it to end and therefore eventually I just gave in and admitted to being in the video."

Their coerced confessions were false, of course, and in September 2002, an agent from Britain's intelligence agency, MI5, arrived at Guantánamo with documentary evidence proving that, just as the detainees had told their interrogators, they were not in Afghanistan, but were living and working in England at the time the video was made.

Still, the nightmare for Rasul, Iqbal, and Ahmed did not end. The torture continued for them and the others imprisoned at Guantánamo. "Soldiers told us personally of going into cells and conducting beatings with metal bars.... Soldiers told us 'we can do anything we want.' We ourselves witnessed a number of brutal assaults upon prisoners. One, in April 2002, was of Juma al-Dossary from Bahrain, a man who had become psychiatrically disturbed, who was lying on the floor of his cage immediately near to us when a group of eight or nine guards known as the ERF Team (Extreme Reaction Force) entered his cage. We saw them severely assault him. They stamped on his neck, kicked him in the stomach even though he had metal rods there as a result of an operation, and they picked up his head and smashed his face into the floor. One female officer was ordered to go into the cell and kick him and beat him, which she did, in his stomach....

"Sometimes detainees would be taken to the interrogation room day after day and kept short-shackled without interrogation ever happening, sometimes for weeks on end. We received distressed reports from other detainees of their being taken to the interrogation room, left naked and chained to the floor, and of women being brought into the room who would inappropriately provoke and indeed molest them. It was completely clear to all the detainees that this was happening to particularly vulnerable prisoners, especially those who had come from the strictest of Islamic backgrounds."

Ahmed said that because he was young and strong he could deal with the physical torture—the routine beatings, the lack of decent food, natural light, exercise or adequate medical treatment. But after 2003 when General Geoffrey Miller took command of Guantánamo, the torture became more psychological, and that was more difficult. Isolation, filthy conditions, forced sleep deprivation up to 180 hours at a time, the repetition of being asked the same questions hundreds of times, withdrawal of reading material, exposure to extreme temperatures, the humiliation of forced nudity in front of provocative women, constant verbal threats from guards and interrogators, forced injections, endless hours of being short-shackled in stress position with no access to a toilet, the horror of not knowing where they were or why or what they were charged with, the inevitable hopelessness that comes when no end is in sight—all these and more were part of the psychological torture designed to "break" the prisoners.

"During the whole time that we were in Guantánamo, we were at a high level of fear," said Rasul. "At the beginning we were terrified that we might be killed at any minute. The guards would say to us 'We could kill you at any time. Nobody knows you're here. All they know is that you're missing and we could kill you—and no one would know.' After time passed, that level of fear came down somewhat but never vanished. It was always there."

Rasul, Iqbal, and Ahmed said that many prisoners had become mentally ill and more than 30 had attempted suicide, some repeatedly. A very high percentage had been put on the antidepressant Prozac or other psychotropic drugs. "For at least 50, so far as we are aware, their behavior is so disturbed as to show they are no longer capable of rational thought," said Rasul and Iqbal.

Just before their release, the three prisoners said that U.S. intelligence officials asked them to sign a confession and become informants on the activities of the Muslim community back in England. The U.S. officials offered good housing and other gifts as a reward, but all three prisoners refused.

The night I met the Tipton Three was a real eye-opener for me. I didn't know much about U.S. torture techniques at the time. I believed most of what the three told us, though I thought to myself that the sexual harassment of religious Muslims sounded exaggerated. Later, Defense

Secretary Rumsfeld's "special interrogation plan" memo was made public. The Tipton Three obviously did not know what Rumsfeld had said in 2002 when he'd written it. But what they reported matched almost exactly with every one of the 17 techniques that Rumsfeld suggested, including sexual humiliation. I knew then that they were telling the complete truth.

The Supreme Court scheduled the oral argument for *Rasul v. Bush* for April 20, 2004. It took us a long time to prepare. Joe, Tom, and I discussed who should present our oral argument. Tony Amsterdam would have been the most brilliant, but by that time he had stopped arguing before the court.

Some in our community thought it would help us to have a straight, conservative lawyer argue the case. I didn't necessarily agree. The Center had chosen Bill Kunstler to argue two flag cases before the court, and he won both of them, five to four. It wouldn't have changed the outcome if Archibald Cox or one of the conservative solicitors general had argued these cases.

But Joe and Tom wanted a respected conservative, and they suggested John Gibbons, a Nixon appointee to the Third Circuit Court of Appeals. Retired for more than a decade, Gibbons had a reputation as a Republican judge who was tough on criminal defendants. But since his retirement, he had defended a number of death-row inmates and argued successfully before the Supreme Court on behalf of one.

From a packed gallery, I watched Judge Gibbons present our oral argument before the court. I won't say it went off without a hitch, but there was nothing embarrassing, no big gaffes. The key question was whether we should argue narrowly that Guantánamo is essentially U.S. sovereign territory since the U.S. has complete control there and that therefore habeas applies. Or, should we argue more broadly that habeas extends to everywhere a person is in U.S. custody? During our preparations, we had knockdown arguments about this. I insisted that we argue for the second, extended habeas jurisdiction.

My view was that if we argued more narrowly, that could limit the kinds of cases the court would review in the future. For example, what if a detainee is tortured in an Afghani prison under U.S. control? Under the more narrow view of habeas jurisdiction, the court would not consider the case because the U.S. does not have sovereignty in Afghanistan. But under the extended view of habeas jurisdiction, the court could consider it.

During the Supreme Court oral argument, one of the justices asked Gibbons, "What if Saddam Hussein is pulled out of a foxhole on the battlefield? Would the court have habeas jurisdiction?" My answer was that the court does have jurisdiction, but it may choose not to exercise it when a prisoner is detained on the battlefield. Others on our team thought I was crazy to insist on this, but Tony Amsterdam convinced them. And so, Gibbons presented this argument to the court.

The second issue the court asked about was, once jurisdiction is established, what happens at the detainee's habeas hearing? What rights does the prisoner have? Gibbons gave them the answer that Tony Amsterdam had developed. "We don't know that," he said. "Right now, this court is determining if there is jurisdiction to hear a habeas petition from Guantánamo. The rights will be determined later."

In his oral argument, Judge Gibbons emphasized that the heart of the case was "the authority of the federal courts to uphold the rule of law. Respondents [the Bush administration] assert that their actions are absolutely immune from judicial examination whenever they elect to detain foreign nationals outside our borders. Under this theory, neither the length of the detention, the conditions of their confinement, nor the fact that they have been wrongfully detained makes the slightest difference. Respondents would create a lawless enclave insulating the executive branch from any judicial scrutiny now or in the future."

The oral argument lasted just a half hour. Afterwards, the legal teams for *Rasul* and *Al Odah* gathered to share a drink. I got up on a table and offered a toast, thanking everyone who had worked so hard to get us this far. Based on the questions the justices had asked, we felt pretty good about our chances. But we had to wait for their decision.

The issue of torture didn't really figure in the oral argument before the court in *Rasul*. But two other related cases, *Hamdi v. Rumsfeld* and *Rumsfeld v. Padilla,* came before the court eight days later on April 28, 2004. Both involved American citizens held indefinitely and without charges in U.S. military prisons as "enemy combatants." The cases asserted the prisoners' rights to legal representation and a fair hearing in a U.S. court.

Deputy Solicitor General Paul Clement argued for the government in both cases. Halfway through the *Padilla* argument, Justice Ruth Bader Ginsburg asked Clement what the court could do if the executive ordered the torture of a prisoner. Clement answered that the military would court-martial anyone who tortured "a harmless, detained enemy combatant" and that the Supreme Court had no authority to intervene in such a situation. Ginsburg then asked, "Suppose the executive says mild torture will help get this information...It's an executive command. Some systems do that to get information."

"Well, our executive doesn't," Clement replied. "And I think the fact that executive discretion in a war situation can be abused is not a good and sufficient reason for judicial micro-management in overseeing of that authority. You have to recognize that in situations where there is a war, where the government is on a war footing, that you have to trust the executive." His message was clear: you have to trust the president.

But within hours of Deputy Solicitor General Clement's smug denial that the administration would ever order torture, CBS's national network program *60 Minutes* broadcast shocking photos it had obtained from Abu Ghraib prison in Baghdad. Within days *The New Yorker* and *Washington*

Post published more images. The photos showed naked prisoners piled on top of each other, a U.S. soldier dragging a naked prisoner on the floor by a dog leash, prisoners forced to dress in women's underwear, naked, hooded prisoners forced to sodomize each other, an electrically wired prisoner forced to stand on a box over water with arms spread out as if in a crucifixion, vicious dogs lunging at helpless prisoners, a smiling U.S. servicewoman posing with a dead body packed in ice, and an American serviceman in blue gloves beating up several handcuffed prisoners lying on the ground. And much, much more.

For the next two months, as the court considered *Rasul* and the other cases, more evidence of torture and humiliation of Abu Ghraib prisoners kept appearing. The connection with Guantánamo was clear. The commander of Guantánamo, Major General Geoffrey Miller, had been brought in to supervise "enhanced interrogation" at Abu Ghraib and had put into effect the same kinds of torture techniques he had used at Guantánamo.

A picture is worth a thousand words. The government's lame denials could not compete with the power of those images. The whole world was witnessing mass torture. How could the court avoid the issue? After the oral arguments I thought we were going to win *Rasul* in any event, but the Abu Ghraib photos insured our victory.

On June 28, 2004, I was in Greece on a much-needed family vacation. The Guantánamo cases had been stressful, and I'd always loved archaeology, so there we were on a tiny island off Crete on an archaeological dig. My son Jake, then 16, had just dug up the most important archaeological find of the year—a six-inch Minoan trident, the only Bronze Age trident ever found in the East Aegean. We were celebrating Jake's good luck when the news of the court's ruling in *Rasul* arrived.

I was so excited I almost dropped the newspaper. In a six-to-three decision, the justices held that the courts had jurisdiction to hear petitions for writs of habeas corpus from the Guantánamo detainees. For me, the best part of the opinion was the majority's discussion of King John at Runnymede in the year 1215 and the importance of the Magna Carta as the basis for habeas corpus. This was really the core of the case: could the executive imprison people at will without any court review? The court gave a resounding no. The justices said, in effect, "We are going to take jurisdiction. We want this government to know that the courts are operative when it comes to offshore detentions."

The majority opinion, written by Justice John Paul Stevens, rejected the *Eisentrager* argument. It said that the habeas statute on its face has no geographical limit—and even if it did, Guantánamo would fit within it. And to my amazement, the court said there was jurisdiction not only under the habeas statute, but also under the Alien Tort Statute 1350, which Tom had insisted on including in his brief.

This was an extraordinary win. And the court re-enforced it on the same day when it also ruled in *Hamdi v. Rumsfeld* that a U.S. citizen held as an "enemy combatant" has a constitutional right to defend himself in a fair hearing.

We were all thrilled. The *New York Times* called *Rasul* the most important civil rights case in 50 years, and we at CCR received letters from people saying that their faith in America had been restored. It was a grand moment.

While it was a remarkable victory, a number of issues were still not settled by the case. These included the nature of the hearing that the Guantánamo detainees would have, the legal basis for detaining them, and the scope of applicable constitutional, international, and treaty rights. Did the detainees need to be charged and convicted in criminal cases, or would some kind of preventive detention apply? We didn't know it then, but these issues would be litigated in Sisyphean fashion without resolution in various court cases for many years to come.

Our team of lawyers acted quickly after the *Rasul* decision. Before Bush could respond, we wanted to get as many cases as possible into federal court and present the administration with a fait accompli. We immediately went before Judge Kollar-Kotelly and asked that lawyers go to Guantánamo to represent detainees in their habeas petitions. The government objected and attached various conditions, such as requiring lawyers who go to Guantánamo to have security clearance and insisting that they could talk to detainees designated as particularly dangerous only if the government could listen in on their conversations.

I didn't have a security clearance and I'd had my fill of the place years before in the Haitian case anyway. Joe had a security clearance, but given the government's heavy restrictions, he was reluctant to go. So Gita Gutierrez, later an attorney at CCR, was the first lawyer to visit Guantánamo. She flew down in June 2004 to represent Moazzam Begg, though she had to sign various orders and operate under all kinds of restrictions. Over the next few years, Gita traveled to Guantánamo 25 times. Both Joe and Tom followed Gita and went many times to meet with their clients. And of course each time one of the lawyers went, their clients would give them new names of detainees who wanted representation.

At the same time, we tried to file as many habeas petitions as we could on behalf of those Guantánamo detainees whose names we knew and whose relatives we represented as "next friends." Clive Stafford Smith had gathered a fair number of names of detainees. We put out a call to lawyers throughout the country to help. Scores came forward, and we set up training sessions at Columbia University on how to file habeas, how to travel to Guantánamo, and how to respond to the special needs of clients who have been tortured.

Within six months, we had 100 lawyers working with us. Eventually more than 600 lawyers from big and small firms worked pro bono through CCR as the attorneys for hundreds of detainees at Guantánamo. I believe the response from these lawyers—who included Republicans and Democrats, progressives and conservatives—will be seen in the future as one of the great chapters in the struggle for fundamental rights in the United States.

The administration responded as we expected. It set up what it called Combatant Status Review Tribunals (CSRTs)—an absurd attempt to evade federal-court review of the detentions. The CSRTs were supposed to determine if a prisoner was an enemy combatant or not. The Secretary of the Navy would appoint a panel of three officers to decide, based on secret evidence from the military and the prisoners. But the burden of proof lay with the prisoners to prove that they were not enemy combatants. They could not have counsel. They could not confront or cross examine their accusers. They could not see the evidence the military presented. They had no means to gather evidence or to bring witnesses. And they had no right to appeal the CSRT's determination.

On a speaking tour in London, I held a joint press conference with Michael Mori, one of the U.S. military's own lawyers. In his uniform, Mori stood up and denounced the CSRT as "a kangaroo court." He went on, "You cannot have unfair, slanted rules. The rules we have for courts martial and for federal court are the ones that we as a society think will convict the right people, not the wrong people. If you convict the wrong people, the right people are still running around."

It's one thing for a civilian like me to denounce the CSRTs, but here was a military lawyer in uniform saying that under this system the wrong people were being held. In more than 90 percent of the cases, the CSRTs simply confirmed the previous designation of the detainees as enemy combatants. But the vast majority of these detainees were still not charged with any crime. The handful actually charged with a specific crime had to appear before military commissions, which were no more fair than the CSRTs.

In 2006, the Supreme Court considered *Hamdan v. Rumsfeld*, in which Guantánamo prisoner Salim Ahmed Hamdan challenged the legality of the military commission that tried him. Hamdan had been charged with supporting terrorism because he had been Osama bin Laden's driver. In another victory for the detainees, the Supreme Court rejected the administration's argument that habeas and the Geneva Conventions do not apply to al-Qaeda detainees. And it went even further, declaring the military-commission system illegal because it violated the Uniform Code of Military Justice, and unconstitutional because it had been set up without congressional approval.

In response, the administration turned to Congress to override the *Rasul* and *Hamdan* decisions by passing the Military Commissions Act of 2006. It abolished the statutory right of habeas for enemy combatants and authorized revised military commissions to resume.

After the Democrats won the 2006 elections and regained the majority in Congress, Tom Wilner and I organized a lobbying effort to restore habeas. Both Tom and I knew many of the Congress members. The Center reached out to 75 top attorneys from many states to come to Washington and talk to their representatives. We prepared a set of materials four inches high and met at Wilner's office to assign who would talk to which representative. We had no problem getting meetings with the senators and representatives. Both Barack Obama and Hillary Clinton issued statements supporting habeas. But in the end House Speaker Nancy Pelosi refused to let the bill come to a vote.

I hated lobbying, and I didn't like going to Washington. After this frustrating experience, I concluded it was naïve to think that popularly elected legislators would risk taking on anything truly controversial. There are a few exceptions, of course. But this confirmed what I already knew—that courts, even conservative or moderate courts, are important. At least they could deal with issues like the Haitian HIV exclusion, abortion, habeas corpus, and the rights of alleged terrorists.

Tom Wilner wanted to challenge the Military Commissions Act and the Detainee Treatment Act of 2005 with a case brought by his original Kuwaiti clients. But Tony Amsterdam and CCR persuaded him that the facts in Guantánamo detainee Lakhdar Boumediene's case were more compelling. Boumediene had been captured in Bosnia—not on a battlefield—and held there on charges that he'd planted a bomb at the U.S. embassy. A court in Bosnia then cleared him of the charges. Not long after he left prison as a free man, U.S. forces kidnapped him in Sarajevo and flew him to Guantánamo.

CCR assigned the case, consolidated with *Al Odah v. United States* under the name *Boumediene v. Bush,* to Steve Oleskey and a team of lawyers from the prestigious Boston law firm of Wilmer, Pickering, Cutler, and Hale to work as co-counsel with Wilner. In 2008, after a complicated legal battle, *Boumediene* resulted in another major victory for detainees. The Supreme Court ruled in a 5-4 decision written by Justice Kennedy that, contrary to the Military Commissions Act, Guantánamo detainees have a constitutional right to habeas corpus and that the review process under the Detainee Treatment Act was not an adequate substitute for the full judicial review that had been affirmed in *Rasul.*

Guantánamo has been a long struggle, much longer than we at CCR and others ever imagined. The landmark decisions *of Rasul, Hamdi, Hamdan,* and *Boumediene* were amazing successes for the detainees and major setbacks for the Bush-Cheney-Rumsfeld administration. Having attorneys present at Guantánamo was what stopped the most overt forms of torture. By the time Bush left office in January 2009, more than 500 of the Guantánamo detainees had been released. My guess is that almost none would have been released without the litigation.

On the other hand, I'm profoundly disappointed that despite Barack Obama's campaign promises and the efforts of our 600-lawyer team, we haven't been able to close the camp. The courts have not been generous at all. We won several good Supreme Court decisions. *Boumediene* basically said, "A detainee has a right to a hearing and a right to be released if the court rules in his favor." But in practice, every time a detainee wins in a lower court and is possibly getting out, the government appeals to the D.C. Circuit Court, which reverses the lower court and stops the Supreme Court decision from being implemented. And the Supreme Court won't do anything to enforce its own ruling. So we're just balled up in the courts in a way that is completely unacceptable.

What's going to close Guantánamo? I don't have an answer. As of this writing, 41 men still suffer imprisonment there without being charged or having a judicial review. They've been there for many years. The detainees have gone on several hunger strikes to bring attention to their plight. It's horrible to think that people are so desperate that the only thing they can do is to punish themselves even further to get control of their own lives. Basically they're saying, "Look, Obama promised. The courts ruled. And now there's nothing left except us and our bodies."

We still do not know what the outcome will be for these and other detainees. Even though the Supreme Court has established habeas rights at Guantánamo, we don't know what the scope of those rights will be. Will the United States in effect have a preventive-detention policy, but with habeas rights? We may eventually close Guantánamo, and that will be an important victory. But what about other detention facilities such as Bagram and the secret sites? Will habeas rights apply to them?

I still think that alleged terrorists must be charged and tried under a criminal law system. But my fear is that, regardless of the outcome at Guantánamo, some basic human rights have been lost. Even though the administration may now be forced to give detainees court review of their status, it has won its argument that it can treat the Guantánamo detainees as "enemy combatants" and imprison them for many years without criminal hearings. It has essentially installed a massive preventive-detention system that now has the imprimatur of the executive and the Congress.

At CCR we believe that we can continue to make a difference by fighting against preventive detention, torture and other abuses at

Guantánamo and secret U.S. prisons around the globe. We think that in the future, Guantánamo—and the legal, political, and moral outrages that it symbolizes—will be viewed the way most of us now view the concentration camps set up in the U.S. for Japanese Americans during World War II. Until that day, it's the obligation of all of us to join in the ongoing struggle for basic constitutional and human rights.

9

NEW PROJECTS

After the Supreme Court's decision in *Rasul v. Bush,* I stepped back and left litigation in the Guantánamo cases to other lawyers at CCR and big outside law firms. I concentrated on administration, recruiting outside counsel to represent the detainees, and fundraising.

In the few years before *Rasul,* the Center had gone through a very difficult transitional period. Compared to the 1960s when everyone made the same salary and decisions were made collectively, by the 1980s CCR's collective had been modified so that lawyers made more than legal workers. The organization had also added an executive director with decision-making power, though s/he could still be overridden by the collective. And I had been appointed as the first legal director, which made me quite nervous because rarely at CCR did anyone direct anyone else.

In the period from 1991 to 1994, grants dried up and CCR faced a devastating financial crisis that threatened to close its doors. To avert disaster, the board took control of CCR's finances, hired a new executive director, Ron Daniels, to lead the organization away from its original collective structure, and let go half the staff. In response, the staff organized a union, and we had a bitter, painful strike. The board supported the union, and the collective was dissolved. I believed these changes were necessary because the collective had become rife with conflict, and differences of class, race, and gender had taken a toll on everything from case selection to salaries and jobs to work rules.

By 2002 CCR had recovered and was working much better, but it was still a relatively small institution. There was a staff of 18, including six attorneys, and the annual budget was around $1.5 million. Soon after we began the Guantánamo cases, I became president of CCR's board. To be honest, I was a good lawyer, but I had very few executive skills. One thing I could see, however, was that the Guantánamo cases represented a unique opportunity for CCR to expand its work and influence.

Growing out of the civil rights movement, CCR had always been dedicated to racial justice. I'd seen myself as a keeper of that flame, a caretaker of the founders' original vision. But in the 1980s and 1990s, the Reagan/Bush/Clinton years, CCR's work expanded into international human rights. We built deep connections with grassroots movements and progressive governments in Latin America and pushed back against the intensifying repression at home. With the Guantánamo cases, everything we'd learned from our previous work in racial justice, resisting repression, and international human rights seemed to come together. CCR had the perfect combination of experience and independence to be able to handle the Guantánamo project. But I knew that if we were going to do it right, we needed more resources.

After our victory in *Rasul*, the Center suddenly grew. By 2006, we had a staff of 29, including several new lawyers hired to work exclusively on Guantánamo, and a budget of $2.6 million. But the rapid expansion wasn't easy. In 2005, we lost our legal director, Jeff Fogel. And Ron Daniels, who'd led CCR as our executive director for 12 years, had become increasingly uncomfortable in the job. Ron was not a lawyer, and his focus, like the Center's, had always been on racial justice. Now we were embarking on the Guantánamo project—the most massive mobilization of pro bono lawyers in American history. The Center was in chaos, with very strong personalities pursuing their own agendas. A change was needed.

NEW PROJECTS

The situation calmed down in 2006 when the board brought in a young Black attorney, Vince Warren, as CCR's new executive director. For seven years Vince had worked at the ACLU specializing in criminal and racial justice, and he was no stranger to the Center either. As a student at Rutgers Law School in 1992, he had participated in our Ella Baker summer intern program, and he had been a member of our board since 1999. Though Vince had no experience as an executive director, he was extremely capable and took the new job very seriously. He hired a new legal director, Bill Quigley, built up our Guantánamo Global Justice Initiative legal team, and expanded our communications and development departments. Chaos abated, and the staff again began to enjoy working at the Center.

Though the Guantánamo cases received more attention, Vince made sure that our ongoing racial justice work stayed on track. The biggest case at the time was *Floyd v. City of New York,* a class-action suit filed in 2008 to stop the New York City Police Department's racial profiling of Black and Latino residents and stop-and-frisk practices. The case was a follow-up to CCR's landmark class-action racial-profiling case *Daniels v. City of New York,* which resulted in the Special Crimes Unit in New York being disbanded. In 1999, four officers in the Special Crimes Unit had been widely condemned for killing an innocent unarmed man, Amadou Diallo, with 41 shots. The *Daniels* case settlement of 2003 required the NYPD to end unconstitutional racial profiling, but data compiled from 2003-2007 showed that racial profiling and stop-and-frisk continued. So CCR's Baher Azmy, Darius Charney, and Somalia Samuel filed *Floyd v. New York*, which ended in a 2013 decision holding the city liable for constitutional violations and ordering broad reforms. As of this writing, the remedial process that the district court ordered has begun and the reforms should be substantial.

Our other ongoing racial justice class-action suit, *United States of America and Vulcan Society v. City of New York,* charged the New York City Fire Department with discriminatory hiring practices. In a city that was 27 percent Black at the time, only 2.9 percent of firefighters in New York were Black. It was the least diverse fire department of any big city in America, largely as a result of a discriminatory written exam used as a screening mechanism in hiring. Brought by Ghita Schwarz, Darius Charney, and co-counsel Richard Levy in 2002, the case was eventually settled in 2014 after a court ruled that the city was liable for racial discrimination. The settlement awarded Black and Latino victims a stunning $98 million, and forced the city to accept new recruitment goals and equal opportunity within the department.

With the Center running more smoothly, I turned my attention to fundraising. When we won *Rasul* in the Supreme Court, our budget was stretched thin. The decision didn't hurt us, but it didn't help immediately either. So I went to see my friend Sara Rios at the Ford Foundation, who had worked at the Center but had left during the strike. Up to this time we were just too radical for Ford. But after two or three meetings with Sara, she called and said, "Michael, we're going to give the Center $200,000 for Guantánamo work."

After this big breakthrough, Guantánamo work became more acceptable to the funding community. The Oak Foundation in the U.K., started by Tony Pilaro, a co-founder of duty-free shops, gave CCR a $200,000 grant. Atlantic Philanthropies, a huge foundation, awarded CCR a $1.5 million grant over a five-year period, with a matching grant at the end.

And then in 2009 I was at the Sundance Film Festival, and something serendipitous happened that would help us expand CCR. I met Tony Tabatznik, a shy, long-haired, ex-South African Londoner with a shaggy gray beard. In his early 60s, Tony had recently sold his second generic pharamaceutical business and now (with his daughter, Lara) headed the Bertha Foundation which, among other things, funded progressive documentary films. I invited him to visit me in our CCR offices in New York, which he soon did. I introduced Tony to Bill Quigley who showed him articles on how activists, storytellers, and lawyers, working together, can change the world—a belief that Tony shared.

I also introduced him to Vince Warren who mentioned that it was the last day of the Ella Baker summer internship program and asked if we would like to join him in the final sum-up meeting of the interns. Two hours later, having listened to these idealistic young law students explain the life-changing power of their Ella Baker experiences, Tony, Vince, and I emerged, moved and in tears. Tony asked me how many of these programs we offered at CCR.

"One each summer," I told him.

"Why don't we do summer, winter, autumn, and spring courses and do them globally?" he suggested—and added that he would love to fund such a program. That was the beginning of CCR's two-year Bertha Fellows program, which trains and places recent law school graduates at progressive legal organizations around the world. I am so proud to have helped pioneer this program that funds more than 100 young lawyers every two years in 17 countries. It is now an integral part of CCR and occupies a special place in my heart.

By 2012 when I stepped down as president, the Center's staff had grown to 50, including 13 staff attorneys and three legal fellows, and its annual budget had increased to more than $6 million. I remained active as president emeritus, but it was time for me to devote more of my energy to two exciting projects that I had gotten involved with a few years before. One was a fledgling radio show, the other a new center for constitutional rights across the Atlantic Ocean.

LAW AND DISORDER

In the summer of 2004, not long after the Supreme Court's ruling in *Rasul,* the Republican Party was scheduled to hold its convention in New York City to nominate George W. Bush for a second term as president.

Hundreds of thousands of non-violent protesters were expected to flood the streets in demonstrations over several days. The New York Police Department announced that in order to keep order, it would employ bomb-sniffing dogs and 10,000 officers in full riot gear and body armor, armed with submachine guns and rifles. In addition, for several months in advance of the convention, the NYPD had infiltrated and compiled dossiers on protest groups in 15 cities.

In numerous speeches, Bill Kunstler had warned us about "the emerging police state." The NYPD's preparations for the convention, combined with the Bush administration's illegal "war on terror," mass surveillance, and blatant disregard for civil liberties, provided compelling evidence that the police state was no longer emerging. It had already arrived.

Michael Smith and I sat down at lunch one day to discuss what we could do. I'd known Michael for 25 years, since we both lived in the West Village, around the corner from each other. When I was elected president of the National Lawyers Guild back in 1982, I asked Michael to work on our magazine, *Guild Notes.* He said yes, and we've been close friends ever since.

You didn't have to be a genius to understand that the courts and Congress were not going to stop the police state any time soon. Nor did the corporate mainstream media, in lockstep with the Bush administration and the police, offer much hope. They had not asked the tough questions or provided the skeptical analysis that the founders of the country had expected from the press.

"We need to find a way to let people know what's really going on," I said.

"How about we start a radio show?" said Michael.

I immediately liked the idea. Michael's close friend Jim Lafferty, president of the National Lawyers Guild chapter in Los Angeles, had already been hosting a respected drive-time program about legal issues that aired on KPFK, Southern California's listener-sponsored Pacifica radio station. Inspired by the Lafferty model, Michael and I informally kicked around various approaches and came up with a concept. Unlike the wildly popular National Public Radio show *Car Talk*, we would not take phone calls from listeners about their individual legal problems. Instead, in a weekly one-hour program, we would interview knowledgeable guests—legal scholars, lawyers, judges, authors, journalists—and use our experience as progressive movement lawyers to discuss legal and political issues currently in the news.

The advantages of radio were obvious. A show could be done on a low budget and could reach millions of listeners. Michael and I would host it ourselves as unpaid volunteers. With the help of an engineer/producer we could record the program and offer it at no charge to radio stations committed to airing radical viewpoints rarely presented in mainstream media.

In such turbulent times, we knew we would have no trouble finding timely subject matter. But deciding on the name of the program was harder. We finally settled on *Law and Disorder*, borrowing the title of a legal column in the *Kingston Daily Freeman*, an upstate New York newspaper, that chronicled local crimes like drug-store break-ins and DWI's. We thought it was apt for the grander criminals on the national stage.

Michael Smith pitched our proposal to the programming committee of our local New York Pacifica station, WBAI. The committee listened but never responded. However, WBAI program director Bernard White was impressed and decided to put *Law and Disorder* on the air for an hour once a month beginning in July 2004.

Before we recorded our first show, we revised the format. Recognizing one of the strengths of *Car Talk*, we figured out that the back-and-forth discussion/banter/repartee between the hosts was crucial to the success of the program. Michael and I were two older Jewish men with similar viewpoints. We decided to bring in more diverse co-hosts, two younger women who had strong legal and political backgrounds but also distinct personalities and experience.

The first person we asked was Dalia Hashad, an advocate in the ACLU's Campaign Against Racial Profiling. In 2004, the height of Bush's wars in Afghanistan and Iraq, much of our program covered legal issues involving the horrifying treatment of Muslims, domestically and internationally, at Guantánamo and elsewhere. We'd seen Dalia, an articulate Egyptian graduate of New York University Law School, interviewed as a guest on *Democracy Now!* She was an outspoken, charming Muslim woman in her late twenties, and we thought her experience and intelligence would add a whole new dimension to *Law and Disorder*.

Soon after, we asked Heidi Boghosian, whom we both knew as executive director of the National Lawyers Guild, to join us. A graduate of Temple Law School, Heidi was a half-Armenian activist lawyer from a younger generation and had focused much of her work on police brutality, government surveillance, and privacy issues. Fortunately for us, she also had studied broadcasting and had both an engaging personality and a marvelous radio voice.

Collectively, we four co-hosts represented three of the most prominent progressive legal organizations in the country—the ACLU, the National Lawyers Guild, and the Center for Constitutional Rights. Dalia later took a job with Amnesty International, and I was also part of a Listserv informational network of hundreds of lawyers working on Guantánamo, human rights, and torture cases. As a result, we had access to many experts in the progressive legal community to invite as guests. In addition, Michael Smith had been very active in socialist political work for many years, and he had extensive contacts in that community.

In July 2004, we recorded our first program in a WBAI studio on the 10th floor of 120 Wall Street. Heidi, Michael, and I sat around an L-shaped table, each with a microphone and wearing a headset. (Dalia was on assignment in California, so she missed that first show.)

NEW PROJECTS

Heidi welcomed listeners. "Here at *Law and Disorder,* we four attorneys and activists will strive to be your eyes and ears, your early warning system, your educators, counselors, and advocates," she said.

On that first show we talked about three important Supreme Court decisions—*Rasul, Padilla,* and *Hamdi*—that had just struck a blow at the Bush administration's so-called war on terror. And we interviewed some of the lawyers who had worked on those cases—Joe Margulies, Donna Neuman, Barbara Olshansky. To set a casual conversational tone, we decided not to write out our questions in advance. Instead, we took a shoot-from-the-hip approach with each of us informally chiming in.

The second show focused on the 2004 Republican convention during which the New York Police Department carried out mass arrests. Police rounded up more than 1,800 people, many of them innocent bystanders, holding them in a crumbling building which one lawyer called "a little Guantánamo on the Hudson." (In 2014, the city settled a class action lawsuit brought by 1,200 protesters, paying the class a total of $6.6 million. The city paid another $6.4 million to 460 individuals.)

After several months, *Law and Disorder* got a regular weekly time slot on WBAI at 10 a.m. on Mondays, following *Democracy Now!* (Later that changed to 9 a.m.) And we raised enough funds to hire as our full-time producer a former U.S. Army paratrooper named Geoff Brady. Geoff was a talented public-radio journalist who'd been freelancing for Free Speech Radio News.

Our program covers a wide range of legal and political topics, but in the early years we focused a lot of our attention on the illegal wars in Iraq and Afghanistan, torture at Abu Ghraib, Guantánamo, and other CIA black sites. This led some of the staffers at WBAI to dub our program "The Torture Show." Or as Dalia joked in one of our outtakes: "Today we report on a series of disasters. Everything that stinks in the world right here in one hour."

MOVING THE BAR

Over the years we broadened our scope and covered diverse top-ics, including the expanding surveillance state, police brutality, the prison industry, drone warfare, the Occupy and Keystone Pipeline pro-tests, Hurricane Katrina, censorship, climate change, human traffick-ing, immigration law, Palestinian rights, and the gradual destruction of democracy and rise of oligarchy through gerrymandering, dark money, and voter suppression.

We interviewed well-known guests, including radical British-Pakistani historian and activist Tariq Ali; former Attorney General Ramsey Clark, who'd led the movement to impeach then-President George W. Bush; and Len Weinglass, who'd represented the Chicago Seven anti-war activists and Daniel Ellsberg in the Pentagon Papers case.

One interview that was most memorable for me was with Mumia Abu-Jamal, the former Black Panther journalist/activist who had been wrongly convicted of killing a Philadelphia police officer and had been in prison since 1981, much of that time on Death Row. Heidi had been active in Mumia's defense committee and had visited him regularly, so she arranged for him to call in to the show from prison in Frackville, Pennsylvania. Rather than focus on his own case, Mumia chose to talk about seven anti-war activists who had broken into an FBI office in Media, Pennsylvania in 1971 and made public documents proving the existence of COINTELPRO, the FBI's illegal spying program against pro-test groups. Mumia said these anonymous activists were precursors of whistleblowers Chelsea Manning and Edward Snowden. Then he quoted Martin Luther King: "Some laws need to be broken because they are fun-damentally unjust."

For those who had never heard him before, Mumia came across as a thoughtful, brilliant, widely read, articulate man, not the brutal cop-killer portrayed in the mainstream media. The interview was interrupted periodically by a recording saying, "This conversation is being monitored by Mahanoy State Correctional Institution." It was a sober reminder of where Mumia had been living for more than three decades.

Some of the best interviews on *Law and Disorder* were with little-known activists. One that particularly moved me was with Shanti Sellz and Daniel Strauss. Both in their early twenties, they had volunteered with the Arizona-based coalition No More Deaths, which provided food, water, and medical aid to migrants in distress as they struggled to cross the desert from Mexico into the U.S.

The couple had been arrested by the U.S. Border Patrol while driving three very sick Mexican men to a Tucson hospital. It was extremely hot, with temperatures well over 100 degrees, and 75 migrants had already died that week. The three men had been lost in the desert for four days and were suffering from hunger, dehydration, severe foot blisters, and vomiting caused by bacterial infections from drinking filthy water from cattle tanks.

The Border Patrol sent the men back to Mexico and charged Shanti and Daniel with human smuggling and conspiracy. The couple argued in court that they were not smuggling, but saving these men's lives. Eventually the charges were dismissed, and No More Deaths continued its work. As Shanti put it, "Humanitarian aid is never a crime."

Five years later, my son Jake and his partner Elena Stein volunteered with No More Deaths, and we interviewed them on *Law and Disorder* as a follow-up to our original story. The situation at the border had worsened—two people died every day crossing the desert from Mexico to the U.S. The water bottles that Jake and Elena placed out in the harsh terrain for those in need were emptied by the Border Patrol, leading to more deaths. But my faith in humanity was restored by hearing these courageous young people willing to go out into the desert to help save lives.

Another key interview featured Henri Alleg, 85, a French journalist who had been arrested in 1957 by French paratroopers during the Battle of Algiers in the Algerian war for independence. He'd been held prisoner for a month in Algeria and endured various forms of interrogation and torture, including waterboarding, electric shocks, and hanging from his feet. As he told us, the French Army had perfected torture and provided a model for the techniques later used at Guantánamo.

Describing the experience of being waterboarded, Alleg said, "It's bringing someone to the brink of death. There's a terrible agony of knowing you're dying." Most people subjected to waterboarding end up talking, but Alleg never cracked. While he was still imprisoned, Alleg wrote a short book describing the torture he'd endured and smuggled the pages out. Entitled *The Question,* the book caused a sensation when it was published in France in 1958. It was reprinted in the U.S. in 2007, thanks to the efforts of New York publisher Ellen Ray, who found Alleg and approached the University of Nebraska Press to re-publish the book. Alleg concluded his interview with some advice: "The American people should be careful not to be led by politicians who speak of human rights and do the exact opposite of what they say."

Occasionally we'd run a segment called "Lawyers You'll Like," in which we interviewed movement lawyers doing important work. We hoped they would inspire young people interested in a career in law. Among our guests were Melvin Wulf, former legal director of the American Civil Liberties Union, and criminal defense lawyer Myron Beldock, who represented the wrongly convicted Yusef Salaam of the Central Park Five and Rubin "Hurricane" Carter, the former boxing champion who served 20 years in prison after being wrongfully convicted of murder.

We also made a special effort to interview women lawyers. For generations, law schools admitted only a handful of women. But recently, the doors have opened and now thousands of accomplished women are literally changing the face of the legal profession. Among the distinguished women lawyers who've been guests on *Law and Disorder:* Mara Verheyden-Hilliard, executive director of the Partnership for Civil Justice Fund, which has won several major First Amendment lawsuits on behalf of citizens in Washington D.C.; Jan Susler, partner in the People's Law Office in Chicago, who has represented Puerto Rican political prisoners and advocated for prisoners' rights; civil rights lawyer Carol Sobel, chair of the National Lawyers Guild's Mass Defense Committee, which has represented Occupy Wall Street and many other protesters; criminal defense attorney Nancy Hollander, lead appellate counsel for whistleblower Chelsea Manning; and defense attorney Lynne Stewart, who represented the accused terrorist, Sheikh Omar Abdel-Rahman, and then herself went to prison when Attorney General John Ashcroft charged her with providing material support to terrorists.

Law and Disorder began broadcasting in 2004 on only one station. But WBAI's powerful 50,000-watt signal reached millions of listeners in the tri-state area. The show was also offered on the Pacifica Audio Port, which allows station managers at affiliates all over the country to download and broadcast it. Each year the show has picked up more stations. As of this writing, 120 radio stations broadcast *Law and Disorder*, and it is also available online via podcast. Our website gets thousands of hits every week, and we receive e-mails from countries as far apart geographically and politically as Argentina, Russia, and New Zealand. All this indicates that listeners all over the U.S. and the globe have a thirst for radical viewpoints on law and politics.

For me, the show is an extension of my work as a lawyer/activist and an important part of my life. The program continues to offer a platform for diverse voices, older colleagues I've admired and younger lawyers I've worked with and sometimes mentored. Heidi, Michael, Dalia, Geoff, and I have become a little family. I look forward to those three hours every week when I can put aside all other responsibilities, get together with my co-host friends and other colleagues, and discuss the events going on around us.

One thing I have learned over the years is that if we are going to create lasting change, we need informed, politically aware, and committed grassroots movements. We cannot rely on the mainstream media. We have to inform ourselves through independent media. That is why I hope programs like *Democracy Now!* and *Law and Disorder* will continue long into the future.

ECCHR

The European Center for Constitutional and Human Rights, a non-profit global legal organization based on the CCR model, was founded in the summer of 2007 in Berlin, Germany.

But ECCHR's origins actually go back to 2004. In June, just as the Supreme Court was about to issue its decision in *Rasul*, CBS's *60 Minutes* released sickening photographs of torture that U.S. soldiers and the CIA had inflicted on prisoners at Abu Ghraib. Even though I knew torture was going on, I was still shocked.

So I talked with CCR's vice president, Peter Weiss, who in 1982 had won the landmark *Filártiga* case that established the precedent of universal jurisdiction in cases of war crimes and crimes against humanity, including torture. Peter and I both realized that even though we had won the *Rasul* case, the torture at Guantánamo, Abu Ghraib, and elsewhere at "black sites" was continuing unabated. President Bush, Vice President Cheney, and Defense Secretary Rumsfeld had all insisted that torture was effective and they had the right to use it. Although the Bush administration had prosecuted a handful of low-level soldiers for committing torture in Iraq, the investigations had been run by the Defense Department, CIA, and other agencies involved in the war crimes. No one in the upper chain of command had been held accountable.

Peter and I agreed that torture would continue until high-level officials in the Bush administration who had authorized it were prosecuted. And the relevant prosecutor, Attorney General Alberto Gonzales, was himself involved in the torture program. So it was clear he would not be filing any criminal charges.

Normally under international law, countries are responsible for investigating their own war crimes. However, if they fail to do so, the international community can step in under the principle of universal jurisdiction. We considered bringing a lawsuit before the International Criminal Court to stop the torture. But we decided it would be futile because the U.S. had refused to ratify the treaty that created the ICC. So we turned to the courts of Europe. In many European countries victims can initiate criminal proceedings and appeal to a court if the government prosecutor refuses to go forward with a case.

We soon found an article by prominent German criminal lawyers Florian Jessberger and Gerhard Werle describing the German Code of Crimes Against International Law. Under this 2002 law, violations of the Geneva Conventions, including torture and inhumane treatment of detainees, are defined as war crimes and crimes against humanity. The code specifically gives German courts universal jurisdiction over these crimes, even when there is no direct link to Germany. In addition, the German code applies not just to anyone who directly commits a war crime, but to the military or civilian authority who orders it, knowingly fails to prevent it, or fails to punish a person who commits it.

Thanks to this law, Germany seemed a promising venue. But to file a complaint there, we would need to work with a German lawyer. I contacted Florian Jessberger, who recommended Wolfgang Kaleck, a German criminal attorney who had experience with cases involving universal jurisdiction.

Since 1998, Wolfgang had been an advocate for the Koalition gegen Straflosigkeit (Coalition Against Impunity). The organization had brought lawsuits in Germany to hold top Argentinian military officials accountable for the murder and disappearance of German and Argentine citizens during the junta's Dirty War from 1976-1983. Under the dictatorship of General Jorge Rafaél Videla, more than 30,000 people in Argentina had "disappeared" and 100,000 had been brutally tortured.

When I called Wolfgang, he explained the strategy he had used, which became a blueprint for the human rights movement around the world. Under universal jurisdiction, he'd obtained from a German court an arrest warrant and an extradition request for General Videla. In addition, various rights groups had secured 100 arrest warrants from Baltasar Garzón, the same Spanish judge who'd issued the warrant to arrest Chilean dictator Augusto Pinochet in 1998.

"The idea of these cases," Wolfgang explained, "was not to try Argentinians in European courts, but to pressure the Argentinian government to launch its own investigations. This is the so-called Videla Effect or the Pinochet Effect."

The strategy worked. From 2003-2005, the new leftist government of Argentine President Néstor Kirchner abolished amnesty laws that had prevented criminal prosecution of military officials for 20 years. It launched investigations into 2,600 former members of the military and others involved in the dictatorship, resulting in more than 550 convictions.

Clearly, Wolfgang was the right lawyer to partner with us. In several phone calls, we agreed that high officials in the Bush administration needed to be brought to justice. I invited Wolfang to meet with Peter and me in CCR's New York office to strategize about how we could initiate prosecutions in German courts. Peter, then 78, had been born in Vienna and in 1941 as a teenager had fled from Nazi-occupied Austria to the U.S. He was tall, thin, dignified, balding, with a gray goatee. I was 61 then and had lost many members of my extended family in the Holocaust. I was a lot shorter than Peter and bald. We were both Jewish. Wolfgang, in his early 40s, was a leftist activist from a younger generation of Germans hoping to leave the horrors of the Nazis far behind them. He'd worked with international solidarity movements since his student days in the 1980s. And I couldn't help noticing that he had a full head of thick brown hair.

Here we were, an odd trio, planning how to bring a criminal complaint in Germany to stop torture and other war crimes carried out by high officials of the United States, the country that had defeated Hitler and the Nazi war criminals in World War II. The irony was not lost on any of us.

At first a bit quiet as he listened to Peter and me propose possible strategies, Wolfgang proved to be energetic and confident, raising all the tough questions. He was open, fun-loving, and had a brilliant mind. We hit it off immediately.

"There's plenty of evidence of torture at Abu Ghraib," I said. "But we have to evaluate several dozen reports from NGOs, the U.N., and internal U.S. military investigations. And we have to draw up dossiers on all the top officials who authorized the torture—military, intelligence, politicians. We'd like to file the complaint right after the U.S. election in November."

"That's only a few months," said Wolfang. "I have a full book of cases I'm already committed to. You must think I'm some kind of maniac to be able to work that fast."

"We'll figure out the legal strategy together and identify the targets of the complaint," said Peter. "Students who work with the Center will do the research and compile the dossiers."

"And my part in all this?" asked Wolfgang skeptically.

"The hard part," I replied, and Wolfgang laughed. "Write the legal analysis and the complaint. Does what happened at Abu Ghraib meet the definition of torture under international and German law? And can German prosecutors take action?"

"Well, you guys have been doing this a long time," said Wolfgang. "I don't have to tell you that the law says national governments are obliged to investigate their own war crimes."

"That's impossible in the U.S. now," said Peter. "It may never happen here. But war criminals have to be held accountable somewhere—if not here, then in Germany."

"Everybody I know in Germany thinks I'd be crazy to bring a case like this," said Wolfgang. "We're almost certain to lose. The U.S. government will pressure German authorities. Even human rights groups like Amnesty International are saying we could destroy the concept of universal jurisdiction and set a very bad precedent."

"I heard the same argument when we brought the *Rasul* case," I replied. "Now all those people who were afraid of a bad precedent are happily claiming victory."

Wolfgang looked thoughtful for a moment. "Okay," he said with a big smile. "Let's do it. So how do we communicate?"

"By e-mail and phone," I said.

"Are we going to be under surveillance?"

"Sure, they'll be listening in, reading whatever we write," said Peter.

"But we're used to that," I added. "And by the way, from now on when you come to New York, you'll be living at my house."

A few months later, on November 30, 2004, Wolfgang filed a 160-page criminal complaint with a German prosecutor on behalf of CCR and four Iraqi detainees who had been brutally tortured at Abu Ghraib. It charged Defense Secretary Donald Rumsfeld, former CIA Director George Tenet, and eight other high-ranking officials and officers with war crimes. (As sitting president and vice president, Bush and Cheney were immune from prosecution.) CCR later added an eleventh defendant, Attorney General Alberto Gonzales, after he admitted at his confirmation hearing that he had helped draft and then approved legal memoranda authorizing torture and inhumane treatment of detainees.

Though pulled together in a rush, the complaint provided ample documentation from the public record that Rumsfeld and other top officials had authorized the torture techniques used at Abu Ghraib—certainly enough to warrant investigation and prosecution under the German code. In addition, this case had important links to Germany. The U.S. military had—and still has—major bases in Germany. The U.S. Army's 205th Intelligence Brigade, which was involved in the torture at Abu Ghraib, was stationed in Wiesbaden. The head of that brigade, Col. Thomas Pappas, was stationed there as well. Lt. General Ricardo Sanchez, former commander of U.S. forces in Iraq, and his deputy, Maj. Gen. Walter Wojdakowski, were both stationed in Heidelberg. Under the German code, it is obligatory to investigate and prosecute alleged war criminals living on German soil.

We were confident we had a very strong case. The problem, as Wolfgang had warned, was that the U.S. had the power to bully the German authorities. We don't know what happened behind the scenes. But we do know that Rumsfeld publicly threatened that he would not attend the important annual Munich Security Conference unless the case was dropped.

A day prior to the Munich conference in February 2005, the German prosecutor dismissed the complaint. His explanation: the U.S. government, which had primary responsibility for its own war crimes, was still investigating those up the chain of command who had authorized torture. Of course, that was utterly untrue. But the ruling stood, and Rumsfeld went to Munich.

Two years later, we tried again. This time Wolfgang had plenty of time to prepare. On November 14, 2006, a couple of days after Rumsfeld resigned as defense secretary, Wolfgang filed our new, more thorough 384-page complaint with the German prosecutor. Then he and I headed over to the Babylon Theater in old East Berlin. We'd organized a press conference at this historic site where anti-fascists had fought against Hitler. When we got there, we were stunned. On the marquee were the words "Menschenrechte Gegen Rumsfeld"—Human Rights Against Rumsfeld. One hundred fifty reporters and NGO activists packed the room, compared with just a handful when we filed our case the first time. In two years, the climate had changed.

"We're not so arrogant as to think we can put Rumsfeld behind bars on the first attempt," Kaleck told the press. "Patience is needed."

The new complaint again charged Rumsfeld, Tenet, Sanchez, Gonzales, and several other top U.S. officials with war crimes. But this time it also charged four top Bush administration lawyers—William Haynes, David Addington, John Yoo, and Jay Bybee—who had drafted memos justifying and authorizing torture. The complaint was brought on behalf of 12 Iraqi citizens who had survived torture at Abu Ghraib and one Saudi citizen who had been detained and tortured at Guantánamo since January 2002.

All of these survivors had their own horror stories to tell. But the torture of the Saudi man, CCR client Mohammed al-Qahtani, could be traced directly to Donald Rumsfeld. At Guantánamo, al-Qahtani had endured a regime of aggressive interrogation techniques, known as the "First Special Interrogation Plan." Authorized by Rumsfeld in an Action Memo dated December 2, 2002 and re-authorized on April 16, 2003, those techniques were implemented under the supervision of Rumsfeld and the commander of Guantánamo, Major General Geoffrey Miller, who was later assigned to Abu Ghraib.

These cruel methods, described by al-Qahtani to CCR lawyer Gita Gutierrez and documented in detail in a leaked interrogation log from Guantánamo, included 48 days of severe sleep deprivation and 20-hour interrogations, forced nudity, sexual humiliation, religious humiliation, beatings, threats to his family, prolonged stress positions, prolonged sensory overstimulation, and threats by military dogs. A December 20, 2005 Army Inspector General Report (the Schmidt Report) concluded that Rumsfeld was "personally involved" in the interrogation of al-Qahtani and was "personally briefed" weekly by Gen. Miller during the interrogations.

NEW PROJECTS

The evidence of torture, documented by the International Red Cross and internal U.S. Army and Defense Department reports, was overwhelming. We had lined up impressive witnesses who were ready to testify, including the former commander of all U.S. prisons in Iraq, Brigadier General Janis Karpinski. And Dick Cheney's argument that waterboarding yielded vital information had already been refuted by the CIA's own Human Resource Exploitation Manual of 1983. It stressed that torture only induces the victim to say what he or she thinks the torturer wants to hear. Similarly, FBI interrogation instructor Joe Navarro stated in a December 2004 internal memo that "the only thing that torture guarantees is pain, it never guarantees the truth."

Although some in the German legal community criticized us for grandstanding, we received so much public support that at one point the German prosecutor called us to complain that his German server had jammed after he received 30,000 e-mails from citizens urging him to prosecute.

In addition, the U.S. Congress had recently passed the Military Commissions Act (MCA), which re-defined war crimes, essentially granting amnesty to officials who had engaged in torture after 9/11. Of course, such a pardon is illegal: under international law, war crimes cannot be pardoned. But the MCA amnesty was clear evidence that the U.S. government had no intention of conducting a serious investigation. That meant it would be very difficult for the German prosecutor to use the legal reasoning of the previous prosecutor to reject our case.

Still, we weren't surprised in April 2007 when the new prosecutor dismissed our complaint, providing another bogus reason: "Prosecution can be refused in the case of acts committed abroad," she wrote in her opinion, "if a perpetrator is neither present in the country nor can be expected to be present. This is the case here." Of course that wasn't true.

We appealed—and lost again. But I felt strongly that Rumsfeld could still be judged in the court of public opinion. Using mostly documents, evidence, and arguments from our two complaints, the CCR staff and I wrote *The Trial of Donald Rumsfeld: A Prosecution by Book*. Formatted like a trial, it was published in 2008 by New Press. I presented an opening statement, followed by evidence for the prosecution. This included the torture log detailing treatment of Mohammed al-Qahtani, Donald Rumsfeld's memos authorizing torture, and the testimony of Iraqi torture survivors from Abu Ghraib as well as survivors from Guantánamo. We also included the Defense Department's Schlesinger Report, a statement from General Janis Karpinski, and shocking photographs of torture from Abu Ghraib.

Next we presented the witnesses and statements for the defense, in their own words. These included Rumsfeld's and Alberto Gonzales's public statements, the original memos written by lawyers Yoo, Bybee, and Gonzales that enabled torture, and Rumsfeld's testimony before the House Armed Services Committee. As CCR wrote in a rebuttal, the defense's evidence proved just as damning as the prosecution's.

The book concluded with an epilogue about the concept of universal jurisdiction, Peter Weiss's brief history of the prosecution of war crimes from Pinochet to Rumsfeld, and Wolfgang Kaleck and Claire Tixeire's analysis of our two German cases against Rumsfeld.

The book documented a policy of torture for the historical record. And just as Richard Nixon's name will forever be linked with lies and coverup, Rumsfeld's name will go down in history linked with torture.

Despite the German prosecutors' dismissal of our complaints, Wolfgang refused to be discouraged. On the contrary, his experiences with the Rumsfeld and Argentine cases had convinced him that he was no longer satisfied doing individual criminal defense work at the law firm he'd co-founded in 1991.

Shortly after we'd filed our second Rumsfeld case, Wolfgang and I took a walk together in Kreuzberg, a countercultural neighborhood that was a hotbed of leftist political resistance in Berlin. As we passed cafés and bars packed with Turkish immigrants, punk rockers, hip-hoppers, and avant-garde artists, he told me that although his law partners admired and supported what he'd done with the Rumsfeld project, they'd suggested that this kind of work didn't fit with the future economics of the firm.

"They're right," he said. "Maybe the law firm isn't the best place for me now. I want to be part of a bigger political project."

For years I'd had a vague dream of starting organizations like CCR in other countries. Now, if a brilliant, energetic lawyer like Wolfgang got involved, it seemed more possible.

"You know, in the U.S., civil liberties organizations like CCR and the ACLU are funded by donations and foundation grants," I said, "so they can take on bigger, more complex political cases."

"We don't have anything like that here," he said.

"That could change," I said. "All it took to start CCR was four committed civil rights lawyers getting together and deciding to do it."

Already I could see the wheels turning in his brain.

A few months later Wolfgang invited me to a meeting at his office with a small group of European lawyers, including Lotte Leicht, director of Human Rights Watch's Brussels office. At the urging of his German friends, Wolfgang said he was thinking of starting a new human rights legal organization in Berlin and asked for our advice. We all encouraged him, but pointed out that if the organization was going to bring cases against the CIA or transnational corporations, it wouldn't make sense to limit it to Germany. We suggested the organization extend its range to include all of Europe. Wolfgang agreed.

That was the beginning of the European Center for Constitutional and Human Rights. Wolfgang left his law firm and became legal director and general secretary, running the organization, which at first consisted of himself, one other lawyer, and an administrator. My role as board chair was largely to support Wolfgang and guide him to possible funders.

Though ECCHR had been inspired in part by the work of the Center for Constitutional Rights, Wolfgang and the board, which included a wide range of respected human rights lawyers, all agreed that it was essential for the new organization to create its own separate identity.

ECCHR's original mandate was to initiate and support strategic litigation against human rights violators in two areas:

1. War crimes and crimes against humanity not only at Guantánamo and Abu Ghraib but also in Sri Lanka, Yemen, Syria, Colombia, Argentina, Chile, and other countries.
2. Exploitation of workers by transnational corporations at every step of the supply and production chain.

Later, as war-related immigration problems intensified in the Middle East and Mediterranean, ECCHR added a third area to its mandate.

3. Violence and violation of the rights of refugees and migrants at European Union borders in the Mediterranean.

From the beginning we knew that to tackle such complex issues, ECCHR needed to develop a wide range of legal mechanisms based on an ongoing dialogue between partners in the North and South. So Wolfgang made a conscious effort to reach out to young lawyers, universities, artists, local experts, and grassroots activist groups as well as affected communities all over the world.

For such an ambitious undertaking, we needed a solid financial foundation. But one of the main funders who had promised a large donation dropped out because of financial losses in the Bernie Madoff scandal, delaying the opening of ECCHR's doors for the rest of 2007. For the first six months, the organization had virtually no funding. To receive even a modest salary, Wolfgang had to borrow from his sister.

Eventually, though, Wolfgang corralled some foundation support, and the fledgling organization opened its doors in January 2008 in a tiny, dark office on Greifswalder Strasse. It kicked off its slate of work by bringing a new case in France against Rumsfeld and the other accused war criminals. Over the next few years, ECCHR and its local partners brought similar cases in Spain, Italy, Belgium, Switzerland, and again in Germany.

Almost all of those cases accusing U.S. officials of war crimes were delayed indefinitely or dismissed. Thanks to the U.S. diplomatic cables that WikiLeaks released in 2010, we now know why seeking justice in these cases has been just as difficult abroad as it has been at home. The U.S. government has put a heavy thumb on the scales of justice in other countries. For example, during the George W. Bush presidency, the U.S. intervened to derail the case of Khaled El-Masri, a German citizen abducted in Macedonia by Macedonian police in 2003. The CIA flew him to a black site in Afghanistan to be interrogated as part of the "extraordinary rendition" program, and after he was strip-searched, sodomized, and tortured for four months, realized they had kidnapped the wrong man. They then dumped Khaled El-Masri on the side of an Albanian road.

Leaked cables from 2007 reveal the extent of U.S. pressure and German collusion in the El-Masri case. U.S. officials warned the German government that if it issued international warrants, relations between the two countries would suffer. In public, Munich prosecutors issued arrest warrants for 13 suspected CIA operatives while Chancellor Angela Merkel's office called for an investigation. In private, however, the German justice ministry and foreign ministry both made it clear to the U.S. that they were not interested in pursuing the case. Later that year, Justice Minister Brigitte Zypries announced her decision not to attempt extradition of the 13 CIA operatives, citing the U.S. government's refusal to arrest or hand over the agents.

Another leaked cable dated 1 April 2009 reveals that the Obama administration attempted to influence the case that ECCHR and its local partners had brought in Spain against six Bush administration lawyers. Our complaint charged that they violated international law by creating a legal justification for torture at Guantánamo and elsewhere. The U.S. cable to the Spanish Chief Prosecutor Javier Zaragoza warns that this complaint "may reflect a 'stepping-stone' strategy designed to pave the way for complaints against even more senior officials." It also bemoans Spain's "reputation for liberally invoking universal jurisdiction." Zaragoza replies that "in all likelihood he would have no option but to open a case." But he does not "envision indictments or arrest warrants in the near future" and will "argue against the case being assigned to Garzón," the tough judge who issued the arrest warrant for Augusto Pinochet.

Apart from ECCHR, local European prosecutors have scored some victories in human rights cases. Successfully resisting U.S. pressure, Italian prosecutors in 2009 won convictions in the cases of 22 CIA agents and a U.S. Air Force colonel who had illegally kidnapped Egyptian cleric Abu Omar off the streets of Milan. They sent him to Egypt where he was imprisoned without charges and tortured for four years. Convicted in absentia, the CIA station chief was sentenced to eight years in prison, and the other CIA agents and the colonel were sentenced to five years.

Even if these agents do not spend a day in jail, these convictions send a powerful message: if you commit human rights atrocities, even on behalf of the most powerful state in the world, you are not guaranteed immunity. If you were a CIA agent, would you kidnap again? Would you waterboard? I certainly don't think these convictions will stop all future torture. But prosecutions act as a deterrent. The Italian courts have taken a powerful first step to put teeth in the expression that "no one is above the law."

The primary goal of ECCHR's cases against Rumsfeld and the other U.S. officials was to prove that universal jurisdiction could be applied not just to low-level torturers or torturers in smaller nations, but to the highest authorities in the world's most powerful nations. I use this simple test to measure equality before the law: If a law cannot be applied to the powerful, of what use is it? We haven't yet won a universal jurisdiction case against the highest authorities of the United States. But we will keep trying.

Our other goal in bringing these cases was to make sure that there will never be a safe haven for torturers and war criminals anywhere in the world. At the very least, the complaints that ECCHR and its partners have filed have had one tangible result: CIA torturers, Donald Rumsfeld, and even George W. Bush are now afraid to travel to certain countries. If they go to Europe, these enemies of humankind know that they risk being arrested, prosecuted, and imprisoned.

From 2008 to 2015, I flew to Berlin twice a year for ECCHR board meetings and in the last few years much more often. I loved these trips. Wolfgang and I became close friends, spending a lot of time hanging out in cafés, drinking wine, and talking politics. Berlin was a vibrant city, and ECCHR was involved with all sorts of cultural institutions and activities. Wolfgang was always taking me to an opening of the latest show at a hip art gallery, a premiere of a new play at a local theater, or a party with fascinating people from all over the world.

But nothing in Berlin was more thrilling to me than to walk into ECCHR's headquarters in the large, light-filled loft it had moved into in 2009 and see the beehive of activity. In just a few years, ECCHR has become a dynamic, cutting-edge human rights organization. Working with its global partners, it continues to bring cases against war criminals. But it has expanded far beyond its initial focus to take on transnational corporate crime and human rights violations involved in migration issues. Here is a sampling of what ECCHR has done:

- Challenged clinical pharmaceutical trials performed without consent on 20,000 girls in India.

- Brought a complaint against the Swiss government for not adequately investigating the murder of a trade unionist in Nestle's plant in Colombia.
- Sued German clothing retailer KiK to establish corporate responsibility and obtain compensation for victims of the fatal 2012 fire at the Ali Enterprises textile factory in Karachi, Pakistan that killed 260 people.
- Filed a case in Germany against a Swiss timber production company for brutal beatings and rapes in the Congo and challenged German and U.K. surveillance firms for their potential complicity in serious human rights abuses in Bahrain.
- Challenged pesticide use in Malaysia, war crimes and sexualized violence in Sri Lanka, sexual slavery during World War II, and drone strikes in Pakistan.
- Filed a complaint against Spain's border authorities for violating the rights of refugees from sub-Saharan Africa and the European Asylum Support Office for unfairly assessing applicants for international asylum at Greece's borders.

ECCHR and its partners have won some of their complaints, lost others, and some are still pending. Regardless of the outcome, ECCHR continues to bring to light human rights violations that have been ignored for too long. But ECCHR also understands that litigation alone cannot bring fundamental change or hold governments and corporations accountable. To achieve these goals, it also supports grassroots organizations, publishes extensively, and holds seminars and workshops all over the globe.

"At ECCHR we don't talk as much about strategic litigation as we did at the beginning," says Wolfgang. "We still engage in litigation and aim for success in court proceedings. But now we describe our work as legal intervention. We use the law and other means in order to have an impact on society, to support local movements, to fight for the oppressed."

NEW PROJECTS

From its threadbare origins, ECCHR has grown rapidly to a strong team of 24 staff lawyers and 12 trainee lawyers. It is involved with litigation and other projects in 50 countries. And it will be a powerful legal force for worldwide human rights long into the future. Thanks to a training program that the Bertha Foundation founded in 2012, ECCHR's offices are always abuzz with the activity of young lawyers and law students from such diverse places as China, India, Colombia, Malaysia, and Europe. Trainees work on ECCHR cases, but also undergo a rigorous curriculum that includes workshops and lectures by internationally renowned guest speakers.

Since 2008, more than 400 human rights lawyers from more than 40 countries have volunteered or been trained at ECCHR. I have had the pleasure of working with many of these young people, and I am very touched that the torch is being passed to a new generation of enthusiastic, skilled, and radical international lawyers. It is reassuring to know that every day ECCHR and its alumni are continuing to work for human rights worldwide, providing the kind of legal advocacy that can and will make a difference.

10
A VISIT TO PALESTINE

If there was one moment when I finally let go of the connection I'd had with Israel since childhood, it came in 2010 on a visit to the occupied territories in the West Bank. For many years before then, I had been speaking out publicly against the occupation. But that was an intellectual position consistent with my anti-imperialist politics. Deep down, like many American Jews, I still had a powerful emotional tie to Israel. That changed forever when, at 66 years old, I finally saw the reality on the ground for myself.

Our trip began in late December 2009 in Cairo, Egypt. My wife Karen and I, and our two children, Jake, age 21, and Ana, 19, had decided to join the Gaza Freedom March (GFM) with 1,400 others to try to enter Gaza, the besieged homeland of a million and a half Palestinians. People from 42 countries had gathered for the non-violent march, which had been endorsed by, among many others, Code Pink's Medea Benjamin, historian Howard Zinn, and writers Alice Walker, Gore Vidal, Noam Chomsky, and Naomi Klein.

We were hoping to focus attention on the unlawful, punishing blockade that the Israeli and Egyptian governments had imposed on Gaza since 2007, and demonstrate to the Palestinians imprisoned in that small strip of land that they were not alone. Specifically, we intended to break the siege by bringing in tons of much-needed medical and food aid.

We did not make it into Gaza. Nor did almost anyone else from the march. Sadly, the Egyptian government (presumably in cahoots with Israel and probably the United States) refused to let us through the Rafah border entrance in Sinai. For five days we participated in the GFM's demonstrations to change Egypt's recalcitrance, to no avail. When we realized we weren't going to get into Gaza, we decided to go to Jerusalem and the West Bank to witness Israel's occupation of Palestine in those areas.

I had been to Israel twice as a child, once in the mid-1950s and once in the early 1960s. Back then, I had no idea that the land I was walking on had just a few years earlier been populated by another people. I knew nothing about Palestinians. Neither my family, nor my teachers, nor anyone in Israel had ever told me about them. My youthful trips to Israel were all milk and honey, and I have wonderful memories of the time I spent in Herzliya, Tel Aviv, Jerusalem, and Eilat. I came back in love with the place.

My disillusionment was gradual and very difficult. It began with the 1967 war in which Israel took the occupied Palestinian territories, Sinai, and the Golan Heights. Of course the Israelis had already taken a lot of Palestine's land and forced 700,000 Palestinians to flee their homes in 1948, but in 1967 I wasn't conscious of that.

I did know that millions of Palestinians were living in the occupied territories, and I had an emerging sense that people have a right to self-determination. Israel's argument that it had to have all of this territory for self-defense when its powerful U.S.-supported military had won the war in six days didn't make sense to me. Intellectually, I knew it was wrong for Israel to act as an occupier. But emotionally, I couldn't yet break with my attachment. I had many relatives in Israel, and I still thought of it as the land of my people.

My broader political understanding developed during the Vietnam War. I began to let go of some of the assumptions I had grown up with— that the U.S. was a moral country doing good for the world's people, and that Israel was a moral nation simply trying to defend itself from ene- mies hellbent on destroying it.

In the 1970s and 1980s, as I did solidarity work, I began to look at what the Israeli government had been doing in the world. It was support- ing apartheid in South Africa. It was training the U.S.-backed Contras who were fighting to overthrow the Sandinista government in Nicaragua. It was arming the U.S.-backed military in El Salvador against the liberation movement. Israel received more U.S. military aid than any country in the world. And in exchange, I realized, it had become the United States' most important ally in the Middle East—a foot soldier for U.S. policies around the globe.

As difficult as it is for me to write this, over time I also came to understand that the Israeli government's constantly repeated refrain that it wanted peace with the Palestinians was actually a false narrative. The truth was that the agenda of Zionism—as articulated by its leaders, from founder Theodor Herzl to Israel's first Prime Minister David Ben- Gurion to more recent Prime Ministers Menachem Begin, Ariel Sharon, and Benjamin Netanyahu—had always been to eliminate Palestinians from the Jewish state of Israel by any means, including terrorism.

So as my family and I embarked on this journey, 50 years after my first trip to Israel, I knew a lot more. Or I thought I did. But nothing had really prepared me for the apartheid state I was about to encounter as we flew to Tel Aviv and then took a car, with a Palestinian guide, into the occupied West Bank cities of Hebron, East Jerusalem, and Jenin.

I don't use the term "apartheid" lightly. What is happening in Israel and Palestine should be apparent to anyone who opens their eyes— checkpoints, a pass system, segregated roads, Jewish-only cities, and the expropriation for Jews of large swaths of Palestinian land. My entire family was shocked. It was all so intentional, so cruel.

When we visited Hebron, it was a city of 160,000 Palestinians. Over a period of two decades, 600 Israeli settlers had gradually moved into the center of the city. The way they did it was to take over an area approximately 30 blocks wide, previously populated by Palestinians. In the middle of this neighborhood, the settlers (supported by Israeli soldiers) ousted Palestinian families from homes they'd resided in for generations and moved into the empty apartment houses.

We visited such a neighborhood. To protect the settlers, Israeli armed guards surrounded the entire area. Though many Palestinians still lived in the district, they were not allowed to drive cars into it. They often had to walk more than a mile around checkpoints to get to their homes. They took food and other necessities in by mule. Only the Israeli settlers had cars and were allowed to drive in. The settlers also had an ambulance, donated by an American from Palm Beach. That ambulance, with a Magen David (a Jewish star) on it, was for the exclusive use of settlers. It could not be used to take a Palestinian to a hospital.

Hebron felt like an armed camp with watch towers overlooking the areas where the settlers lived. Small contingents of Israeli soldiers were on every corner, guarding each of these little enclaves. The Palestinians who remained faced constant harassment from the settlers and the Israeli soldiers. We saw one Palestinian open market located below a hill on which there was a Jewish settlement. A protective wire mesh covered the market—a necessity to protect Palestinian shoppers from bottles and garbage that settlers threw down from above.

Even young Jewish children could throw rocks at Palestinians with impunity. We were there with our host, a young Palestinian man, and settlers threw rocks at my children. The Israeli guards did nothing to stop them. Our host had a head full of scars from the times he had been attacked by settlers hurling rocks, and another man we met had a bullet still embedded in his head where he had been shot by Israeli soldiers.

One Palestinian woman told us that the massacre of February 25, 1994 still haunted Hebron's residents. On that day, the Jewish holiday of Purim, Baruch Goldstein, a fanatical Brooklyn-born settler and member of the extremist Jewish Defense League, entered Hebron's Tomb of the Patriarchs during a Muslim prayer service. He opened fire with an assault rifle, killing 29 innocent, unarmed Palestinians and wounding 125 before he was wrestled to the ground and beaten to death.

Shaken by what we'd seen in Hebron, we spent a few days in East Jerusalem. There we joined a demonstration against evictions in Sheikh Jarrah and witnessed Israel's open gobbling up of land in East Jerusalem and its environs. We saw Palestinian houses demolished in neighborhoods that Israel had designated as Area C—areas that were to be purged of Palestinians and illegally placed under complete Israeli control. We visited the homes of people whose houses had been demolished, rebuilt, then demolished again and again.

By contrast, we then visited Ma'ale Adumim, a Jewish "settlement" about two or three kilometers east of the city. You can see it from a hill in East Jerusalem. "Settlement" is a word the media uses all the time. But Ma'ale Adumim was actually a suburb of 50,000 people. The Israelis call it a "dormitory community." In the U.S. it would be called a "bedroom community." In an utterly parched land, it was a lush green oasis with a swimming pool as big as I've ever seen. And, of course, no Palestinians were allowed to live in that "settlement."

It was obvious that the Israelis were clearing East Jerusalem of as many Palestinians as they could. Beyond that, they were building these suburban "settlements" many kilometers outside of the city boundaries. Their plan was to incorporate them into what the Israelis call the "Jerusalem envelope."

All of this expropriation of occupied land taken by conquest during the 1967 war is illegal under international law. Article 49 of the Fourth Geneva Convention of 1949 prohibits nations from moving their population into territories occupied in a war. And it is, of course, absolutely devastating to the Palestinians who lived there.

Israel's unapologetic land-grab and inhumane treatment of Palestinians in the West Bank seemed unbelievable, almost surreal, to someone like me who had grown up embracing the idealistic dream of a Jewish homeland. But there was no avoiding the truth. My wife, my children, and I saw it with our own eyes. What I still don't understand is how anybody in the world today, whether Jewish or not, can accept or defend these illegal, brutal policies.

Leaving East Jerusalem, we next drove two hours north to Jenin, passing checkpoint after checkpoint. We visited the Jenin refugee camp, established in 1953, that had been so devastated by Israeli soldiers in April 2002 during the second intifada. We met refugees there who had been displaced twice. Initially, they were pushed out of their homes during the 1947-48 war. Then, after the second war in 1967, they were pushed out again into different camps—there are many in the West Bank. And all these years later, in 2010, they were still living in a refugee camp.

Run by the Palestine Authority, Jenin was different from other West Bank cities we had visited. Pictures of Palestinian "martyrs" hung from the lampposts, and armed Palestinian military men patrolled the street corners. While I always felt safe, this was clearly a militant Palestinian city.

After driving around awhile, we parked our car in front of a beautiful building constructed out of Jerusalem limestone. It felt like an oasis. This was the home of the Jenin Freedom Theatre, founded in 2006 by Juliano Mer-Khamis, the son of Israeli communists (Jewish father, Arab Christian mother) who identified himself as "100 percent Palestinian and 100 percent Jewish."

A big, affectionate bear of a man, Juliano hosted us for what proved to be a remarkable day. In the 1980s his mother Arna had set up learning centers and a theatre for Palestinian refugee children in the Jenin camp. Juliano documented his mother's work in the 2004 film *Arna's Children* and then followed in her footsteps by starting the Jenin Freedom Theatre, a community center that works with young people from the refugee camp who have tremendous anger and frustration after seeing their relatives and friends injured, killed, and jailed during Israeli incursions.

"We are not trying to heal their violence," said Juliano. "We try to channel it in more productive ways." The theatre is part of the resistance movement, according to Juliano, helping children and young adults to explore their feelings through poetry, dance, music, plays, and photography.

Juliano introduced us to a young man who taught photography at the theatre. Many of his students were teenage boys and girls, and their large color photos were mounted in an exhibition hall. We asked the teacher how it was for the teenagers when they returned to their homes in the camp. He said it was difficult, especially for the girls. They were doubly or triply oppressed—within their families, by the Israelis, and sometimes by the Palestinian government as well. The photographs of their difficult reality moved my daughter Ana so much that she asked the teacher to send them to her. Later she reproduced and presented them at an exhibition at her college.

While the theatre criticizes the Israeli government and its supporters, it doesn't pull punches when it comes to the Palestine Authority either—as we found out when we saw its play based on George Orwell's book, *Animal Farm*. In this version the human oppressors were the Israelis and the animals were the Palestinians. As the animals revolt and take power, they eventually oppress their own people. The political message could not be missed. The Palestine Authority, which many in the West Bank view as corrupt, had become the oppressor.

I asked Juliano how the Palestine Authority let him get away with it. "The officials come to performances and sit in the front row," he said. "Sometimes they laugh, sometimes they don't, but they let me and the theatre alone."

After the performance, we had a long lunch with Juliano and his lovely Finnish wife, Jenny Nyman, who fundraised for the theatre and had

recently had a baby. Juliano talked about his early life when he'd voluntarily enlisted in the Israeli army and been imprisoned for refusing orders
to frisk an old Palestinian man. In his ebullient style, he regaled us with
stories and thoughts about his later acting career, his radical independent
politics, and the power of theatre and art to transform people's lives.

A little more than a year after our visit, Juliano, age 52, was assassinated in his car in front of the Freedom Theatre. His young son was
sitting in his lap. At the time, his wife was pregnant with twin boys, who
were born a month later. No one was ever charged with the murder.

When I told my daughter Ana about Juliano's death, her eyes filled
with tears. She could not understand why anyone would murder a man
who was using art to heal people and to try to resolve violent conflicts
peacefully. I had no answers for her.

Now, as I remember Juliano, I think of this wonderful man and his
child who will never get to know and love him. I also think of the hundreds of young people, like those we met at Jenin, who may no longer be
able to move beyond their rage and frustration to a more hopeful future
where Juliano believed his theatre could take them.

Before our late-night flight back to New York City, we had one last
day in Jerusalem. A few days earlier, I'd suggested we visit Yad Vashem,
Israel's memorial to the Holocaust. But I was ambivalent for myself and
my family. This was not because I did not care about the Holocaust. I
cared deeply. My family lost many, many relatives in Tykocin, Białystok,
and Vilna. For members of my family who grew up in Cleveland, trips
to the killing camps in Europe were a rite of passage. As a 13-year-old
in 1956 I had been to a dark, cave-like Holocaust memorial in West
Jerusalem. In later years I made pilgrimages to Holocaust memorials in
New York, Washington D.C., and Berlin. To this day, the Holocaust and its
horrors remain a fundamental part of my identity.

So why was I ambivalent? Would visiting Yad Vashem somehow justify, if not for me, then for my wife and children, some of what we had just

seen in Hebron, East Jerusalem, and Jenin? Would it make the case for a Jewish state in Israel? My generation was raised on the narrative that Israel was necessary to save the Jewish people from the Holocaust—and to protect Jews from another Holocaust in the future. Wasn't that the very reason for having the major Jewish Holocaust memorial in Israel, at the foot of Mt. Herzl, a mountain named after the founder of Zionism?

In the end, I left my doubts behind and trusted my wife and kids to come to their own conclusions. So we made our pilgrimage to Yad Vashem on a sunny morning in late January.

Like so many visitors, we walked through the memorial in a stupor of horror. Display by display, we saw the documented history of the murder of six million Jewish people. Ghetto by ghetto, we witnessed the vile efficiency of the Nazi project. It was one of the most relentless indictments of human cruelty we had ever seen.

For my children, it was one of the first times they had immersed themselves in the history, documents, and words of the Holocaust. They spent hours listening to the testimony, viewing the videos, and asking questions. Occasionally, there were references to Zionism since it was part of the history of Jews in Eastern Europe. But it was not until the end of the formal exhibits that the "logic" of connecting the Holocaust to the founding of the state of Israel was made explicit: the musical theme at the end of our journey through Holocaust history was *Hatikvah* ("The Hope"), Israel's national anthem.

We then went into the Hall of Remembrance, a large round space with a deep pit carved out of its center, its walls lined with volume after volume of the names of the murdered. Off to one side was the computer room with a data base of the names that are known. My children immediately went to the computers and looked up our murdered relatives. Many had died at the Auschwitz concentration camp. Others had died of typhus within days of liberation from the camps. Others still were killed in the 1941 massacre in the Łopuchowo forest in Tykocin, Poland.

Three thousand men, women, and children from that village dug their own graves with the assistance of the local population and were slaughtered by the Einsatzgruppen, the German security service, during what has been called the Holocaust by Bullets. Thirty-seven members of our family were murdered in Tykocin.

As we left the museum—a triangular, elongated, windowless, cold concrete structure—we walked toward the picture window at the end. The beautiful view again reinforced the narrative: from the Holocaust to the state of Israel.

But as we stepped out into the light and onto a terrace overlooking the hills of Israel, I realized that in the distance below us lay the site of the former Palestinian village of Deir Yassin, where 150 men, women, and children were massacred by Zionist terrorists in April 1948. And suddenly I felt betrayed.

As saddened and horrified as I was by what we had just seen at Yad Vashem, I was struck by the contradiction of having the museum in Israel. This was a country forged from the theft of other people's land and homes, a nation whose treatment of Palestinians had echoes of what we had just seen: walled-in ghettos, stolen houses and land, a segregated population. It was an irony not lost on my family.

Yad Vashem should be a history lesson for us all, but it's a lesson that seems to be lost on many descendants of the Holocaust's victims. The history of genocide conveyed at Yad Vashem was unspeakably horrifying. But I felt the museum was using the powerful narrative of the Holocaust to try to make visitors accept, or at least justify, something that was unacceptable: the apartheid state that is today's Israel.

Earlier on our trip to Hebron our Palestinian guide had asked me whether I really believed that six million Jews had been killed in the Holocaust. Angered by his doubts, I answered him unequivocally: six million Jews had been murdered. But the visit to Yad Vashem helped me understand his skepticism. From his perspective, the Holocaust has been used to justify the daily violation of his people's human rights—and the world's failure to stop it.

These words have been painful to write. It's very difficult for me to raise questions about a memorial to the most horrific event in Jewish history. But I do not accept that Jewish sorrow should be used to hide or justify the sorrow of others. To truly remember and honor the lessons of the Holocaust would be to end the apartheid system that is the Israel of today. That would be a day of true hope.

PALESTINE LEGAL

After we returned to the U.S. in 2010, I couldn't stop thinking about what we'd seen in the West Bank. The disturbing images flashing through my head left me enraged. It was clear that Israel is not going to change from inside. It will change only when it is forced to by the rest of the world. That is why the Boycott, Divestiture, and Sanctions (BDS) movement, launched in 2005, is so important and also why Israel is so determined to silence it.

Inspired by the boycott campaigns of the 1980s that led to the end of apartheid in South Africa, the BDS movement pressures universities, investment banks, and other institutions to divest from or boycott companies that are complicit in human rights abuses in Israel and the occupied territories. On the *Law and Disorder* radio program, I interviewed Omar Barghouti, one of the founders of the BDS movement and author of the book *BDS: The Global Struggle for Palestinian Rights.* A calm, brilliant, and persuasive activist intellectual, Barghouti laid out the three goals of the BDS movement: the end of the 1967 occupation, the end of systematic racial discrimination in Israel, and the right of return of Palestinian refugees to Palestinian land in accordance with U.N. Resolution 194.

While the occupied territories get a lot of attention, Barghouti emphasized that BDS is just as concerned with the unequal two-tier system in Israel, one for Jews and the other for Israeli-born Palestinians who make up 20 percent of the population. "Israel has at least 30 laws that discriminate in a systematic way against indigenous Palestinian Arab citizens of Israel," he said. "If full equality for these citizens would destroy Israel, as some argue, what does that say about Israel? Did ending apartheid destroy South Africa? Did ending slavery and segregation destroy the U.S. South?" To those who dismiss BDS as ineffective, Barghouti pointed out that it will take time. "In less than six years we have achieved more than our comrades in South Africa did in 20 years," he said.

Barghouti was right. By 2011, student groups supporting Palestinian rights were sprouting up on university campuses all over the U.S. Many had successfully passed student body resolutions and referenda in support of BDS.

Israel had always known that it was vulnerable to international boycott. It responded swiftly. In a 2010 paper, the Reut Institute, an Israeli think tank, characterized the BDS campaign as a "delegitimization challenge" and an "existential threat" to Israel. The institute recommended that Israel sabotage and attack those who question Israel's policies.

In October 2010, the Jewish Federations of North America and the Jewish Council for Public Affairs launched the Israel Action Network, a $6 million campaign to counter activities that "delegitimize" Israel. It backed lobbying, public relations, and watchdog groups whose goal was to vilify and silence Palestinian rights advocates by labeling them as anti-Semitic or pro-terrorist.

The result of their efforts, to cite just a few examples from 2011, was that 10 students at the University of California Irvine were convicted on criminal charges for protesting a speech that the Israeli ambassador to the U.S. had made on their campus. In Olympia, Washington, several food co-op members initiated a lawsuit against their own co-op board that had voted unanimously to boycott Israeli goods. And at Rutgers

University, Hillel and the Anti-Defamation League accused students who had been fundraising for the U.S. Boat to Gaza—which tried to break the blockade—of providing material support for terrorism. Rutgers prevented them from donating the money they raised to the non-profit organization of their choice.

These attempts to target the First Amendment-protected free speech of Palestinian rights activists infuriated me, especially since I'd recently seen for myself Israel's treatment of Palestinians in the West Bank. I called a small meeting to explore what could be done about the desperate situation in Palestine. Attending were several experienced lawyers and activists: Maria LaHood, counsel in several Palestinian rights cases for CCR; Jamil Dakwar, director of the ACLU's Human Rights Program; and Columbia University professor Rashid Khalidi. By far the youngest in attendance was Rashid's daughter, 32-year-old lawyer Dima Khalidi, who had been an Ella Baker summer intern at CCR in 2007.

My first experience working directly with Dima was in 2009 when she and Rashid alerted me to the Simon Wiesenthal Center's plan to build a so-called Museum of Tolerance on top of the ancient Muslim Mamilla Cemetery in Jerusalem. Some of Rashid and Dima's own ancestors and many historical figures were buried in that cemetery. I was livid that the Wiesenthal Center had the gall to even consider building on top of the graves of generations of Palestinians—and that Israel's Supreme Court had allowed the project to proceed.

I gathered a group of lawyers—Len Weinglass, Maria LaHood, Michael Smith, Richard Levy, Michael Kennedy—to discuss strategies to stop the desecration of the cemetery. But we couldn't find a viable legal path to take. Fresh out of law school, Dima volunteered to draft a complaint to United Nations human rights officials asking them to intervene. We had no illusions that Israel would pay attention to what the U.N. would do. But we wanted the U.N. to document the violations, to publicize the issue and bolster opposition in the U.S., Palestine, and Israel. Human Rights Council resolutions did express concern at the desecration of the cemetery and called on Israel to stop its "illegal activities therein." Despite these resolutions and continuing public opposition from Palestinians who view the site as sacred, the project proceeded, digging up hundreds of remains and hiding evidence. (Editor's Note: The museum is still under construction and is scheduled to open in 2019.)

Two years later, we were meeting again to brainstorm about how to confront Israel's impunity on Palestinian issues. Jamil pointed out that several international human rights groups—including CCR, ECCHR, the ACLU, Amnesty International, and Human Rights Watch—were working on lawsuits to make Israel accountable for its human rights violations in the occupied territories. Bringing another lawsuit seemed redundant and a probable dead end.

"Why don't we focus on what's happening to Palestine activists in the U.S.?" I suggested. I knew that CCR had been receiving many calls from these activists whose advocacy efforts on behalf of Palestinians were being suppressed in various ways.

We were all well aware that Israel and its surrogates—the Brandeis Center, StandWithUs, the Zionist Organization of America, the Anti-Defamation League, the American Israel Public Affairs Committee, the Jewish Federations of North America, the Jewish Council for Public Affairs, the American Jewish Committee, among many others—were actively trying to suppress voices opposed to Israeli policy. The most obvious was Hillel International, the largest Jewish campus organization in the world, which openly prohibited its affiliates from hosting speakers supportive of BDS. This orchestrated campaign was an obvious assault on the right to dissent and freedom of speech.

Rashid emphasized the urgency of having lawyers to turn to, noting that the intent was to crush the movement and to chill academic work around Palestine.

A VISIT TO PALESTINE

"We've done something like that before," I reminded everyone. "Back in the '80s, CCR and the Lawyers Guild started the Movement Support Network to defend Central America solidarity activists from government harassment and spying."

The group concluded that we needed to do some research, and Dima volunteered. In the next few months she spoke to dozens of lawyers and activists in the U.S., Europe, and Palestine. Her study confirmed what we had suspected: activists everywhere were under attack for defending Palestinians' human rights. They felt threatened and needed legal protection.

Dima wrote a proposal to start a new non-profit legal organization. Its mission would be to defend Palestinian-rights activists in the U.S., protect the right to dissent, and build public support for Palestinian rights. Though the organization would be independent, its legal work would initially be done with CCR as co-counsel and have the benefit of supervision and support from CCR attorneys. I took the proposal to Tony Tabatznik, and the Bertha Foundation agreed to provide initial funding.

Originally called Palestine Solidarity Legal Support and later shortened to Palestine Legal, the fledgling organization began in 2012 with just two attorneys: Dima in Chicago as its director and Liz Jackson in the San Francisco Bay Area. For the first year, they both worked out of their homes as they reached out to the Palestine solidarity community, opened an intake line where activists could report incidents or ask for help, and developed a know-your-rights training program for students.

In 2013, the group officially launched. Word-of-mouth spread, and soon Palestine Legal was receiving dozens of calls from activists for Palestinian rights who were being harassed or intimidated. The harassment, mostly on college campuses, took many forms, including accusations of anti-Semitism and pro-terrorism, cancellations of pro-Palestinian speakers and events, lawsuits, threats and prosecutions against activists, and firing of professors who spoke out against Israeli policies.

While Palestine Legal routinely helped with these complaints, it also wrote *amicus* briefs in both the Irvine 11 and Olympia Food Co-op cases, conducted know-your-rights workshops, and published a legal and tactical guide for Palestinian rights activists and students.

As the movement for Palestinian rights grew steadily through 2013, high-level Israeli government figures, led by Prime Minister Benjamin Netanyahu and wealthy benefactors such as Sheldon Adelson and Haim Saban, participated in strategic meetings to oppose Palestine activism, particularly BDS campaigns. As a result, Israel stepped up its attempts to suppress voices critical of its policies. The Jewish Agency for Israel announced that it would commit $300 million to this effort and "would combine donor dollars from the United States with Israeli government funds to create what is likely the most expensive pro-Israel campaign ever."

But Israel's expensive PR blitz wasn't enough to overcome the world's revulsion at Israel's ruthless attack on Gaza in July 2014. In 51 days, Israeli forces carried out more than 6,000 air strikes and fired 50,000 tank and artillery shells, killing 1,462 Palestinian civilians, a third of them children, and wounding nearly 10,000. No match for the Israeli army, Palestinian armed groups launched 4,881 rockets and 1,753 mortars towards Israel. Sixty-seven Israeli soldiers and six civilians were killed and 1,600 injured. More than 5,500 Gazans were imprisoned, including 164 children held without charges.

I was appalled, as were tens of thousands of protesters around the world who poured into the streets in solidarity with the Palestinians. Students for Justice in Palestine groups sprouted up on campuses. The BDS movement gained momentum and began to achieve major successes. The Presbyterian Church (USA) voted to divest from Caterpillar, Hewlett-Packard, and Motorola Solutions—three enormous companies that "supply Israel with equipment used in the occupation of Palestinian territory." The Bill Gates Foundation sold its entire stake in G4S, a

UK-based corporation that provided surveillance systems to Israeli prisons. Faced with plummeting revenues and stock prices, several big corporations, including SodaStream and the French company Veolia, abandoned their operations in illegal West Bank settlements as a result of BDS campaigns.

The more effective the movement was, though, the more Israel escalated its assault on anyone who criticized its policies. The most publicized case involved Steven Salaita, who had resigned as a tenured English professor at Virginia Tech University, sold his house, and accepted a new tenured job that the University of Illinois at Urbana-Champaign had offered him. After Salaita sent out several enraged tweets about Israel's assault on Gaza, pro-Zionist groups and wealthy donors accused him of anti-Semitism and pressured the university to terminate his contract. Two weeks before classes began, the university caved in, and Salaita was left without a job. Represented by CCR, Salaita filed a lawsuit against the university, which eventually agreed to a settlement awarding him more than $800,000. However, he has been unable to find work at an American university ever since. Salaita's experience affected me deeply, and Karen and I held a fundraiser for him at our home.

Salaita was only one of many professors targeted for criticizing Israeli policies. In the fall of 2014, the AMCHA Initiative, an Israel advocacy group, issued a blacklist of more than 200 Middle East Studies professors it declared to be "anti-Israel."

Another of the casualties was Sari Nusseibeh, the Palestinian president of Al-Quds University in Jerusalem, which had a partnership with my alma mater, Brandeis University in Massachusetts. I knew President Nusseibeh, a widely respected scholar who spent his entire life working for a peaceful solution between Palestine and Israel. We both served on the advisory board of the International Center for Ethics, Justice, and Public Life at Brandeis. After a student rally at Al-Quds in which demonstrators stepped on Israeli flags, Brandeis President Fred Lawrence suspended Nusseibeh from our board and ended the 10-year partnership with Al-Quds.

However, the Brandeis faculty sent three of its members to Jerusalem to investigate what had happened. They reported back that in response to the rally President Nusseibeh had issued a statement that the students' actions "violated university policy and principles." He urged "students and others to act in a way that promotes mutual respect, peaceful coexistence, and the exchange of ideas."

Evidently, that wasn't good enough for President Lawrence. After he suspended Nusseibeh and ended the relationship with Al-Quds, I resigned in protest from the ethics board. In a letter to Lawrence, I explained that his precipitous actions were unacceptable. They not only wrongly damaged Sari Nusseibeh's dignity and reputation, but damaged far more the reputation of Brandeis itself.

In 2014-2015, the attacks on Palestinian rights activists by pro-Israel advocacy groups escalated further. Calls to Palestine Legal flooded its intake line. As an advisory board member, I urged Dima to publish the incidents she had compiled in her initial research, together with the record of incidents Palestine Legal had documented since then through its intake line. Beyond its legal work, it seemed to me, Palestine Legal could become an important advocate by compiling a systematic record of the incidents reported to it every day and publishing it in an easily accessible report.

In September 2015, Palestine Legal and CCR co-published the report entitled *The Palestine Exception to Free Speech.* In my view, it is a must-read for anyone who believes in preserving the First Amendment in the U.S. It shows that when it comes to the issue of Palestine, the rights to free speech and academic freedom have been severely eroded.

The statistics speak for themselves. Between January 2014 and June 2015, Palestine Legal responded to 292 incidents of censorship, punishment, or suppression of the rights of Palestinian activists. [Editor's

Update: In 2017, Palestine Legal responded to 308 incidents of suppression of U.S.-based Palestine advocacy, a 19 percent increase from 2016. In 2018, it responded to another 289 incidents. Over five years, from January 1, 2014 through December 31, 2018, it responded to a total of 1,247 incidents.]

More than 85 percent of those incidents targeted students and professors on more than 65 U.S. college campuses. The report outlines the tactics—including event cancellations, administrative disciplinary actions, firings, lawsuits, and false and inflammatory accusations of terrorism and anti-Semitism—that Israel advocacy groups are using against activists. It also contains testimony from some of those who have been targeted and an appendix documenting more than 50 campus-related case studies.

The report detailed how Israeli advocacy organizations have been using baseless legal complaints to try to suppress free speech. For example, the Brandeis Center, the AMCHA Initiative, and Zionist Organization of America have all filed complaints against universities, alleging violations of Title VI of the Civil Rights Act of 1964. They claimed that speech critical of Israel creates a hostile educational environment for Jewish students. Palestine Legal and others have refuted that false argument, and so far it has been rejected by the Department of Education, which is in charge of adjudicating such complaints, and by the courts.

However, Israel advocacy groups have turned to an even more dangerous tactic: lobbying for anti-BDS bills or executive orders in various states. As the *Palestine Exception* report notes, 11 of these measures were introduced in 2014 and another 16 in the first half of 2015. (Editor's Update: As of 2019, anti-BDS legislation has been enacted in 27 states.) Even though the Supreme Court has long held that political boycotts are a First Amendment-protected form of free speech, these laws take a direct shot at the right to boycott. For example, some prohibit state contracts with organizations that support BDS. Others require state pension funds to divest from companies that boycott Israel.

Palestine Legal has provided legal support and analysis to activists opposing these unconstitutional laws. In 2016, local coalitions supported by Palestine Legal defeated anti-BDS bills in Maryland, Virginia, and Massachusetts. In New York, activists successfully stopped two anti-BDS bills in the legislature before Governor Andrew Cuomo signed an anti-BDS executive order.

As the movement for Palestinian rights grows worldwide, Israel's attempts to suppress and silence it are intensifying. To deal with the increased case load, Palestine Legal has grown. It now has five attorneys and three support staff working out of Chicago, Berkeley, and New York.

As an advisory board member, I was privileged to join these bright, energetic, courageous young people at a staff retreat in Chicago in the summer of 2015. I saw them in action as they strategized and planned for the challenges ahead. They recognize that the battle for Palestinian rights is going to be long and difficult. They know that the stakes are high. It is not just Palestine that is in jeopardy, but also the U.S. Constitution's First Amendment. Palestine Legal is committed to defending and protecting both.

I don't know when, how, or if the conflict between Israelis and Palestinians will be resolved. But I do know that BDS and the global movement for Palestinian rights—thanks in large measure to the support they receive from Palestine Legal—are gaining strength and having a positive impact.

ROOTS

Shortly after Israel launched its 2014 assault on Gaza, I took a long-planned roots trip to Germany and Poland, accompanied by my wife and children, my sister, my brother, and my niece. I had traveled to Poland in the 1980s and again in 2008. But my children had never been to Warsaw, where my mother's mother was born, or to Białystok, where my father grew up. I wanted to share these places with my family.

I'd recently become interested in genealogy. With the help of Dr. Alex Friedlander, my brother Bruce, my sister Ellen, and I had filled in our extended family tree. The awful truth was that 101 members of our mother's and father's families had been murdered in the Holocaust. Several years before, I'd taken my wife and kids on the emotional, thought-provoking visit to the Yad Vashem memorial in Jerusalem. But they had never been to a Nazi death camp. Though I dreaded going, I wanted my children to know the reality of what had happened to their ancestors.

Our trip began in Wannsee, Germany, where Nazi leaders had conceived the Final Solution to the Jewish Question—their genocidal extermination plan for the Jewish people. In Berlin, we visited the house where my great uncle, Elias Shpet, had lived with his wife Emma. In September 1939, as part of their campaign against foreign-born Jews, the Nazis had detained Elias, then 60 years old, and sent him to a work camp at Sachsenhausen. In January 1940, after five months of hard labor under unspeakable conditions, Elias died there. The Nazis sent his ashes to Emma. (This was before they began mass cremations and mass graves in the death camps.) She buried the remains in the Jewish Weissensee cemetery. On an earlier trip to Berlin I had found Elias's grave. It was unmarked and overrun by weeds. Profoundly moved, I went to a stone mason and ordered a new gravestone for him.

For two years after Elias's death, Emma had remained at their home in Berlin. Then the Nazis sent her to their death camp at Chełmno. She was killed there in 1944. To commemorate Elias and Emma, I had ordered two *stolpersteine*—stones bearing brass plates inscribed with the names and dates of Nazi victims. The *Stolpersteine* Project was initiated by the German artist Gunter Demnig in 1992. Its goal is to remember individuals at the last place where they freely chose to live before the Nazis killed them.

On our trip to Berlin, my family and I witnessed the ceremony placing the *stolpersteine* in front of the building where Elias and Emma Shpet had lived. It was in a modest neighborhood in the former East Germany. A small group of neighbors huddled around as the stones were placed in the ground. And I found myself weeping for these two relatives I'd never known.

In Warsaw, on a cold, rainy day we visited the cemetery where my mother's grandmother was buried. It's a sprawling place with more than 100,000 graves, all overgrown and in disrepair. Somehow my son Jake found the small tombstone marking the grave of my great-grandmother. It was pocked with bullet holes. Jews from the Warsaw ghetto had taken cover behind it and other gravestones as they tried to escape the Nazis' gunfire.

We also went to a memorial at the site of the Warsaw ghetto uprising. In 1943, when the Nazis tried to send the Jewish residents of the ghetto to the Treblinka death camp, the Jews armed themselves and fought back. For several months they resisted. In the end, the Nazis burned the ghetto to the ground, killing 13,000 Jews.

In Białystok, we walked on the street where my father lived as a boy. We had a photo of the Ratner family's house and searched for a long time, but we didn't find it. The house had been torn down many years before.

Our trip ended with visits to the killing camps at Auschwitz and Treblinka. We'd seen photos and read about these places. But being there was far more gut-wrenching. Auschwitz has been restored the way it was as a work and death camp. As if in a trance, we walked inside the decaying brick buildings, and my mind's eye caught fleeting glimpses of the unimaginable suffering that had taken place there. The train station where cars jammed with terrified Jews had arrived. The haunting, abandoned train tracks. The piles of worn shoes. The ghostly killing chambers. The canisters of Zyklon B poison gas. The desperate scratch marks of fingernails on walls. The ovens. The mass burial grounds.

Treblinka was a death camp that the Nazis deliberately hid from the world. No work was done there, just extermination. After an uprising in which approximately 60 Jewish prisoners escaped, the Nazis destroyed the entire camp. We only know what happened at Treblinka from the accounts of the few who escaped. Over a period of nine months, most of Poland's Jews were rounded up and sent there. Upon arrival, they were killed, cremated, and buried in mass graves.

Treblinka is about ten miles from Białystok in the middle of nowhere. When we visited, we were the only ones there. We walked into a beautiful forest. Then we came upon a large clearing in the woods that extended for acres and acres. This was the mass grave where the remains of nearly one million Polish Jews were buried.

There is a memorial at Treblinka, a Soviet-era monument consisting of ragged stones sticking out of the ground, each marked with the name of a city or village where the victims had lived. My brother Bruce and I walked through the memorial silently, arm in arm, shaking our heads, tears in our eyes. When we came upon the stone marked Białystok, we stopped and stood for a long time, thinking and feeling. Who knows how many of our family had been murdered here?

As we left, we were all in shock. We cried. Nobody spoke. The magnitude of the horror was beyond words. It took me a long time to recover and try to make some sense of what we'd seen. I kept thinking about the phrase "Never again." I'd heard it repeated by Jews my entire life. The meaning was clear: never again should there be a Holocaust, never again should the Jewish people be victims of genocide.

Overcome by what I'd seen at Auschwitz and Treblinka, I now understood on a gut level the power and importance of "Never again" to Jews, and particularly to Holocaust survivors and their families. But for me, those two words have a broader meaning. They mean that never again should genocide happen—period. My work as a human rights lawyer stems directly from heeding the admonition "Never again," whether that "never" is for Jews, Armenians, Native Americans, Cambodians, Rwandans, Palestinians, indigenous peoples, or any other people on this earth.

The scale of the Nazi Holocaust may be unparalleled in history. But all people are capable of unspeakable acts against their fellow human beings. To all those acts—whether it's torture at Guantánamo, the killing of Tutsis in Rwanda, or the methodical strangulation of Gaza —we must also say "Never again."

My trip to Poland in 2014 confirmed what I'd concluded after my trip to Yad Vashem in 2010. The Holocaust cannot be used to justify terrible acts by anyone, including the state of Israel. That is why I, an American Jew whose family lost many members in the Holocaust, can say today that I am very proud to be part of Palestine Legal and the international movement for Palestinian rights.

11
VIVA CUBA LIBRE!

Other than the days on which my wife Karen gave birth to our two children, no day in my life has been more memorable and moving than July 20, 2015.

I woke before dawn on that Monday morning, my mind racing with a mix of excitement, anticipation, and adrenaline. I put on my best gray blazer, a blue shirt, and a flashy tie. I was ready to go to Washington D.C. to witness an historic moment. On this day, after 54 years of being closed, the Cuban embassy in Washington, D.C. and the U.S. embassy in Havana were scheduled to reopen, marking a long-awaited thawing of diplomatic relations between the two countries. I had worked hard to get to this moment, along with many others, but it had been such a long time coming that I wasn't sure I'd ever see it in my lifetime.

On January 3, 1961, when I was 16 years old, President Dwight Eisenhower had severed U.S. relations with Cuba, as the CIA prepared for the disastrous Bay of Pigs invasion that was to come a few months later. Flags were lowered and the embassies in both countries were shut down. In 1977 President Jimmy Carter opened the door a crack, allowing the former Cuban embassy in Washington, a grand limestone building at 2630 16th St., to house a Cuban interests section administered by the Swiss government. For the next 38 years, the interests section could issue passports and visas, but there were still no formal diplomatic relations between the U.S. and Cuba.

Throughout this entire time, the U.S. government had tried to overthrow the government of President Fidel Castro. The Cuban revolution had survived the Bay of Pigs invasion, the assassination of Che Guevara, and the CIA's numerous unsuccessful attempts to assassinate Castro himself. The U.S. had also tried to isolate Cuba in Latin America and the Caribbean, demanding that it be removed from the Organization of American States (OAS) and leading the overthrow of progressive governments in Brazil, Argentina, Bolivia, Uruguay, and Chile that supported Cuba. Perhaps the most devastating assault was what the Cubans call *el bloqueo,* or the blockade. After the Castro government nationalized Cuba's oil refineries, the U.S. imposed a commercial, economic, and financial embargo on Cuba. It was a crippling blow. In 1959, when the revolution seized power, 85 percent of Cuba's trade was with the U.S. By the end of 1961, the percentage of its trade with the U.S. had plummeted to zero.

Fifty-four years later, *el bloqueo* was still in effect, but the revolutionary government, now led by Fidel Castro's younger brother Raúl, was still in power. A new generation of progressive governments in Latin America had recognized Cuba and welcomed it back into the OAS. In 2014, at the OAS meeting, President Obama came to the realization that it was the U.S., not Cuba, that was becoming isolated. He understood that something had to change, and in a symbolic gesture, he shook hands with President Raúl Castro. As Obama put it, "We can't keep doing the same thing for five decades and expect a different result." With the help of Pope Francis, representatives of the two governments began meeting in secret. And finally, in a 45-minute phone call, Pope Francis, President Obama, and President Castro hammered out an exchange of political prisoners and agreed to ease travel, banking, and communications restrictions on both sides.

That agreement was an historic step toward normalizing diplomatic relations between the two countries. In an address from the White House cabinet room, Obama said, "Through these changes, we intend to create more opportunities for the American and Cuban people and begin a new chapter among the nations of the Americas."

Early on the morning of July 20, Michael Smith and I boarded a high-speed train from Penn Station in New York to Union Station in Washington, D.C. As the co-authors of two books about the murder of Che Guevara and as longtime activists in the Cuban solidarity movement, we had the honor of being invited by the Cuban government to witness the embassy's reopening ceremonies.

Our Che books resulted directly from the enactment of the Freedom of Information Act (FOIA) in 1967 and President Clinton's executive directives in the early 1990s expanding FOIA to allow the release of some previously withheld national security documents. I had long admired Che Guevara for his courage in fighting against international capitalism and U.S. corporate power in particular. In 1984, with the help of Ann Marie Buitrago and Ellen Ray of the Fund for Open Information and Accountability, CCR and I made a request under the FOIA for all FBI files relating to Che. A year later we received two large boxes of documents. In 1997, on the 30th anniversary of Che's murder, we published our first book based on these files, *Che Guevara and the FBI.*

The FBI files included documents from a range of U.S. agencies that shared information, including the CIA, National Security Council, State Department, and Foreign Broadcast Information Service. They run from 1952 when the FBI opened its first file on Che to 1968, nearly a year after he was murdered in Bolivia. The files describe him as "fairly intellectual for a Latino," revealing more about the Bureau's racist stereotypes than about Che. But most of the documents concentrate on Che's movements and associations. The spy agencies saw him as a serious threat to the United States, a dangerous role model for revolutionaries worldwide.

They clearly wanted Che dead. Although the documents we had for the first book raised our suspicions, they did not show any evidence of assassination plots against Che.

In 2007, a decade after we published the first book and with no additional request, I received another box of documents from the government. We could only surmise that someone on the inside wanted the public to know the full story of Che's death. Our second book, *Who Killed Che? How the CIA Got Away with Murder,* was based on the new set of documents and interviews we conducted, including with Che's widow Aleida March, Ulises Estrada, former head of Cuban intelligence for Latin America, and Gustavo Villoldo, a Cuban exile the CIA had sent to Bolivia disguised as a Bolivian soldier in order to track down Che. We also gleaned information from several books published in the interim, including CIA operative Félix Rodríguez's *Shadow Warrior* and Jorge Castañeda's *Companero: The Life and Death of Che Guevara.*

The official story put out by President Lyndon Johnson's staff was that Che had been wounded in combat, captured, and finally executed by a Bolivian counter-insurgency force. This narrative offered the White House plausible deniability and steered any responsibility away from the CIA. As for the Bolivian government, it claimed Che had not been executed but died from combat wounds.

Our analysis of the documents, together with the context provided by the interviews and other books, left no doubt that the U.S. Army Green Berets trained, armed, and directed the Bolivian Army unit that tracked down Che in the jungle. A Bolivian soldier pulled the trigger, but the orders to murder Che were issued as part of a deal the CIA had made with Bolivian President René Barrientos: if the CIA found Che, Bolivia would kill him. The CIA and the U.S. government were ultimately responsible for Che's assassination.

The Cuban government appreciated our efforts to set the historical record straight. Both books, originally published in the U.S., were translated and distributed widely at low cost in Cuba, and *Who Killed Che?* was featured at the 2014 Havana Book Fair.

When Michael Smith and I arrived in Washington, we took a cab to the embassy, an impressive two-story stone mansion built in 1917. At 9:30 a.m. it was already 90 degrees, with the mercury rising. The sun shone down from a cloudless blue sky, and the sweltering air was thick with humidity. It felt like a sauna.

But Cubans were used to heat, and the atmosphere on the embassy grounds was electric. A crowd of 700 invited guests milled around out front. Several hundred more bystanders watched from the street. In snappy suits and elegant dresses, the guests may have looked like they were dressed for a gala at the Gran Teatro de la Habana, but it felt like a festive Cuban street party. Everyone was excited, talking, laughing, kissing, embracing, sweating.

"I've been dreaming of this day ever since I became a socialist in college," said Michael.

I'd been dreaming of it for a long time, too. As I looked at the crowd in front of the embassy, my thoughts drifted back to the late 1960s when I was in college and law school. Like many students back then, I'd seen the poster that seemed to be on everyone's walls. It had a romantic image of the defiant revolutionary Che in a beret, with his famous quote "Let me say, at the risk of appearing ridiculous, that the true revolutionary is guided by great feelings of love." It was a sentiment that combined what many of us in the 1960s were feeling: the need for revolutionary change and the need for compassion. Che instantly became a hero of mine.

But I didn't fall in love with the country of Cuba until I volunteered for the Venceremos Brigade in 1976 and spent two months working in construction and traveling there (see chapter 6). The special allure of Cuba captured my heart immediately—its joyous people, laughing, dancing, playing music in the streets, inviting me into their homes for meals; its physical beauty from beaches to jungle to mountains; its exciting capital of Havana adorned by Deco-era architecture, colorful 1950s American cars, and the majestic Malecón walkway by the sea.

Ever since then, I realized, my life and career have been closely intertwined with this magical island in the Caribbean. Over the years at CCR, I've helped defend many people who'd gotten into trouble by defying the U.S. government's travel ban and embargo against Cuba (see chapter 7). The most important case I worked on in the '80s also involved Cuba—the Haitian HIV-positive refugees had been kept out of the U.S. and sent to the U.S. Naval Base at Guantánamo Bay (see chapter 8). In the early 2000s, I spent most of my time representing prisoners at Guantánamo (see chapter 9). And along with others at CCR, I had been involved in the defense of the Cuban Five, who'd been wrongly convicted of conspiracy to commit espionage in Miami, when in fact what they'd been doing was trying to stop right-wing Cubans' terrorist attacks on Cuba. Len Weinglass had been their lead attorney, and Margaret Ratner Kunstler and I had written an *amicus curiae* brief supporting them. Now, as part of the agreement between Obama and Raúl Castro, the last of the Cuban 5 had been released back to Cuba.

Through all of this, my love for Cuba's people and my respect for its revolution have only grown deeper. For me, as a person who became involved in political movements in the '70s, Cuba was perhaps the most important revolutionary country in the world. And it remains so today for many people because it rejected the values of western capitalism that so many had embraced—private profit, the selfish interests of the individual, the aspiration to unlimited wealth for a few at the expense of the many. Against all odds Cuba showed the world what a revolutionary government committed to socialism, education, health, and the well-being of its people could do. It became an example for every revolutionary movement worldwide.

Domestically, it leveled the playing field. After the revolution, the gap between rich and poor narrowed dramatically. Before the revolution, 73 percent of the land was owned by 9 percent of the people, mainly investors from the U.S. Under international law, Cuba had a right to nationalize its own property and was required to compensate the previous owners. Under the new agrarian land reform laws, it offered compensation based on evaluations the U.S. owners had provided for tax purposes, but the U.S. landowners refused. The Cubans then nationalized the land. Farms were limited to 3,333 acres and real estate to 1,000 acres. The government expropriated land that exceeded those limits and redistributed it to more than 100,000 peasants and communes in 67-acre parcels. Under new housing laws, the government destroyed shanty towns and built new government housing to replace them. Eviction and real estate speculation were prohibited, rents were limited to 10 percent of household income, electricity was free, and half of urban rental tenants were converted to homeowners.

The government provided free education from kindergarten through doctorate level based on ability. In 1961, the Year of Education, the government sent literacy brigades into the countryside as teachers and in one year increased literacy levels from 60 percent to 96 percent— one of the highest rates in the world. In 1953, only 53 percent of children were enrolled in school. By 1986, 100 percent were enrolled.

Despite the embargo, no one starved. Every household received government-subsidized monthly food rations. And every Cuban got free high-quality health care. Average life expectancy rose from 55.8 years in 1950 to 79 years in 2012, while infant mortality plummeted to 4.83 deaths per thousand births in 2013, lower than in the U.S. And in 2005, Cuba's ratio of 67 doctors per 10,000 population—compared with only 24 per 10,000 in the U.S.—was the highest in the world.

Yes, there were problems. The economic embargo, the collapse of the Soviet Union, increasingly severe hurricanes, bureaucratic incompetence, and some bad government policy decisions caused a lot of suffering and frustration. Discrimination against gay people was widespread, though that has improved somewhat in recent years. The kind of free speech, dissent, and elections we're used to in the U.S. didn't exist.

But the priority for revolutionary Cuba has always been economic and social rights for all. I agree with that priority. I want to see children living in decent housing, getting an education, having health care, and participating in society, not begging on the street. And that's the example Cuba provided domestically.

Internationally, Cuba has not only been a model for revolutionary movements and governments, but Cubans have put their own lives on the line in other countries. On the eve of Angola's independence in 1976, Cuba sent 25,000 troops to support the People's Movement for the Liberation of Angola against the invading South African army. Fighting side by side with Angolan leftists and anti-apartheid activists, those Cubans helped defeat the South African army. That victory marked the beginning of the end of apartheid.

Cuba's international solidarity efforts have never stopped. When I worked in Central America in the 1980s, I saw with my own eyes Cuba's support for the revolutions in El Salvador, Nicaragua, and Grenada. If there were disagreements among the leaders, they would meet in Havana to try and work them out. When there were earthquakes in El Salvador, Cuba sent doctors to help. More recently Cuba has sent doctors to help the people of Venezuela, South Africa, the Gambia, Guinea-Bissau, Mali, and many other countries. As of 2015, Cuba has more than 25,000 doctors working in 68 countries worldwide.

Cuba has been an example for all of us. Despite its flaws, the Cuban revolution has shown us how to put socialist ideas into practice, how to sacrifice and take risks in order to make profound changes in the social order and in people's individual lives. That is the reason I have proudly worked for more than four decades to support the Cuban revolution.

Over the years, I visited Cuba many times for work, research, book launches, and pleasure. On these trips I made many friends in Cuba and in the solidarity movement around the world. As we waded into the crowd in front of the embassy, many of those friends greeted Michael and me. It was as sweet a reunion as I could imagine.

Ricardo Alarcón, former Cuban foreign minister, president of the National Assembly, and for 30 years Cuba's permanent representative to the United Nations, was the first to give Michael and me a hearty hug. He'd been a friend for many years and had written the introduction to our second book about the death of Che.

We turned around, and there to give us kisses was Code Pink co-founder Medea Benjamin. One after another, we embraced old friends from the solidarity movement—Michael Krinsky, Cuba's lawyer in the U.S.; Cuban-American lawyer José Pertierra; Peter Kornbluh, director of the National Security Archive's Cuban Documentation Project; Estela Vázquez, executive vice president of 1199 Service Employees International Union; Sandra Levinson, director of the Center for Cuban Studies in New York, who'd been arranging trips to Cuba and supporting Cuban cultural exchange for decades; actor Danny Glover; and so many others. *Democracy Now!* host Amy Goodman circulated through the crowd, broadcasting live, microphone in hand.

Several courageous members of the U.S. Congress who had supported Cuba over the years were also there—Senator Patrick Leahy of Vermont, and Representatives Barbara Lee of California and Raúl Grijalva of Arizona.

Joining all these guests was a delegation of more than two dozen Cuban officials from Havana, led by Foreign Minister Bruno Rodríguez and Cuba's chief negotiator, Josefina Vidal. The delegation also included one of Cuba's most beloved musicians, Silvio Rodríguez, whose lyrical, impassioned songs and pure voice had accompanied the revolution since the early days of the Nueva Trova (New Song) movement in the 1960s.

At precisely 10:30 a.m., a military band played a brass fanfare, and the official ceremonies began. As the crowd hushed, the Cuban delegation walked out and lined up near the flag poles. Another fanfare. Then three Cuban soldiers marched out in full-dress white uniforms with red-white-and-blue sashes and gold epaulets. They halted in front of the flagpole and unfolded the Cuban flag. As they raised it, the band played the Cuban national anthem. Everyone in the crowd was singing, tears streaming down their cheeks. "*Viva Cuba!*" someone shouted. And then others joined in, "*Viva Cuba libre!*"

I looked up. For the first time in 54 years, the Cuban flag—blue and white stripes with a white star on a triangle of red—was proudly flying at the Cuban embassy in the United States. And though I'm not usually a flag-waver, tears of joy were streaming down my cheeks, too.

After the flag-raising ceremony, everyone moved inside the embassy. For its reopening, the Cubans had restored it to its former splendor, featuring an opulent marble stairway, elegant high ceilings, stained-glass windows, and freshly painted walls decorated with photos of Cuba.

We filed into the grand ballroom for a speech by Bruno Rodríguez, Cuba's calm, bespectacled, foreign minister. Behind him, draped on the wall, was the same Cuban flag that had been lowered from the embassy in Washington in 1961. It had been returned to Cuba and kept in a museum there until this moment. In the audience were scholars, religious leaders, activists, businesspeople, lawyers, diplomats, members of Congress, all of whom Rodríguez thanked for working "so hard for so many years so that this day would come."

People who don't know Cuba might have expected a sugar-coated talk about this special moment and the renewed friendship between the two countries. But instead Rodríguez spent most of his speech talking about the painful history of the relationship between Cuba and the United States.

He began with Cuba's most celebrated liberation fighter, the poet José Martí, best known in the U.S. for writing the words to the song "Guantanamera." Martí had visited the United States and written a book praising what he believed was a wonderful, fascinating, and important country. However, Martí warned Cubans to be careful when dealing with the U.S., a world power that could devour and absorb a small island like Cuba.

Rodríguez then talked about the Platt Amendment, "imposed in 1902 under a military occupation" by the U.S. as a condition of Cuba's independence. It essentially allowed the United States to intervene in Cuban affairs whenever it wished and "led to the usurpation of a piece of Cuban territory at Guantánamo," where the U.S. military base remains today.

Rodríguez continued through the litany of the U.S.'s shameful support of dictators in Cuba, including the last one, Fulgencio Batista, and its endless attempts to sabotage and overthrow the revolutionary Castro government.

"Today an opportunity has opened up to begin working to establish new bilateral relations quite different from whatever existed in the past," concluded Rodríguez. "The Cuban government is fully committed to that. But only the lifting of the economic, commercial, and financial blockade which has caused so much harm and suffering to our people, the return of our occupied territory of Guantánamo, and the respect for Cuba's sovereignty will lend some meaning to the historic event we are witnessing today."

At the end of his speech, the 58-year-old foreign minister invited everyone to celebrate upstairs in a big room they'd named for Ernest Hemingway. The famous American author had lived in Cuba for many years. He'd known Fidel Castro and supported the revolution. On one wall of the room, above a dark oak bar, the Cubans had hung an enlarged facsimile of Hemingway's signature. On another wall was a photo of Fidel and Hemingway together.

Michael and I headed for the bar, which was set up with hundreds of *mojitos* made with Cuban rum. It was a joyous occasion, and the drinks and Cuban music made it even more jubilant. I was only sorry that a number of my friends who'd worked so long for this day had not lived to see it.

The mood in the room ranged from buoyant to euphoric, and most everyone I talked to seemed optimistic about the future. "Today marks a growing-up day for the United States," said Representative Raúl Grijalva. "We are finally going to act like adults in our own hemisphere, quit being punitive with Cuba." Representative Barbara Lee, who has traveled to Cuba more than 20 times over the years, said, "This is a great day. We have a long way to go to lift the embargo, but we're going to keep working on that, and we'll see that day, too."

"What about closing Guantánamo?" I asked.

"I don't know," she answered. "But I think all issues are on the table now. That's the beauty of having diplomatic relations."

I glanced across the room, and in a corner I spotted a crowd of people gathered around an elderly Cuban man who was seated. I made my way over to them and stood nearby to listen. The man said he was 86 years old. He was one of only three people still alive who had joined with Fidel Castro and 135 other rebels when they unsuccessfully attacked the Moncada Barracks in Santiago de Cuba on July 26, 1953. He'd also been with Fidel, Che, and the group of 82 rebels who sailed from Mexico on the small boat, the *Granma,* and landed in Cuba on November 25, 1956. One of only 20 to escape to the Sierra Maestra, he was there for the beginning of the guerrilla movement that ended in January 1959 with the triumphant march into Havana. Amazingly, he'd also been a member of the Cuban military force that repelled the CIA's Bay of Pigs invasion in 1961.

This man had fought every battle and not only miraculously survived, but like the revolution itself, had triumphed. Looking at him, I realized that he was the living embodiment of the Cuban revolution. Someone asked him what he was feeling on this special day.

"Same way I felt the day we won at the Bay of Pigs," he replied.

"And how did you feel then?" someone asked.

"Fidel said it better than me," he said. "It's in a book. You can find it." And he returned to his *mojito*.

I never did get that remarkable man's name. But returning to New York on the train that night, I got on the internet and found a quote from Fidel following Cuba's Bay of Pigs victory.

"We are at a decisive moment in our history," Fidel had said. "Tyranny has been defeated. The happiness is immense. However, there still is much to be done. Let's not deceive ourselves believing that from now on everything will be easy. Perhaps everything from now on will be more difficult."

Those words seemed as relevant on July 20, 2015 as they had been when Fidel spoke them in April 1961. It was a beautiful day, and thankfully president Obama had begun the long-overdue process of restoring relations between Cuba and the U.S. But the embargo remained in effect, and Guantánamo was still a prison controlled by the U.S.

Was this really the beginning of a new era? Obama's actions might simply represent a change of methods, the softer glove of imperialism. He'd done something similar with Iran, agreeing not to use military force there. Instead, the U.S. would assert its influence and domination of the region through diplomacy. Certainly this softer approach was better for Cuba. But it did not signal a new United States government saying that it would take its place as an equal partner in the world community. No, the U.S. was still at the top of the world's pyramid. It would continue dominating other countries and regions economically, culturally and, if necessary, militarily.

I was also well aware that whatever progress had been made under Obama could easily be reversed in the future by a more bellicose, interventionist President or an extreme right-wing Congress. I had no illusions. I had worked for 45 years as a lawyer and activist in the struggle for justice, peace, human rights, and an end to U.S. global imperialism. The movements I'd been part of had made progress on many fronts, but had also suffered many defeats, setbacks, and disappointments. In my legal practice, I'd lost many more cases than I'd won. We are all human, and the temptation to get discouraged or to give up entirely was always lurking. It would be all too easy to ignore injustice and pursue a life of individual comfort and daily pleasures.

But whenever I felt my commitment flagging, I looked to Cuba as a beacon of hope to lift my spirits. The Cuban revolution had provided an example of how to stand up to oppressive power and create a different, more humane world. It had shown all of us that it was possible not just to fight against a seemingly invincible international corporate capitalism, but to win.

That is why I felt so inspired and energized on July 20, 2015. It was a victory for Cuba, a cause for celebration, and a culmination of so much of my life's work. Victories like this don't happen often. And they can take a long time—in this case, 54 years. But they sustain us for the long haul, and we need to savor them.

I know how much more remains to be done. We have a long road ahead to reach the peaceful, just, environmentally sustainable world we all want to live in. But looking back on my life, I realize we've already come a long way. I have no doubt that some sweet day in the future, especially with the help of a new generation of idealistic young people who are willing to work, sacrifice, organize, and fight, we will get there.

Venceremos!

ABOUT THE AUTHOR

MICHAEL RATNER (1943-2016) was a New York-based civil rights attorney and a lifelong socialist. He was president of the National Lawyers Guild and the Center for Constitutional Rights and the author of several books including *The Trial of Donald Rumsfeld: A Prosecution by Book, Against War with Iraq, Guantanamo: What the World Should Know,* and (with Michael Smith) *Who Killed Che?: How the CIA Got Away With Murder.*

CPSIA information can be obtained
at www.ICGtesting.com
Printed in the USA
BVHW031826210721
611788BV00003B/18